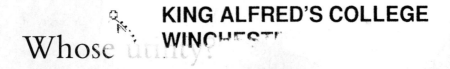

Whose unity?

Public Policy and Management

Series Editor: Professor R.A.W. Rhodes, Department of Politics, University of York.
Series Advisers: Professor Peter Jackson, University of Leicester and Professor Mike Connolly, University of Ulster.

The effectiveness of public policies is a matter of public concern and the efficiency with which policies are put into practice is a continuing problem for governments of all political persuasions. This series contributes to these debates by publishing informed, in-depth and contemporary analyses of public administration, public policy and public management.

The intention is to go beyond the usual textbook approach to the analysis of public policy and management and to encourage authors to move debate about their issue forward. In this sense, each book both describes current thinking and research, and explores future policy directions. Accessibility is a key feature and, as a result, the series will appeal to academics and their students as well as to the informed practitioner.

Current Titles Include:

Whose utility?

The social impact of public
utility privatization and regulation
in Britain

John Ernst

Open University Press
Buckingham · Philadelphia

Open University Press
Celtic Court
22 Ballmoor
Buckingham
MK18 1XW

and
1900 Frost Road, Suite 101
Bristol, PA 19007, USA

First Published 1994

Copyright © John Ernst 1994

A catalogue record of this book is available from the British Library

ISBN 0 335 19267 X (pbk)   0 335 19268 8 (hbk)

Library of Congress Cataloging-in-Publication Data

Ernst, John, 1951–
    Whose utility? : the social impact of public utility privatization
and regulation in Britain / by John Ernst.
        p.   cm. – (Public policy and management)
    Includes bibliographical references and index.
    ISBN 0–335–19268–8 : £40.00 ($85.00 U.S.). – ISBN 0–335–19267–X
(pbk.) : £15.99 ($34.00 U.S.)
    1. Public utilities–Government policy–Great Britain.
2. Privatization–Great Britain.   I. Title.   II. Series.
HD2768.G74E76   1994
363.6'0941–dc20   93–38812
                                                                          CIP

Typeset by Dorwyn Ltd, Rowlands Castle, Hants
Printed in Great Britain by St Edmundsbury Press, Bury St Edmunds, Suffolk

To Herbois

We may pick a thousand sallets ere we light on such another herb

Contents

Acknowledgements

This book relies substantially on the work of those who have gone before and on the assistance and on the knowledge and insights of colleagues in the field; without whose help I would have stood little chance of understanding the complex and rapidly changing field of public utility services in Britain. Most of the people with whom I have had contact in Britain over the past four years have made a contribution, in one form or another, to the end product of this research. But there are a few individuals who should be given specific mention. Brenda Boardman, Martin Fitch and Teresa Perchard have been important influences on the research. Pat Conaty, Neil Ritchie, Ron Campbell, Barbara Montoute and Diana Scott have been very helpful contributors. The staff of each of the three regulatory bodies have given freely of their time and information.

Jonathan Bradshaw has been a critically perceptive guide and friend throughout. Bronwyn Herbert, Coralie McLean, Ian Gibbs, Autumn Yu, Lars Inge Terum, Alison Holdsworth, Tony Fowles, Meg Huby and Veronica Pearson have been sources of great support and encouragement.

I have been the beneficiary of twelve months financial support under the CVCP Overseas Research Studentship scheme, and a semester's study leave from the Victoria University of Technology (financed through the Commonwealth Staff Development Fund), for which I am very grateful.

I also owe a great debt of gratitude to my colleague, Louise Glanville at the Social Work Unit, Victoria University of Technology, for without her willingness to fill the teaching and administrative breach left by my absence I would have been unable to return to the UK to complete this study.

Abbreviations

ACE	Association for the Conservation of Energy
AMA	Association of Metropolitan Authorities
BG	British Gas
BT	British Telecom
CBI	Confederation of British Industry
CEGB	Central Electricity Generating Board
CPRE	Council for the Protection of Rural England
CSCs	Customer Service Committees
CSUA	Competition and Service (Utilities) Act
DoE	Department of the Environment
ECC	Electricity Consumers Council
ESI	Electricity Supply Industry
FES	Family Expenditure Survey
GCC	Gas Consumers Council
GHS	General Household Survey
HoC	House of Commons
HoL	House of Lords
MMC	Monopolies and Mergers Commission
NACAB	National Association of Citizens Advice Bureaux
NAO	National Audit Office
NCC	National Consumer Council
NCVO	National Council for Voluntary Organizations
NRA	National Rivers Authority
OFFER	Office of Electricity Regulation

OFGAS	Office of Gas Supply
OFT	Office of Fair Trading
OFTEL	Office of Telecommunications
OFWAT	Office of Water Services
PUAF	Public Utilities Access Forum
RECs	Regional Electricity Companies
RWAs	Regional Water Authorities
SSAC	Social Security Advisory Committee
WAA	Water Authorities Association
WSA	Water Services Association

Introduction

One of the most important areas in which there should have been more prolonged and persistent debate and discussion in the 1980s was precisely around the question of the social effects or social consequences of free market policies – or around the issue which classical economists refer to as the question of social cost.

Taylor (1990a: 6)

Sadly, there is no reason to expect the political process to lead to the right pattern of privatization. Unless we are luckier or more careful than we are likely to be, political pressures will tend to retain for the public sector functions where privatization would make sense, and to privatize tasks that would be better left to government.

Donahue (1989: 13)

Privatization seems to have made its initial entry into the lexicon of political ideas with the publication of Peter Drucker's book *The Age of Discontinuity* in 1969, and for more than a decade it has formed a dominant *leitmotif* in the policy-making of the Thatcher and Major Governments. One of the most significant manifestations of privatization policy in Britain has been the denationalization of public enterprises. From relatively modest beginnings during the period 1979–83, with the divestiture of a number of state-owned firms operating in competitive markets, such as British Aerospace, Britoil, Cable & Wireless, National Freight Corporation and Amersham International, the privatization programme reached deep into the post-war fabric of the State with the sale of the public utilities – British Telecom, British Gas, the water authorities and the electricity supply industry – from 1984 to 1991.

Privatization policy in Britain has been driven by a diverse set of political and economic objectives, which range from the ideological (i.e. 'rolling back the frontiers of the state' and popular capitalism) to the pragmatic (e.g. generating additional public revenue). Not all of these objectives, as we will see, have been equally important, and a number of them appear contradictory. But despite the chameleon character of the programme, where different objectives have been emphasized in line with shifting political and economic imperatives, privatization policy has been enacted according to a more or less coherent ideological agenda, involving a substantive redrawing of the boundaries of the State and the market in contemporary society.

The phenomenon of privatization has not been confined to Britain, of course, with governments of varying political hues in Western industrialized countries embracing the precepts of privatization. The World Bank and the International Monetary Fund have become global sponsors of privatization by encouraging developing and Eastern European countries to adopt divestiture and privatization policies as the primary instruments of economic surgery and reform (Starr 1989; De Oliveira and MacKerron 1992; Kikeri et al. 1992). The internationalization of privatization has become increasingly well documented, with writers like Cook and Kirkpatrick (1988), Fraser (1988), Letwin (1988), MacAvoy et al. (1989), Ramanadham (1989), Ott and Hartley (1991), Glennerster and Midgley (1991) and Whitfield (1992), providing useful, if in some instances markedly different, accounts of this late twentieth-century global phenomenon.

The pervasiveness of privatization as a major item on the public policy agendas of governments throughout the world seems to suggest that the current period represents a pivotal point in the history of the modern State. In effect, we appear to be witnessing a process of transformation in the way that the State, and its constituent parts, views itself and is viewed by influential external interests and arguably, by its citizenry. The post-war consensus concerning the explicit responsibility of the State for strategic parts of the industrial economy (such as energy policy and coal production) and for physical infrastructure provision (like transportation, telecommunications, energy and water services) has been progressively displaced by a very different set of views about the nature of the role of the State *vis-à-vis* industrial activity and infrastructural development.

The transfer of the water and energy utilities to the private sector illustrates, in clear relief, this historic shift in political and economic thinking, as these industries occupy not only a fundamental position in the economic and social development of society at large, but they also exert a direct and powerful influence on the lifestyles of every household in Britain.

The sale of the gas, electricity and water utilities to the private sector has not led, however, to a disengagement of the State from the arena of public utility services. Despite it relinquishing ownership and production functions, the State has been required to maintain a significant presence as a regulator of public utility activity. The influence of public regulation on the provision of essential services under private monopoly or quasi-monopoly conditions forms, therefore, a new and important field for policy analysis in this country.

The British Government's privatization programme since 1979 has attracted a considerable degree of academic attention, although to date, this interest has been primarily directed at the economic and, to a lesser extent, the political dimensions of the programme. The advent of industry-specific regulatory agencies has likewise stimulated a developing literature, but here also the focus has been heavily oriented towards economic analysis.

However, the public utilities occupy too important a place in society to continue to cede almost monopoly control of the discourse on utility industry policy and regulation, to the discipline of economics. The energy and water utilities make a fundamental contribution to individual and social well-being and questions concerning the distribution of utility services directly intersect with major issues of social policy. Yet, surprisingly, little analysis of the public utility phase of the privatization programme has been undertaken from a social policy perspective. Indeed, the literature on social policy and the public utilities generally, is extremely scant. Energy is better served in this respect than water, but even in the former, only two major works have been published on the subject in Britain over the last decade, namely Jonathan Bradshaw and Toby Harris' *Energy and Social Policy* (1983) and Brenda Boardman's *Fuel Poverty, From Cold Homes to Affordable Warmth* (1991). Nor, up to this point, has a concerted effort been made to evaluate the impact of utility privatization and regulation on domestic consumers in general, and on low-income consumers in particular. This is likely to be a reflection of the short history of the public utilities under privatization. But even in those studies that have attempted to assess the outcomes of the privatization programme thus far (Bishop and Kay 1988; Chapman 1990; Roberts et al. 1991; Whitfield 1992), only cursory attention has been given to the important question of how privatization has affected ordinary consumers. The central aim of this book is to fill this major gap in the literature and in our understanding of how privatization of the energy and water industries has operated in practice.

It is still too early to provide a conclusive account of how domestic consumers have fared under privatization, but the restructuring of the public utilities has been in place sufficiently long enough to give a clear indication of the extent to which the new regime is acting either to the advantage or the disadvantage of consumers. This book analyses the impact of gas, electricity and water privatization up to the end of 1992, which constitutes an appropriate point at which to reflect on the outcomes of the initial phase of the utility privatization programme. In each of the utility industries, there is a very real sense that the first act has drawn to a close and that there are likely to be significant changes in the plot, and possibly even the players, as the next act unfolds. The catalysts for these probable changes include the Monopolies and

Mergers Commission investigation into the gas industry, the reviews of the water and electricity price controls by the industry regulators, and the Government's review of energy policy in the wake of its controversial proposal to close many of the country's remaining coal mines.

This book focuses centrally on the impact of privatization and regulation on primary areas of service provision for domestic consumers, namely:

- tariffs and systems of charging
- debt and disconnection practice
- service standards and consumer protection
- mechanisms for consumer representation

It also includes an assessment of the broader distributional consequences of the sale of the public utilities (in Chapter 3). It is particularly concerned throughout to examine the way in which the new structures of ownership and regulation have affected access to energy and water services by low-income households in Britain.

Because of the significant negative externalities associated with the provision of energy and water services, privatization has been attended by considerable concern about the nature and quality of private sector stewardship of the environment. Although an analysis of the environmental effects of the privatization of the water and energy utilities is largely outside the scope of this work, the interaction between aspects of environmental policy and social policy is alluded to on a number of occasions, particularly where this is directly relevant to equity and distributional issues.

In seeking to evaluate the outcomes of the utility privatization programme, the researcher is immediately confronted with the problem as to what constitutes the most appropriate 'frame of reference' for conducting such an evaluation. A 'before-and-after' approach, involving a direct comparison of the service systems of the public utilities under nationalized and subsequently, privatized regimes, would be instructive, but is made difficult due to the absence of comparable data. Juxtaposing outcomes with the objectives explicitly set for the privatization programme is a useful way of testing the efficacy of privatization in its own terms, and it utilizes the orthodox methodology of goal-oriented evaluation. However, it may not capture the full array of consequences of utility privatization, as the field of analysis is fundamentally driven (and constrained) by the logic and rationale of the designers of privatization policy. The application of exogenous evaluative criteria – like equity – is therefore likely to be required if the researcher is to get anywhere near tapping the depth of the 'privatization affect', particularly in regard to its social impact. Elements of each of these three modes of evaluation are employed, although emphasis is given to the latter two approaches.

This analysis of the impact of privatization and regulation has been informed by the use of a wide range of primary and secondary sources. Extensive use has been made of documentary material from government agencies, the regulatory bodies, the utility companies and community sector organizations.

This has been complemented by interviews with key informants in the community and consumer sector, the regulatory bodies and the utility industries. The author has also been a participant observer, over several years, in a number of the key fora set up in England and Wales to represent the interests of low-income consumers of utility services, including the Public Utilities Access Forum and the National Right to Fuel Campaign. The burgeoning literature on the economic aspects of privatization and public utility regulation has provided an important part of the conceptual framework used in the book.

Chapter 1 gives a summary account of the major events in the privatization of the gas, electricity and water industries in Britain, and a detailed review of the legislative and regulatory framework, particularly in relation to consumer affairs. It also documents, for the first time, the attempts made by the community and consumer sector to influence the legislative process, using primary source material, obtained through interviews with individuals involved in the campaigns and parliamentary briefing papers. Many of the issues raised, unsuccessfully, by the community and consumer sector at the outset, were to become recurrent problems in the implementation of the new structure of utility provision and regulation.

Privatization connotes a paradigm of utility services as 'commodities' like any other. In Chapter 2 it is argued, however, that this is not the case and that energy and water services have a composite of features, i.e. essentialness, inelasticity of demand properties, natural monopoly provision and externalities, which distinguish them from other services purchased by ordinary consumers in the marketplace. The social and economic characteristics of the utility industries mean that they inevitably intersect with significant areas of public policy. The distinguishing characteristics of utility services necessitate an overlay of strong public regulation. In the past, this was seen to be best achieved through public ownership. However, privatization offers an alternative model of public utility management and regulation. Chapter 2 also looks at the British model of utility regulation and discusses the *modus operandi* of the British energy and water regulatory bodies.

The British privatization programme has been characterized by multiple economic and political objectives, and Chapter 3 sets the scene for the empirical analysis of the outcomes of gas, electricity and water privatization in the remainder of the book by examining these objectives. Privatization of the public utilities has resulted in concrete changes in the relationship between individual consumers and utility providers. It has also had broader distributional effects, and as part of an analysis of how the ordinary citizens of Britain have fared under gas, electricity and water privatization, it is necessary to examine these macro-distributional outcomes. Chapter 3 does this through using primary and secondary source material to explore the issues of public utility assets sales, share ownership and distribution, company profits, executive salaries and employment.

Chapters 4, 5 and 6 form the empirical core of the book. They directly address the question of how domestic consumers have been affected by the

1

The process and structure of public utility privatization in Britain

Introduction

The gas, water and electricity industries were privatized, in succession, over a period of five years by the Conservative Government – British Gas in 1986, the regional water authorities in 1989 and the electricity supply industry (ESI) in 1990–91. Despite having a number of attributes in common, the three public utilities had quite distinct structural and operational histories. The different features of the industries, in conjunction with a range of external political and economic factors, presented the Government with different issues and problems in steering the privatization of each of the industries through the legislative process.

As well as adapting the utility privatization model, originally used in the privatization of British Telecom in 1984, to the particular characteristics and conditions in each industry, the Government also seemed to utilize an element of 'policy learning' in its management of the programme, with some – but by no means all – of the lessons of earlier privatizations being applied to those occurring later in the programme. This is most noticeably the case in relation to the promotion of competition and to aspects of regulation.

This chapter will examine the process of privatizing the gas, water and electricity supply industries between 1986 and 1991, giving particular emphasis to the legislative provisions and structures introduced for the economic and social regulation of the three utilities. It will provide a synoptic, rather than a detailed, account of the major events in the history of the privatization of each of the three utilities, and it will give close attention to the involvement of community sector and consumer organizations in the legislative process. This is partly because good general accounts of the privatization process in these industries exist elsewhere. See, for example, gas (Vickers and Yarrow 1988), electricity (Green 1991, Roberts et al. 1991) and water, from different perspectives and different points in time (Kinnersley 1988; Cook 1989; Ogden 1991; Richardson et al. 1992). But also, in the context of this book, it is more important to detail the regulatory framework developed at the time of privatization – particularly as it relates to domestic consumers, and to identify the sorts of issues that organizations representing the interests of consumers were seeking to place on the policy-making agenda at the outset, rather than to simply reiterate the known history of utility privatization. The involvement of the community sector has been largely overlooked in published accounts of the privatization programme in Britain, which have tended to focus, by and large, on the economic aspects of privatization and regulation.

The privatization of British Gas

Background

> Merely to replace state monopolies by private ones would be to waste an historic opportunity. So we will take steps to ensure that these new firms do not exploit their powerful positions to the detriment of consumers or their competitors. Those nationalised industries which cannot be privatised or organised as smaller and more efficient units will be given top-quality management and required to work to clear guidelines.
>
> *The Conservative Manifesto 1983*, p. 17

The privatization of the gas industry in 1986 has been perceived generally as a major opportunity lost. This is because it involved the straightforward metamorphosis of a public monopoly supplier, the British Gas Corporation, to a private monopoly supplier, British Gas plc, without any significant attempt to restructure the industry, or to introduce competition into the domestic gas market.

Unlike in the earlier privatization of British Telecom and in the privatization of the water and electricity industries subsequently, the way to the sale of British Gas had not been paved by a clear election manifesto commitment, nor a White Paper outlining the details of the new structure for the gas industry in Britain. Indeed, as the quotation above shows, the 1983 *Conservative Party Manifesto*, argued against the very structure that was introduced in the gas industry when it was privatized.

Several months after the election of the Thatcher Government to a second term of office in mid-1983, the Secretary of State for Energy, Peter Walker, established a departmental working group to examine the options for privatizing the British Gas Corporation. According to Lord Belstead, in his

Second Reading speech on the Gas Bill in the House of Lords, this working group carried out 'the most careful scrutiny of the regulatory systems in a number of other countries and a full review of the existing and past arrangements for the control of the gas industry and other utilities here in Great Britain' (House of Lords, 10/4/86, col. 370).

In April 1985, the Secretary of State for Energy sought, and gained, Cabinet approval for the introduction of legislation to privatize the British Gas Corporation. The policy choices available to the Government for the future structure of the privatized gas industry in Britain included (i) the retention of the unitary and monopoly structure of the British Gas Corporation, (ii) the separation of the transmission and supply functions into two businesses and (iii) the sale of the twelve area boards of the Corporation as separate companies. In the event, the legislation made provision for the Government to sell its 100 per cent stake in a unitary British Gas plc – a company which looked little different from its nationalized predecessor, with the exception of the earlier divestment of the British Gas Corporation's on-shore and off-shore oil fields and the removal of its status as the sole authorized gas utility.

The Government's arguments for retaining the existing model were premised centrally on a recognition of the natural monopoly characteristics of the domestic gas industry, as the following excerpt from the Secretary of State for Energy's Second Reading speech on the Gas Bill illustrates:

> It has been argued that splitting the corporation into area boards serving different parts of the country would achieve greater competition. I carefully examined this possibility, and looked into the advantages and disadvantages that it would bring. Under such an arrangement, each consumer would, as is now the case with electricity, face a single supplier in their area. Breaking up the corporation would also put at risk economies of scale through the integrated transmission and distribution system that has been developed, which allow best practices to be spread rapidly through all parts of the country.
>
> House of Commons, 10/12/85, col. 776

The Secretary of State also argued that significant structural change would be attended by marked variations in gas tariffs throughout the country and would cause 'disruption to consumers and industry'. Interestingly, these arguments have gained a new resonance in recent times, as a result of the referral of British Gas to the Monopolies and Mergers Commission (see Chapter 4).

Whatever the merit of the arguments in favour of a unitary model, the privatization of the gas industry manifestly contradicted the restructuring and competition objectives explicit in both the Government's election manifesto and the privatization programme as a whole. The failure to achieve these objectives in the sale of British Gas, in all but the most limited of ways, has been variously attributed to the negotiating power of Sir Denis Rooke (the then Chairman of the British Gas Corporation), the indifference of the Secretary of State for Energy to the Government's privatization agenda, a desire to

Figure 1.1   Key events in the privatization of British Gas.

Apr 1983:	Conservative Party election manifesto (pp. 16–17) promises to abolish 'the Gas Corporation's statutory monopoly of the supply of North Sea gas to industry' and to increase competition in, and attract private capital to, the gas industry
Sep 1983:	Secretary of State for Energy sets up departmental working group to examine options for privatizing British Gas Corporation
Apr 1985:	Secretary of State for Energy presents paper to Cabinet recommending privatization of British Gas Corporation
May 1985:	Government announces intention to privatize British Gas Corporation
Dec 1985:	Second Reading of Gas Bill in House of Commons
Apr 1986:	Second Reading of Gas Bill in House of Lords
Apr 1986:	British Gas incorporated as public limited company
Jul 1986:	Gas Act 1986 enacted
Aug 1986:	Transfer of British Gas Corporation's assets to British Gas plc Director General of Gas Supply appointed
Dec 1986:	Flotation of British Gas

maximize the financial returns to the Government through selling the industry intact, and an imperative to complete the sale ahead of the upcoming General Election in 1987. Certainly, the board and senior executives of the British Gas Corporation appear to have played a pivotal part in shaping the outcomes of gas privatization (National Audit Office 1987; Vickers and Yarrow 1988), and this pattern of executive influence on the 'privatization settlement' was to be a recurring feature in the public utility privatization programme.

The key events in the privatization of British Gas are set out in Figure 1.1.

Regulatory framework

The framework adopted by the Government for the regulation of British Gas was substantially based on the prototype developed for British Telecom. As is the case with all of the privatized utilities, the statutory instruments for the regulation of the industry consist of two parts: the primary legislation or enabling Act, and the operating licence. The economic regulation of the monopoly gas supplier, contained in the licence, was framed around the price control formula $RPI - X + Y$ developed by Professor Stephen Littlechild in 1984, where RPI is the retail price index, X (the 'efficiency factor') was set at 2 per cent and Y provided for the full pass-through of gas purchase costs to consumers. Because of the retention of the unitary, single firm, structure of the industry, the second critical dimension of economic regulation – the promotion of competition – was effectively excluded from the regulatory regime, although under sections 3 and 19 of the Gas Act 1986, British Gas lost its previously-held exclusive right to supply gas through pipes.

Responsibility for the economic regulation of British Gas and the enforcement of the terms of its licence, along with a duty to protect the interests of consumers, was vested in the Director General of Gas Supply. As well as being given a general duty to protect consumers, the Director General was also specifically required to 'take into account, in particular, the interests of those who are disabled or of pensionable age' (s. 4(3) Gas Act 1986). However, most importantly, the Director General of Gas Supply's general and specific duties to protect the interests of consumers was made secondary to his primary duties of (i) securing the satisfaction of 'all reasonable demands for gas', and (ii) securing that authorized suppliers of gas 'are able to finance the provision of gas supply services' (s. 4, Gas Act 1986). A similar set of regulatory priorities (where social regulation is subordinate to economic regulation) also exists for the water and electricity regulators, despite the fact, as will be seen, that organizations such as the National Consumer Council and the Consumers' Association argued strongly against this, particularly during the passage of Water Bill.

In addition to the creation of an Office of Gas Supply, the legislation provided for the setting up of an independent national consumer body (with offices in each of British Gas' regions) – the Gas Consumers Council – to investigate complaints and, if necessary, to make referrals to the Director General of Gas Supply. Remarkably, the Council was given powers in a number of areas which exceeded those given to the Director General of Gas Supply, such as the scope to investigate matters affecting contract as well as tariff customers and a mandate to deal with complaints related to gas appliances.

The establishment of a national, industry-specific consumer body working independently of, but in conjunction with, the regulator was unique to gas privatization. This model was not replicated in either of the subsequent privatizations, despite the fact that in the electricity industry – as with gas – a national body representing consumers had been in existence for many years prior to privatization. The reason for the retention of a national consumer body in the case of gas and not electricity is probably related to the fact that the (about to be abolished) National Gas Consumers Council (with the support of the National Consumer Council) argued for a national forum independent of the regulator and that Sir Denis Rooke apparently lent his influential support to the lobbying for an independent consumer body. Neither of these conditions applied in the period leading into and during the privatization of the electricity supply industry.

Despite the apparent superiority of the model of consumer representation put in place during the privatization of British Gas, the overall framework for economic and social regulation in the gas industry was, on most criteria, the weakest of the regulatory regimes introduced in the three utility industries. Many of the weaknesses in the system of regulation being devised were recognized by community sector and consumer organizations involved in the campaign on the Gas Bill as it progressed through the House of Commons and the House of Lords in late 1985 and early 1986.

Community sector campaign

Unlike later privatizations, and most especially water privatization, the involvement of the community sector in activity surrounding the formulation of the primary and secondary legislation for the privatization of the gas industry was relatively low key. It also lacked the cohesion and coordination evident in the water privatization campaign. The absence of policy documents foreshadowing the privatization legislation (in the form of Green and White Papers) and a lack of campaigning experience on an issue of such complexity, may partly explain the character of the community sector's response to the Gas Bill.

Most of the community sector organizations involved in lobbying over the Bill adopted a pragmatic approach, i.e. they sought not to challenge privatization *per se*, but to influence the shape of the regulatory environment that would attend the privatization of the gas industry. This essentially pragmatic engagement with the policy-making process was also characteristic of the sector's *modus operandi* in the subsequent water and electricity privatizations. However, there were some organizations involved in lobbying over the Gas Bill and other privatization legislation – of which the National Right to Fuel Campaign was a leading example – that adopted what could be described as a 'dual-pronged' strategy: outright opposition to privatization as a principle, was complemented by a set of 'second-best' proposals aimed at improving the regulatory regime and at advancing the interests of low-income consumers.

The community sector campaign (or more accurately, individual campaigns) to influence the gas privatization legislation was directed primarily along three fronts, namely:

1. Identifying the inherent flaws in the proposed system of economic regulation.
2. Exposing the paucity of regulatory protection for low-income consumers.
3. Arguing for energy efficiency obligations/incentives for British Gas.

The National Consumer Council (NCC) took much of the running in the first area, arguing in its briefings on the Second Reading of the Bill and to the Standing Committee on the Gas Bill that, because of the absence of competition in the structure of the privatized gas industry, consumers were unlikely to receive much benefit. In the absence of competition it was imperative, the NCC pointed out, that the regulatory bodies be given 'real teeth . . . with proper powers and proper funding' and that 'trying to save money by reducing the power of the regulator is short sighted. The inefficiency of a utility is passed on to its consumers' (NCC Second Reading Briefing on Gas Privatization, undated, p. 2). The NCC concluded that the powers being given to the Director General of Gas Supply were less than the already circumscribed powers given to the Director General of the Office of Telecommunications. The NCC's call for a stronger regulatory presence in the privatized gas industry was imitated by other community sector organizations, like the National Right to Fuel Campaign (which also advocated the appointment of a 'Gas Ombudsman' with the power to award compensation), and the trade association-cum-energy efficiency lobby group, the Association for the Conservation of Energy (ACE).

On the primary instrument of economic regulation, the price control formula, the NCC argued that it was seriously deficient in that (a) the full pass-through of gas costs provided no incentive for British Gas to purchase economically and that consumers, not the company, would bear the brunt of any poor purchasing decisions ('If British Gas slips up in signing a long-term contract with its suppliers and makes a bad deal, it is the shareholders, not the consumers, who should shoulder the costs') (p. 4), (b) it took no account of a possible decline in standards of service and (c) that the structure of the formula 'allow[s] the industry to reduce prices on services that are subject to competition, while raising prices on those that are not. This tends to mean that prices to big business go down, while prices to householders and small businesses go up' (p. 3).

The NCC arguments were apparently given very little credence by the Government of the day, for none of these issues was addressed in the legislation. But, although their impact at the time was minimal, it is interesting to observe that these matters have been very much at the core of the regulatory agencies' engagement with British Gas over recent years. This has been illustrated in the OFGAS Tariff Review in 1991, the Office of Fair Trading injunction to British Gas to separate its transmission business and to reduce its dominance of the contract market, and the referral of the company to the Monopolies and Mergers Commission in July 1992.

The second strand of community sector action on the Gas Bill and the draft licence was directed at exposing the possible dangers that low-income consumers of gas might face in their dealings with a profit-oriented monopolist, and at introducing a set of formal protections for this group of consumers in the privatization legislation. Although under the draft licence, British Gas was required to produce and publish codes of practice on debt and disconnection and on customer service there was, as the NCC pointed out 'nothing in the licence about what they should contain' (NCC Comments on the Gas Bill and draft licence to Standing Committee on the Gas Bill, 9/1/86, p. 4). In the view of organizations such as the Child Poverty Action Group and the National Right to Fuel Campaign, codes of practice requirements in the licence afforded insufficient protection and they argued for statutory codes of practice as part of the primary legislation. In large part, scepticism about the efficacy of non-statutory codes of practice was conditioned by experience of the operation of the voluntary, and substantially unenforceable, codes of practice introduced in the fuel industries in the mid-1970s.

As well as the introduction of statutory codes of practice, the National Right to Fuel Campaign sought the abolition of British Gas' right to disconnect (contained in the Public Gas Supply Code of Schedule 5 of the legislation) and argued that the industry should be obliged to recover its debts through the courts or a tribunal, that controls should be placed on the amount by which the standing charge could be increased each year, and that 'British Gas have a statutory duty to consider the welfare of disadvantaged gas consumers and to ensure that policies do not exacerbate their problems' (*Fuel News*, Vol. 4, 1985). In the event, only one of these proposals met with any success – the level of annual increase in the standing charge was fixed to increases in line with movements in the retail price index.

The third and final area around which community organizations attempted to influence the legislative and regulatory framework for the operation of British Gas concerned energy efficiency. In making their case, the National Right to Fuel Campaign, the Association for the Conservation of Energy and others, emphasized the seeming incongruity of energy efficiency principles and practice with a privatized energy industry, released from the public accountability and policy constraints of government, and operating under a price control formula explicitly biased in favour of maximizing gas sales. It was argued, therefore, that the only way in which this 'market failure' might be corrected would be through placing a statutory obligation on British Gas for ensuring the efficient use of energy. Detail of the actual mechanics of how this obligation might be defined, monitored and enforced by the regulator was less precise. The ground on energy efficiency was to be revisited three years later during electricity privatization, with only marginally more success.

The issues relating to low-income consumers and energy efficiency which were raised during the passage of the legislation in 1985–86 made, with the minor exception of the standing charge, little discernible impact on the Government's policy decisions at the time. Yet, as in the case of the NCC's critique of the system of economic regulation, their pertinence and relevance has been confirmed over the short history of the privatized gas industry, as will be seen in later chapters.

The privatization of the regional water authorities

Background

The sale of the ten regional water authorities in England and Wales was unequivocally the most contested part of the Thatcher Government's privatization programme. This was reflected in the strong, and largely successful, extra-parliamentary campaign to change the Government's original plans for the organization of the industry in the private sector, and in the failure of the Government, throughout the entire process of water privatization, to win broad public support for the sale. For most of this period, between 70 and 80 per cent of people interviewed by opinion pollsters expressed negative views about water privatization. Nevertheless, the Government completed the sale of the water authorities in December 1989.

The character of the privatization programme generally has been evolutionary and opportunistic and this is exemplified nowhere better than in the sale of the water industry. The story of the idea of water privatization 'arriv[ing] on the agenda suddenly' (Richardson et al. 1992) and the way that 'the government and water authorities stumbled into it' (Kinnersley, 1988) has been documented fully elsewhere and therefore will only be sketched in outline here.

It is generally accepted that the precipitating event in water privatization was a dispute between the Government and the Thames Water Authority in early 1985 over the accelerated repayment of loans and a consequential increase in water charges. In the subsequent House of Commons debate on the issue, the Minister for Housing and Construction announced that the Government 'will be examining the possibility of a measure of privatization in the industry' (House of Commons, 7/2/85, col. 1142).

Following the dissemination of a hastily put together and poorly-drafted (according to Kinnersley, 1988) discussion paper by the Department of the Environment, which drew an indifferent response from the water industry, the Government released the White Paper 'Privatisation of the Water Authorities in England and Wales' (HMSO, 1986b) outlining its plans for the sale of the ten regional water authorities. Along with enunciating the rationale for privatizing the industry (which made little mention of the environmental imperatives that were to occupy such a prominent place in the Government's arguments in 1988–89), the White Paper set out the proposed privatized industry structure and the system of economic regulation to be introduced.

The publication of the White Paper attracted, almost immediately, a strong negative response. A response, not directed primarily at the principle of privatization as such, but at the core proposal that the integrated river-basin management model introduced under the Water Act 1973 – involving the organization and management of water resources and the water-related environment around river basin catchment areas – be retained and that the privatized water companies continue to perform *both* a water production and an environmental regulation function.

The existing system of integrated water management was viewed as generally successful, but strong apprehension was felt about private profit-making bodies performing the critical environmental management responsibilities explicit in the integrated model. Also, as the water authorities themselves were major contributors to water pollution (e.g. through sewerage discharges), there was concern that the advent of private water companies with regulatory responsibilities would serve to deepen the inherent conflict of interest involved in combining production and environmental policing functions.

In the face of concerted opposition from organizations as diverse as the CBI, Council for the Protection of Rural England (CPRE), Country Landowners Association, Green Alliance and the water-sector trade unions (plus, according to Richardson et al. 1992, the new Secretary of State for the Environment, Nicholas Ridley) and doubts about the legality of private water authorities being constituted as 'competent authorities' under European Commission environmental law, Nicholas Ridley advised the House of Commons that the tabling of water privatization legislation would be indefinitely deferred.

A solution to the conflict of interest implicit in privatized companies performing a dual production and regulatory function was subsequently found at the expense of the integrated river-basin management model. As part of its 1987 election manifesto, the Government announced that, upon re-election, it intended establishing a separate water environment watchdog to complement the privatized water authorities. Following the election, this was formalized in the Department of the Environment paper 'The National Rivers Authority: The government's policy for a public regulatory body in a privatized water industry' (July 1987), where it was indicated that the new authority would subsume, *inter alia*, the pollution control, water resource management, discharges consents, flood defence and land drainage functions of the regional water authorities.

The plans for the creation of an independent water environment regulatory body were greeted with wide approval, although the Water Authorities Association (representing the ten water authorities) expressed disagreement with the decision to abandon the integrated management approach. This was to be, however, the only major disappointment for the water authorities in the privatization process. In their analysis of the water privatization policy-making process, Richardson et al. (1992: 172) conclude that 'the WAA lobbying was very effective indeed. The NRA issue was a defeat, but the rest of the [financial settlement] package, as was privatization itself, represented a very good deal for the industry'.

The reversal of the original blueprint for the privatization of the water authorities in 1986–87 was the nadir of the Government's water privatization project. After this initial setback, for all the moral outrage expressed about the notion of expropriating a 'public good' like water for private profit, regardless of a deep, but latent, popular opposition to the sale, and notwithstanding the unhelpful interventions of the European Commission over the timetable for meeting environmental obligations, the Government experienced remarkably few problems in completing its legislative programme for water privatization. Only once did the Government appear to lose its sang-froid, when in March 1989, the Prime Minister ostensibly rebuked the two ministers responsible for water privatization, Nicholas Ridley and Michael Howard, for not handling the process well enough (*The Sunday Times*, 5/3/89).

The major landmarks in the legislative journey towards privatization of the water industry are summarized in Figure 1.2.

Under the legislation introduced into the House of Commons in November 1988, the ten regional water authorities were converted to public limited companies with responsibility for the provision of water and sewerage services within their designated regional areas. Technically, two companies were created out of each regional water authority, one generic holding company

Figure 1.2   Key events in the privatization of the water industry.   .

Feb 1985	Government announces that it 'will be examining the possibility of a measure of privatization in the [water] industry'
Apr 1985:	DoE releases discussion paper on water privatization
Feb 1986:	White Paper 'Privatisation of the Water Authorities in England and Wales' published
Jul 1986:	Privatization of water industry postponed
May 1987:	Commitment to privatize water industry and to create National Rivers Authority contained in Conservative Party election manifesto
Jun 1987:	Conservative Government re-elected
Jul 1987:	Plans for revised framework for water privatization and for the creation of a National Rivers Authority published
May 1988:	Public Utility Transfers and Water Charges Act enacted empowering water authorities to transfer property to other bodies corporate and sanctioning the introduction of water metering trials
Dec 1988:	Second Reading of Water Bill in House of Commons
Apr 1989:	Second Reading of Water Bill in House of Lords
Jul 1989:	Water Act 1989 enacted Director General of Water Services appointed
Sep 1989:	Transfer of Regional Water Authorities' assets to successor companies Instruments of Appointment (licences) come into effect Transfer of water resource and environmental management functions to National Rivers Authority
Dec 1989:	Sale of the ten Water Holding Companies
Jul 1991:	Consolidating Acts, including Water Industry Act 1991, enacted

(unregulated) and one with specific water and sewerage undertaker functions (regulated). It was formally accepted that water and sewerage provision was dominantly a natural monopoly and the regional water and sewerage companies were set up as monopoly providers within their geographical boundaries. In lieu of substantive competition, a form of proxy competition involving comparisons of the performance of each of the companies was the 'second best' solution adopted. The way in which this 'yardstick competition' might work in the water industry was first outlined by the author of the RPI − X price control, Professor Stephen Littlechild (Littlechild 1988).

Yet, arguably in deference to the ascendancy of competition as the ruling principle rather than because of any realistic expectation of practical achievement, a nominal element of competition – relating to 'inset appointments' – was contained in the Bill. 'Inset appointments' enable, at least in theory, water and sewerage undertakers to compete for large customers outside their area, who are not already serviced by a water and sewerage company (e.g. a new large residential or commercial development). Measures have been introduced subsequently to extend the scope for companies to compete for the business of large customers (through changes made to the Water Industry Act 1991, via the Competition and Service (Utilities) Act 1992). The legislation also made provision for the (then) 29 statutory water companies, supplying around 25 per cent of water to consumers in England and Wales, to convert to public limited company status, if they so desired.

Regulatory framework

The regulatory regime proposed in the Bill and subsequent draft licences, shared the broad contours of the systems introduced in the privatization of the telecommunications and the gas industries, but also it was marked by some quite distinct differences. One obvious difference, which will not be discussed at length here, relates to the fact that the function of the economic regulator (Director General of Water Services) was complemented by the existence of the so-called quality regulators (i.e. environmental and water quality regulators), the National Rivers Authority, HM Inspectorate of Pollution and the Drinking Water Inspectorate. The intersection of the different interests and constituencies represented in these four regulatory bodies has raised particular problems in the overall regulatory environment of the water services industry, which is touched on in Chapter 4.

As with gas, in the absence of competition between water companies, the price control formula becomes the primary lever for the economic regulation of the industry. Although because of the existence of over 30 water companies, the Director General of Water Services has an ability to undertake performance comparisons not available to his counterpart in the gas industry. The price control formula set for the water industry was RPI + K, where K represented the amount that water companies were allowed to increase charges *above* the rate of inflation, to offset the substantial injections of capital required to upgrade the infrastructure and to meet existing environmental obligations (totalling an estimated £26 billion at 1989 prices). The level of K set for the first five years varied between companies, but the national average was 5 per cent. The companies were also given the right to seek interim adjustments to K to take account of 'a relevant change of circumstance' arising from factors such as unanticipated costs associated with meeting additional European Commission environmental obligations, the costs associated with the introduction of domestic metering, and increases in national construction industry costs above those assumed in the initial setting of K.

The Director General of Water Services was given two primary duties, one of which was to ensure that the water companies could operate profitably:

to secure that the functions of a water undertaker and of sewerage undertaker are properly carried out as respects every area of England and Wales
. . . and to secure that companies holding appointments . . . as water
undertakers or sewerage undertakers are able (in particular, by securing
reasonable returns on their capital) to finance the proper carrying out of
the functions of such undertakers.

s. 7 Water Act 1989, changed subsequently to s. 2 Water Industry Act 1991

The Director General's secondary duties included a general provision to
protect the interests of customers and to take specific account of the interests of
the disabled and pensioners. The Director General has an additional duty,
resulting from a House of Lords amendment during the Third Reading of the
Bill, to protect the interests of customers and potential customers in rural areas
in respect of charging for water services.

The legislation provided for the setting up of ten regional Customer
Service Committees (CSCs), with responsibility for dealing with complaints
and for advising the Director General on matters related to the interests of
consumers. In contrast to the structure of consumer representation established
under the Gas Act 1986, the consumer bodies in the water industry were
attached to the Director General's office (e.g. the Director General makes the
appointments and funds the committees) and the bodies were structured on a
regional rather than national level. As will be seen below, the power given to
the Director General of Water Services with respect to the management and
work of the CSCs was a major area of concern to consumer organizations
during the passage of the legislation.

The water legislation also made explicit provision, for the first time in
the regulated industries, for a *measure* of quality regulation. This may possibly
have been the result of concerted ongoing advocacy of community sector and
consumer organizations, in tandem with a recognition of the difficulties
confronting OFTEL and OFGAS, in the absence of significant powers in this
area. Along with the traditional requirement that the companies establish
codes of practice in particular areas of customer service (of which more will
be said in the section that follows), the Director General of Water Services
was required to establish two sets of enforceable standards: the first, for
overall standards of performance that the companies would be expected to
attain, and the second, for service standards that 'ought to be achieved in
individual cases'. In the latter, it was envisaged that a small financial penalty
would be levied (and payable to the consumer) for failure on the part of a
company to meet the specified service standard. This Guaranteed Standards
Scheme was announced, with much fanfare, by the Minister for Water and
Planning, Michael Howard, during the passage of the Water Bill. The Minister described it as:

a no-nonsense, no-quibble scheme to provide a spur to management for
good commercial manners and quick recompense to customers for the
inconvenience that they have suffered. It will be a new remedy for the

customer. It will be in addition to existing legal rights. It will be but one of the many advantages that will accrue to the customer as a result of privatization.

House of Commons, 8/12/88, col. 524

Community sector campaign

Amongst the three utility privatizations, the sale of the water industry witnessed the most concerted community sector campaign aimed at influencing the post-privatization regulatory model. The same appears to be true for other activist sectors in the British polity, for example, the environmental and trade union movements (Ogden 1991).

The reason why the activity of the community sector was more concentrated and cohesive during the passage of the Water Bill is not immediately apparent, although it is possible to speculate on some of the probable contributory factors. First, the general political climate that accompanied the privatization of the water industry raised the prospect that the Government's plans might be more vulnerable than had hitherto been the case, giving rise in turn to the hope that appropriately targeted action could lead to success. The fact that the Government had experienced a significant defeat in its first approach to the sale, along with wide-ranging popular and media scepticism about the water privatization process, probably strengthened activist resolve and contributed to a new sense of political efficacy. In the upshot of events, the Government's fragility was more illusory than real, but this was not apparent for much of the time in 1988 and 1989.

Second, the experience of political lobbying in the earlier privatizations had reinforced the need for a collaborative and coordinated campaign, involving a cross-sectional and broadly-based political alliance. The agenda for change in the water privatization process was wide enough, and without the tensions implicit in earlier campaigns, for a coalition to be forged for the first, and only time, between community and consumer organizations, environmental groups, local government peak bodies and the industry trade unions.

Finally, and this is relevant only to a comparison with the involvement of the community sector in the Electricity Bill, the timing of the passage of the two pieces of primary legislation for water and electricity privatization (both were introduced into Parliament in late 1988) was such that the organizations concerned were effectively forced to make tactical choices about where and how they would deploy the bulk of their campaigning effort. In the event, the community sector directed more of its attention to the Water Bill than to the contemporaneous passage of the electricity privatization legislation.

Figure 1.3 identifies the major community sector groups involved in the water privatization campaign; it also indicates the issues for which they took particular responsibility.

The general strategic position of the community sector organizations lobbying around the Water Bill was summed up by one of the NCC

Figure 1.3 Community sector involvement in the Water Bill.

- Association of Metropolitan Authorities Social Services group: charges, metering and disconnections
- National Association of Citizens Advice Bureaux: disconnections, billing and payment procedures, metering
- National Consumer Council: consumer representation, consumer protection, standards of performance
- Consumers' Association: price regulation, consumer representation and the regulators powers
- National Council for Voluntary Organizations: coordinating and parliamentary liaison function

campaigners as 'working for what you can win rather than what you want . . . realistically we had to focus on some pretty small areas' (interview, July 1989). In seeking to influence the legislation, the alliance focused primarily – but not exclusively – on the passage of the Bill through the House of Lords. This was argued on the grounds that:

> the huge majority of the Government in the House of Commons dictates everything and there is no real pressure on the Government in the Commons . . . the ethos in the House of Lords is different, it's a place where people still listen to debates and where votes can be won . . . although the Government can overturn this, it can cause embarrassment if they do so.
>
> Interview with AMA campaigner, September 1989

The issues identified by the coalition of community sector organizations as the major ones upon which to focus in their campaigning were:

1. Payment methods and disconnection.
2. Consumer representation.
3. Duties of Director General of Water Services.
4. Service standards and redress.

Each of these issues will be considered briefly in turn, including the response of the Government to the arguments raised by the coalition.

1. Payment methods and disconnection

The advent of metering trials in a number of areas throughout the country, in combination with the prohibition on charging for water according to rateable value after the year 2000 under section 80 of the Water Bill, raised fears that the newly privatized water companies would introduce the compulsory metering of domestic properties. Early data from the metering trials indicated that 'water bills for large families on low incomes, in low rateable value properties [were] increasing by as much as sevenfold' (Fimister 1989b). In addition, it was anticipated that the water companies would take up the power available to them in the legislation and directly pass on to domestic consumers the costs of meter installation (estimated at between £150 and £200 per property). Because of this, the community sector organizations proposed that a statutory requirement be placed 'on the water companies to offer consumers at least one option for paying for water which does not involve metering' (AMA Briefing to the House of Lords).

It was also suggested that, in light of the budgeting problems of low-income households arising from the traditional practice of the water authorities of levying charges in standard half-yearly or yearly cycles, that provision be made in the Bill for consumers to pay by more regular instalments. Also, that consumers be given a choice of a range of flexible payment options similar to those made available by the fuel utilities. In response, the Government gave no ground on the metering issue, but the Minister for Water and Planning indicated that he would encourage the water companies to adopt a more imaginative and customer-sensitive approach to water billing.

Disconnection from water supply was, relative to the standards of the fuel industries, a relatively rare occurrence. However, there was evidence that the level of water disconnection for debt had risen sharply over the years leading into privatization (amongst the regional water authorities from less than 2000 in 1981 to over 9000 in 1987–88). Concern about the prospect of increasing disconnections in an area with such acute personal and public health implications, was reinforced by the experience of gas privatization, where the level of disconnections had escalated between the period 1985 and 1988. As this was an area of fundamental importance to low-income consumers, as well as being one where a high degree of public and political sensitivity existed, the community sector alliance decided to put considerable effort into the issue of water disconnections.

A tactical decision was taken to present two distinct lines of argument: the first, carried by the AMA Social Services group, that the power to disconnect domestic customers for debt should be abolished, and the second, argued by NACAB and NCC, that disconnections for water debt should not be allowed to occur without recourse to county court action, and that this should be enshrined in a statutory code enforceable by the Director General of Water Services. An AMA campaigner in interview with the researcher (18/8/89) stated: 'We never thought we'd achieve our position but we hoped that in pushing our position that the NACAB line might win acceptance.'

As anticipated by the campaign members, the no disconnections argument was rejected by the Government. Lord Hesketh, Parliamentary Under-Secretary, Department of the Environment concluded, for example, that it was:

> advocating what amounts to a free water policy. In the experience of the water industry, a small minority of customers choose not to pay their water charges even after a county court order has been obtained . . . for

this minority the water undertakers must retain their right as a last resort to disconnect supply.

House of Lords, 18/5/89, col. 1300

However, earlier the Government in concert with the Water Authorities Association and the Water Companies Association, had produced a revised code of practice which specified that water disconnections for debt would not occur without reference to the county court, *except* for those customers who had previously appeared before the court for the recovery of water charges, or where a payment agreement between a customer and water company had been broken (irrespective of whether this had involved county court action or not). It was subsequently argued by the coalition, ultimately with success in the House of Lords, that the exemptions contained in the draft code excluded the very people most likely to be in need of a court assessment of their level of indebtedness and that it discriminated against consumers with multiple debts. In the same House of Lords debate where Lord Hesketh had rejected the call for an abolition of the power to disconnect, the Government indicated that it would remove the exemptions and that the code on disconnections would form part of the licence conditions [subsequently Licence Condition H] which would be enforceable by the Director General of Water Services. The changes effected in disconnection policy were generally perceived by members of the coalition as *the* major achievement of their Water Bill campaign.

2. Consumer representation

Consumer representation is . . . a partisan activity. Regulation and consumer advocacy, are not, therefore the same thing.

Consumers' Association (1989b: 9)

The ability of the new Customer Service Committees (CSCs) to represent the interests of domestic consumers effectively was directly challenged by the community sector coalition involved in the Water Bill campaign. Their discontent about the provisions for consumer representation fell under two broad headings, i.e. the absence of a national consumer forum equivalent to that established in the gas industry and concern that the CSCs were being set up in a way that would make them the creatures of the Director General of Water Services rather than being independent agents promoting the consumer interest. In the latter, it was argued *inter alia* (i) that the members of the CSCs should be appointed by the Secretary of State and not the Director General in order to ensure independence and public accountability, (ii) that the CSCs should have control over the appointment of their own staff and budgets, and not be beholden to the Director General for these essential resources, (iii) that the Director General should not hold 'censorship' powers over the reports of the CSCs, (iv) that they should be given the scope to advise agencies other than the Office of Water Services on matters of importance to consumers (such as the National Rivers Authority, the Monopolies and Mergers Commission and the European Commission), and (v) that provision should be made for representation of low-income and disabled consumers on the CSCs. The National Consumer Council encapsulated the coalition's position on the issue when it stated:

> We believe that the effectiveness of a CSC as a robust, independent consumer voice will be severely muted if it is unable to express its views independently of the Director General to, for example, the MMC and the European Commission . . . The Director General's role is to maintain a balance between the interests of the industry, the shareholders and consumers, and it would be entirely inappropriate for him to have editorial control over the publications of the CSCs.
> NCC Briefing, House of Lords, Report Stage of the Water Bill, June 1989

The Government rebutted the coalition's case by stating that those amendments aimed at increasing the autonomy of the CSCs 'would drive a wedge between the customer service committees and the director general' (Lord Hesketh, House of Lords, 15/5/89, col. 977) and by arguing that the nexus between the CSCs and the Director General actually enhanced the power of the former, as the 'committees carry that much more weight in their investigations of complaints through such an association. Any divorce between him and those committees would therefore weaken rather than strengthen them'.

Minor victories were achieved, however, in guaranteeing that the Director General would be obliged to set up CSCs in the first place (the 'may' in the original legislation was changed to 'shall'), that the CSCs role be broadened to include a general policy review function, and that their meetings be opened up to the public. But the unsatisfactory nature of these outcomes, for the organizations involved, is illustrated in the NCC's admission that:

> [we] have also failed to ensure that the CSCs are independent of the Office of Water Services. We must conclude that the government is determined to limit the effectiveness of the CSCs.
> NCC, House of Lords, Third Reading Briefing, June 1989

3. Duties of Director General of Water Services

The priority given to the duties of the Director General in the enabling legislation is of fundamental importance to the operation and scope of the regulatory regime. If his/her mandate for ensuring that the interests of consumers are protected, in relation to matters such as charging, debt and disconnection and service quality, is given equivalent status to those powers relating to the financial operation of the privatized utilities, then the Director General is in a position to arrive at a reasonable balance between the interests of the key stakeholders in the industries. In particular the regulator would have the ability to rule in favour of consumers or the 'public interest', even though this might conflict with, or bear negatively on, the interests of management and shareholders. If, however, the regulator is given superordinate responsibility for protecting the commercial interests of the privatized companies (representing a clear imperative to conclude in favour of shareholders and management when conflicts arise), the 'consumer watchdog' function is legally and operationally shackled as a consequence.

As shown earlier, in the Water Bill tabled in Parliament, the duties of the Director General were firmly prioritized, with the consumer protection function occupying a subsidiary position. However, in a widely-leaked unpublished draft of the Bill, provision had been made for the Director General to apply equal weight to the duties of consumer protection and advancing the interests of company shareholders.

During the passage of the Bill through the House of Commons Standing Committee, and later in the House of Lords, the National Consumer Council and the Consumers' Association argued vigorously against the apparent change in the Government's thinking on the duties of the regulator and pointed out the contradiction between the framing of these duties and the statement in the 1986 White Paper that '[the] Director General's principal duty will be to safeguard the interests of the customers' (HMSO 1986b: para. 57). In proposing an amendment in the House of Lords, aimed at balancing the duties of the regulator, in May 1989, the NCC expressed the core of the concern:

> If left unamended the companies will not be prevented from overcharging or providing a low standard of service, because the Director General will be required to put the profitability of the water and sewerage companies above the interests of the protection of consumers.
>
> NCC Briefing Paper on Amendment 77A, May 1989

In the debate on the amendment, tabled by the Labour peer Lord McIntosh of Haringey, the Government argued that the financial performance of the water companies and the interests of consumers were inherently interwoven:

> [if] a service cannot be properly carried out that is not in the interests of the consumer. The consumer is right up front . . . The creation of this dual framework is quite deliberate. It reflects the paramount importance for customers that companies are able to carry out their functions properly, and to do this they will need to be able to finance those functions and earn a return on capital. For that reason the duties in subsection (2) are a necessary precondition to the others. Similar, but not identical, structures are provided in the Gas and Telecommunications Acts and in the Electricity Bill.
>
> Earl of Caithness, House of Lords, 4/5/89, cols. 354 and 355

The amendment was subsequently withdrawn.

4. Service standards and redress

The arguments put by members of the community/consumer alliance in the general area of service standards and redress were (i) that the codes of practice needed to be enshrined in statute (based on the view that licence-based codes

of practice would be virtually unenforceable), (ii) that the Guaranteed Standards Scheme was substantially limited to 'administrative matters' and did not
cover key areas of service performance such as water quality and (iii) that an
effective complaints procedure was required. The alliance made little headway
on any of these issues, and on the major question of the legal status of the codes
of practice, the Government claimed that:

> [operating] through a licence condition provides more flexibility than
> would a statutory code, recognising the continuing role of the Director
> General in policing this and other aspects of the framework of regulation
> we are introducing . . . It is not, however, a soft option: an undertaker
> cannot be appointed unless he meets the requirements I have described.
> Letter from Michael Howard (Minister for Water and Planning) to
> Chris Patten, 20/1/89

Two other matters advocated by the community sector – unrelated to service
standards – but of importance to tenants, were more successful. The Director
General was given the power to set the maximum price for the resale of water
and the provision making tenants liable for water charges if they had not been
paid by the landlord was removed.

The privatization of the electricity supply industry

Background

> The privatisation of the electricity supply industry was both the biggest
> and most successful of all the Government's privatisations. It marked
> another major milestone in the remarkable Conservative programme of
> popular capitalism and private enterprise.
> Conservative Research Department (1991: 157)

If the sale of the water authorities was the Government's most controversial
privatization, the sale of the electricity supply industry (ESI) was its most
complex and troublesome. The scale of the Government's plans for the privatization of the ESI, announced in its White Paper, 'Privatising Electricity'
(HMSO 1988a) in February 1988, prescribed the most radical restructuring of a
utility industry to date, involving the vertical and horizontal separation of a
traditionally highly integrated industry.

The monolithic Central Electricity Generating Board (CEGB), responsible for electricity generation and transmission, was to be broken up into three
distinct parts. It was proposed that the generating infrastructure of the CEGB
be split between two new companies: GEN. 1 (later to become National
Power) with 70 per cent of generating capacity, and GEN. 2 (later PowerGen)
with 30 per cent of generating capacity. The decision to allocate the generating
resources (i.e. power stations) of the CEGB in this uneven fashion was premised on a recognition that the larger generating company would be required

to carry the liability of nuclear generation. The transmission network of the CEGB was to be established as a functionally and operationally separate entity, owned and managed conjointly, not by the generators, but by the regional electricity companies (National Grid Company). The 12 existing area electricity boards, responsible for the distribution and supply of electricity to end-users, were to be sold as 12 separate public limited companies. At the same time as the Government published its blueprint for the ESI in England and Wales, the Secretary of State for Scotland announced that electricity in Scotland would also be privatized. But in contrast to the proposed ESI structure south of the border, the Scottish industry was to be sold as two vertically integrated companies, with generation, transmission, distribution and supply functions intact (Scottish Hydro-Electric and Scottish Power). This scenario for the future of the ESI in Britain was formalized with the tabling of the Electricity Bill in the House of Commons in December 1988.

In comparison with the earlier utility privatization legislation, the Electricity Bill made provision for the introduction of an unprecedented level of competition. The two non-natural monopoly dimensions of the electricity industry – generation and supply – were to be exposed to full competition over the medium term. New entrants to electricity generation and supply were to be encouraged through the granting of operating licences, and through the opening up of the common carriage networks to 'second tier' operators. The purchasing of electricity from the generators was to occur through a form of electricity spot market, known as the Pool (and run by a subsidiary of National Grid Company). It was believed that the combined impact of these structural changes would result in a more efficient ESI, supplying electricity at a lower cost to consumers. However, because the Regional Electricity Companies (RECs) were allowed to retain their monopoly franchise for supply to users of medium and small quantities of electricity until 1994 and 1998 respectively, the gains accruing from this new competitive structure would initially be directed mainly to large industrial and commercial users of electricity. Yet even so, the small user stood to gain some benefit from the lower costs of purchasing wholesale electricity in this new competitive market, if the newly competitive generation market functioned effectively and if the savings made by the RECs in purchasing electricity were actually passed on to consumers.

But within this quasi-competitive framework, the legislation and draft licences contained some distinctly non-competitive features. These included the limitations placed on the generating companies' ability to enter the supply market (limited to an average of 15 per cent of demand for the first four years and 25 per cent for the four years thereafter) and conversely, the limits applied to the amount of generation activity that the RECs could undertake (15 per cent of total capacity).

Most controversial of all the competitive constraints, however, was the requirement that the RECs purchase a proportion of their electricity from nuclear sources until 1998, under the Non-Fossil Fuel Orders, and the provision that the extra costs associated with purchasing nuclear power be retrieved through the application of a so-called fossil fuel levy on electricity prices. The level of the levy set by the Secretary of State for Energy at the time of privatization was 10.6 per cent. In justifying this premium on electricity prices – estimated to be about 3 p per kilowatt-hour (House of Commons Energy Committee 1992a) – to subsidize the nuclear industry, the Secretary of State for Energy, Cecil Parkinson, argued that:

> The consumer will pay no increased costs beyond those he would have paid under the existing structure. Our proposals will simply identify costs which had previously remained hidden. The fact that these costs will be identified does not mean that there will be an increase. It simply means that they will be identified and subject to scrutiny, not rolled up in the bulk supply as at present.
>
> House of Commons, 12/12/88, col. 686

Irrespective of whether Parkinson's argument held any weight or not, the institutionalization of this level of cross-subsidy to one sector of the industry was a highly ironical outcome for a programme designed to create a competitive electricity supply market and ostensibly operating according to economic pricing principles.

The Government was to face an even deeper irony after the Electricity Act 1989 was given Royal Assent. The Conservative Party's long-standing commitment to the development of Britain's nuclear power industry had been reinforced by the industry's contribution to the defeat of the Coal Miners' Strike in 1984–85. In the run-up to privatization, a number of economic and energy commentators (for example, Helm 1987, 1988b; Bunn and Vlahos 1988; Vickers and Yarrow 1988) questioned the CEGB's calculations of the cost of nuclear power and identified some of the possible problems that might be encountered in any attempt to sell the nuclear generation sector in the marketplace.

Seemingly oblivious to this mounting critique of nuclear power as a saleable commodity, the Government held to its belief that the sector could be sold, as long as it was bundled with the major generating company (National Power) and if a sufficient level of public subsidy could be guaranteed to partially underwrite the massive decommissioning costs of the nuclear industry. But finally the increasingly close analysis of the economics of nuclear power by the City, in the summer and autumn of 1989, forced the Government first to withdraw the ageing Magnox stations from the sale and ultimately, in November, to withdraw nuclear power completely. The irony of the capital market dealing a body blow to the Government's favourite energy sector was further compounded by the associated announcement that the nuclear sector, unfit for private consumption, would be retained in public ownership, under the guise of Nuclear Electric and Scottish Nuclear.

The consequential change to the original blueprint for electricity restructuring resulted in three generators in England and Wales (National Power with 50.2 per cent of net capacity, PowerGen with 32 per cent and Nuclear Electric with 14.2 per cent) and three in Scotland (with the addition of Scottish Nuclear). In hindsight, the exclusion of the 'nuclear burden' from the privatization

Figure 1.4   Key events in the privatization of the electricity supply industry.

May 1987:	Commitment to privatize the electricity supply industry (ESI) contained in Conservative Party election manifesto
Feb 1988:	White Papers 'Privatising Electricity' and 'Privatisation of the Scottish Electricity Industry' published
May 1988:	Public Utility Transfers and Water Charges Act enacted empowering electricity boards and Electricity Council to transfer property to other bodies corporate
Dec 1988:	Second Reading of Electricity Bill in House of Commons
Apr 1989:	Second Reading of Electricity Bill in House of Lords
Jul 1989:	Electricity Act 1989 enacted
Sep 1989:	Director General of Electricity Supply appointed
Nov 1989:	Withdrawal of nuclear generation from the ESI sale programme and creation of Nuclear Electric and Scottish Nuclear
Mar 1990:	Transfer of Central Electricity Generating Board and Area Board assets to successor companies Licences come into effect
Dec 1990:	Sale of the 12 Regional Electricity Companies (and National Grid)
Mar 1991:	Sale of National Power and PowerGen (60 per cent of shares)
Jun 1991:	Sale of Scottish Power and Scottish Hydro-Electric

equation at the outset would have given the Government far greater scope for breaking up the generating sector into smaller units. This, rather like the privatization of British Gas, is now viewed as an opportunity lost:

> When the CEGB was abolished, the opportunity to divide its existing stations among more than three successor companies was missed, and so greater competition can now only come about through new companies building new stations or the two main generators selling stations.
>
> House of Commons Energy Committee (1992a: s. 38)

The Government experienced other problems along the way, such as the 'on again, off again' and finally aborted, trade sale of PowerGen to Hanson Holdings during the summer of 1990, and the Iraq crisis (with its reverberating effect on the stock market); but despite extending the timetable for the sale of the RECs by six months, the Government completed the entire sale of the ESI in Britain by June 1991. Figure 1.4 summarizes the major events in the sale.

Regulatory framework

Given the complex structure of the ESI, it is hardly surprising that the system of regulation introduced under the Electricity Act 1989 was also likely to be characterized by a degree of complexity. The Director General of Electricity Supply was given substantial economic regulation powers in those domains of the ESI where natural monopoly elements prevail, i.e. transmission, distribution and, for the sub-1 MW market, supply. His powers in relation to generation and the Pool – where competition theoretically prevails – are somewhat more oblique. Discussion in this section will concentrate primarily on those areas of regulation most immediately affecting the interests of domestic consumers.

As in the other regulated utilities, the ubiquitous RPI – X price control formula was introduced as the central mechanism for economic regulation of the ESI. With a measure of poetic justice perhaps, the inventor of the device, Professor Stephen Littlechild, was appointed Director General of Electricity Supply, with responsibility for making it work. The price formula, with different constituent elements, was applied to the areas of transmission charges, distribution charges and supply charges to sub-1 MW consumers. Wholesale electricity purchasing charges were not subjected to price control, as these are notionally regulated by the law of supply and demand through the Pool, although in reality most wholesale purchasing actually occurs outside the Pool under 'contract for differences' or through direct sales arrangements.

The complicated array of pricing prescriptions built into the operation of the privatized ESI were additionally compounded by the introduction, under Condition 3C of the Supply Licence, of a 'supplementary' supply charge for the sub-1 MW sector, operable up to April 1993. The 'supplementary' price cap was devised with the aim of limiting electricity tariff increases to the rate of inflation, and was inserted by the Secretary of State for Energy following political anxiety about the movement in prices in the early years after privatization. The X factor for transmission and supply charges was set at zero (i.e. without an efficiency saving), and for distribution charges it was set for each of the RECs, across a range from zero to *plus* 2.5 per cent (with an average of 1.3 per cent).

The duty of the Director General of Electricity Supply to protect the interests of consumers was accorded, consistent with the other regulators, secondary status:

> A curiosity of the regulatory system is that among the Director General's three primary duties is the duty 'to secure that licence holders are able to finance the carrying on of their activities which they are authorised by their licences to carry on' . . . whereas his duty 'to protect the interests of consumers of electricity' is only a subsidiary duty to be exercised subject to the primary duties. This is a strange way of ensuring that 'the customer, not the producer or distributor, comes first, which was one of the principal declared aims of electricity privatisation.
>
> House of Commons Energy Committee (1992a: s. 134)

His duties with respect to the generality of consumers was supplemented with specific duties to protect the interests of electricity consumers in rural areas and the disabled and pensioners.

Amongst the repertoire of powers given to the Director General was the ability to set overall standards of performance and standards of performance in individual cases (Guaranteed Standards of Performance) for the RECs. The Director General was also given a number of additional powers, which his regulatory colleagues originally did not have. These included the power to determine disputes and to make orders for the settlement of disputes carrying the weight of a county court judgment and wider information collection and publication powers.

A similar model of consumer representation to that in the water industry was introduced, i.e. regional Consumers' Committees under the jurisdiction of the Director General. This was later supplemented by an amendment to the original Bill providing for the convening of a National Consumers' Consultative Committee, chaired by the Director General and composed of the chairmen of the Consumers' Committees. Under the amendment the national committee was given a potentially wide-ranging brief, 'to keep under review matters affecting the interests of consumers of electricity generally' (s. 53 (2)(a) Electricity Act 1989) and was required to meet at least four times each year. This amendment was achieved largely as a result of the successful advocacy of the National Consumer Council.

Community sector campaign

The community and consumer sector's endeavour to influence the passage of the electricity privatization legislation did not really gather pace until the Electricity Bill was debated in the House of Lords. Nor did it have the same sense of united purpose that characterized the water campaign. The focus on the House of Lords seems to have had less to do with strategic considerations and more to do with the fact that during the passage of the legislation through the Commons the overstretched resources of the sector were almost exclusively focused on the Water Bill. In addition, a fallacious assumption was made that the Electricity Consumers Council (ECC) would make much of the running on the Bill. The passivity of the ECC in the campaign, as well as its failure to support the continuation of a national structure of electricity consumer representation post-privatization (see below), was for some activists one of the most disappointing aspects of the campaign. In an interview with electricity privatization campaigners, July 1989, it was stated that:

> . . . the ECC just sat there and watched . . . their silence was deafening . . . their leadership took a different view of regulation to us. The chairman believed that it is basically a technical activity and therefore there is no need for consumer regulation.

During the passage of the Bill through the House of Lords, organizations such as the National Right to Fuel Campaign, the National Consumer Council, Age Concern, Winter Action on Cold Homes, NACAB, and the Association for the Conservation of Energy, concentrated on a set of issues not dissimilar to

those at the forefront of earlier lobbying: disconnection, consumer representation, standards of performance and energy efficiency.

Much of the sting had been taken out of the disconnection issue by the
alacrity with which the Government 'imported' into the regulatory framework
of the ESI, the Condition 12A modification to British Gas' authorization by
OFGAS earlier in the year. Under the terms of this modification, British Gas
was obliged, prior to taking disconnection action, to offer consumers in default
a pre-payment meter 'where safe and practical to do so'. When the Government disclosed that it intended inserting a similar provision into the supply
licences of the RECs (later to become licence Condition 19),
the community sector countered with the argument that while the OFGAS
measure represented a considerable advance, it did not go far enough.

In order for this protection to apply, the utility company needed to make
contact with the defaulting consumer. And evidence from British Gas was
already showing that thousands of consumers were still being disconnected
because of failure to make contact with the customer in default (described as
the 'no contact' problem). The alternative, in the view of the NCC and the
National Right to Fuel Campaign was to place the RECs under an obligation
to supply, but not necessarily on credit terms. In order for this to be commercially workable, the two organizations proposed what amounted to a policy of
compulsorily installing pre-payment meters for consumers in debt. It was suggested that if a customer defaulted on payment, the electricity companies
should be required to install a pre-payment meter, whether contact had been
made with the consumer or not. The Government, with some justification,
rejected this approach on the grounds that the imposition of a pre-payment
meter without regard to the wishes of the consumer would represent a severe
invasion of privacy. The NCC responded that it did 'not think that installation
of pre-payment meters as an alternative to disconnection is an invasion of
customer privacy, indeed it could be the only means by which a customer
retains access to an essential supply' (NCC, House of Lords, Report Stage
Briefing, June 1989: 4). The Government remained unconvinced.

The well-trammelled ground over the arguments for a national independent consumer body was traversed again, but with only slightly greater success
than in the water campaign. The decision by the Electricity Consumers Council to abolish itself ahead of the enabling legislation, weakened the case for the
establishment of a national body of electricity consumers. The NCC was
successful, however, in having the inferior fallback provision on the formation
of an *ad hoc* National Consumers' Consultative Committee added to the Bill.

In welcoming the power of the regulator to set guaranteed standards of
performance, the campaigning organizations argued that the proposed areas to
be covered by the scheme were too limited, in that they did not cover many of
the areas of service delivery most germane to domestic consumers. In order to
give some real teeth to the concept of quality regulation, it was suggested that a
system of financial penalties or some form of price formula adjustment should
be available to the regulator for breaches in the overall performance standards.

Neither of these matters gained Government support at the time, but they have been pursued, in part, by the regulator in more recent times.

The amendments on energy efficiency, particularly that promoted by the Association for the Conservation of Energy (ACE), came closest to giving the sector a major victory in the electricity privatization legislative process. As in the case of gas, the price control formula provided in-built incentives for the companies to maximize the sale of electricity and contained no off-setting mechanism for promoting energy-efficient practice. Using research on the American experience of regulation, ACE proposed that a US-like clause on 'least-cost planning' be inserted in the Bill. This would have forced the companies to explore the cost-benefit of energy efficiency alternatives to capital investment in new generating capacity and would have empowered the Director General to penalize companies through the price control formula if they failed to do so. The amendment was successfully negotiated through the House of Lords despite the fact that it was 'technically deficient', as the regulator 'did not have the power to give capital investment approval and so could not refuse it' (Roberts et al. 1991: 77). But it was rejected by the Government when the Bill returned to the House of Commons. In lieu of the original amendment, the Government added the rather nebulous clause that the Director General:

> determine such standards of performance in connection with the promotion of the efficient use of electricity by consumers as, in his opinion, ought to be achieved by . . . suppliers.
>
> s. 41 Electricity Act 1989

This effectively gave the regulator an energy efficiency promotion function, but without the complementary enforcement power to back it up. In the view of a leading advocate of the amendment, its defeat reflected 'the power of the vested interests and industries supporting the anti-conservation status quo', whereas another campaigner, less closely associated with the amendment described its flawed drafting as 'an absolute disaster'.

Conclusion

From this account it can be seen that the Government introduced a number of structural changes to the model of utility privatization over the course of the programme. This is illustrated most distinctly in the juxtaposition of the complex, disaggregated model of the ESI with the unitary model of British Gas. Yet from the perspective of the domestic consumer, for all the competition-oriented refinements introduced between the privatization of British Gas and the privatization of the electricity supply industry, the broad statutory and organizational framework for the three utilities was substantially similar, notwithstanding the incremental modifications made to the regulatory regime over this period.

It is clear from an analysis of the three community sector campaigns, that although some successes were achieved, most of these were of a relatively minor nature. On the major issues – such as those concerning the priority to be accorded to the interests of ordinary consumers in the regulatory system, the balance between equity, service quality and company profitability considerations, and the ability of domestic consumers to achieve a strong independent voice – the community sector campaigns had a limited impact. At least at the time. Against this backdrop it is difficult to contest the conclusion drawn by the organization that played a leading part in the three campaigns – the National Consumer Council – that while 'the interests of consumers have been given increasing emphasis as the programme has progressed, the overall impression is that they have largely been treated as a residual of other policy considerations' (NCC 1989a: 18).

The community sector was not alone in its impotence, of course. One of the more striking aspects of the history of the Government's utility privatization programme is the way that it emerged from the legislative process almost completely unscathed. But then given the Government's resolve to complete the project, its parliamentary dominance, over the period 1986 to 1991, and the powerful coalition of utility industry and City interests supporting the

Table 1.1   The structure of public utility privatization in Britain.

Providers	Regulators*	Consumer representation
1. *Gas (Dec 1986)*		
British Gas plc	Office of Gas Supply	Gas Consumers Council (central and regional)
2. *Water (Dec 1989)*		
10 Water and sewerage companies 23 Water only companies (England and Wales only)	Office of Water Services National Rivers Authority HM Inspectorate of Pollution Drinking Water Inspectorate	Regional Customer Service Committees
3. *Electricity (Dec 1990–Jun 1991)*		
Generating companies National Power, PowerGen and two publicly-owned nuclear electricity companies National Grid (transmission) 12 distribution companies and two integrated companies in Scotland	Office of Electricity – Regulation	Regional Consumer Committees

* Non-ministerial government departments, financed through utility companies' licence fees.

original terms of the privatization settlement, this is neither particularly surprising nor inexplicable. Following Hill et al. (1989), the process of privatizing the three utilities could be seen as an expression of 'élite policy-making'.

Despite being substantially unsuccessful during the passage of the utility privatization legislation, the community sector campaigns have been largely vindicated over time. Many of the issues raised before an unreceptive political audience in 1986 and 1988–89 have become residual and recurring themes and problems in the regulation of the public utilities ever since, as later chapters reveal.

The organizational structure established through the three pieces of primary legislation is illustrated diagrammatically in Table 1.1.

2

Public utility services, public policy and regulation

Introduction

The commercial character of energy and water services has been given increased emphasis and impetus in Western economies over recent years. Although the ascendancy of commercial objectives over social objectives has long been a feature of the organization and management of public utilities in Britain and elsewhere, the commercialization of public utilities could be seen to have reached its apotheosis in the privatization programme of the British Conservative Government from 1984. Measures by governments in other countries to liberalize and 'corporatize' the utility industries are similarly premised on a driving belief in the incontestable dominance of commercial considerations in public utility practice.

The emergence of a highly economistic formulation of public utility practice has been paralleled by the promotion of the view that public utility services are, first and foremost, commodities that can and should be traded like any other product in the market economy. Directly or indirectly, this 'commodification' of utility services, has had a substantial impact on ideas about the most appropriate way to organize and manage the industries concerned. It has also had a decisive impact on the long-standing debate about the scope of public utility responsibility for 'non-commercial' objectives and activities, particularly those in the area of social policy.

Under the conceptualization of public utility services as 'merely another set of commodities', there is ostensibly little justification, in market economies, for the industries concerned to be owned and managed outside the private sector, or, at an absolute minimum, to be insulated from the disciplines and efficiency criteria of the private market. The belief in the unrivalled facility of the market to act as a mechanism for commodity production, distribution and consumption – much invoked by New Right ideologues over the past 15 years or so – has been lent additional credibility by the dissolution of command economies in the late twentieth century.

Most significantly, the commodity view of utility services predetermines the scope of producer/supplier responsibility *vis-à-vis* their consumers. If utility services are of the same fundamental character as the array of products purchased by customers in the conventional market place, it follows that the suppliers of these services have no more, nor less responsibility for customer care than is applicable in the market place generally. This requires the operation of a customer service regime, expressive of the principles and statutory obligations of fair trading, and the use of customer relations approaches (including possibly, the promotion of access to supply for groups such as the elderly and disabled) essentially designed to gain commercial advantage over competing firms or industries. It certainly does not require – and indeed usually proscribes – that attention be given by the utility industries to access, equity and distributional impacts as they affect different classes of consumers. These considerations are seen to fall exclusively within the policy domain of government, as is deemed to be the case with other essential commodities, like housing, clothing and food.

Yet can energy and water services reasonably be viewed as commodities like any other? Do they have internal and external properties that differentiate them from other goods and services traded in the general market place? And if they are more than 'mere commodities', what are the broad implications of this for public policy? These are the questions that form the substance of the first part of this chapter.

The introduction of a regulatory system is an explicit public policy response to the unique composite of social and economic characteristics that differentiate public utilities from other industries in the economy. Public regulation is required in order to offset the limitations of applying conventional market principles and market processes to the utility sector and in order to provide protection for ordinary consumers. In the second half of the chapter, the framework of public regulation introduced for the privatized gas, electricity and water industries in Britain, is critically examined.

The social and economic characteristics of public utility services

The essentialness of utility services

Universal access to clean water and safe and reliable supplies of energy is generally recognized as one of the fundamental quality-of-life benchmarks in late twentieth century society. Water and energy represent two of the vital ingredients in the physical and social infrastructure of all contemporary

Figure 2.1   Public perceptions of the importance of public utility services.

Public utility-related services occupied primary places on the list of publicly-defined necessities derived from MORI surveys undertaken as part of the 'Breadline Britain' series in 1983 and 1990. The top five standard of living items (with percentage of survey sample classing them as necessities) were:

	1983	1990
Heating to warm living areas of the home during cold weather	97%	97%
Indoor toilet (not shared with another household)	96%	97%
Damp-free home	96%	98%
Bath (not shared with another household)	94%	95%
Beds for everyone in the household	94%	95%

Other utility-related items also rated highly as necessities (1983 figure first, followed by 1990 figure): refrigerator (77%; 92%), washing machine (67%; 73%), television (51%; 58%) and telephone (43%; 56%). (Mack and Lansley 1985: 54; Frayman 1991: 4.)

A European Commission study on the *Perception of Poverty* in 1989 (Commission of the European Communities 1990: 10), found that across the 12 member states, 94 per cent of the sample of people interviewed rated 'having running water, electricity and one's indoor toilet' as 'absolutely necessary'; 71 per cent of people also rated 'having basic equipment such as refrigerator or television set' as 'absolutely necessary'.

societies, albeit that in many developing nations, this infrastructure is still in an appallingly rudimentary form.

At an individual and household level, water and fuel (for lighting, cooking and warmth), occupy a status similar to that of food and shelter, i.e. they are literally necessary for sustaining life. Because of their centrality to individual and collective well-being, water and energy are usually defined as essential services and as 'basic necessities'. This is illustrated in Figure 2.1.

Associated with the essentialness of water and energy services is the fact that they are, in many instances non-substitutable; that is, there is a real or practical absence of alternative means for meeting water and energy-related needs. This is most clearly evident, in the substantive sense, in the area of water services, where there are no realistic and hygienic alternatives to running water for meeting the requirements of household washing, cleaning, food preparation and disposal of human waste. The possibilities for product substitution are greater in domestic energy use, because of the product rivalry that exists within the energy market in areas like space and water heating and for the running of certain appliances. However, for a large number of households the prospect of substituting gas for electricity – or vice versa – as the fuel source of heating or cooking, is foreclosed, in a practical sense, due to the high conversion costs involved (e.g. the purchase and fitting of new appliances, multiple supply charges, etc.). In the case of lighting and for appliances other than those used for heating and cooking, there are presently no technically or socially viable substitutes for electricity.

The composite of essentialness and non-substitutability in water and energy, clearly differentiates them from most other consumption goods traded and purchased in the orthodox market place. Because of the product character of water and energy, the scope for individuals to exercise purchasing choice amongst an array of similar commodity alternatives (as in the case of food, for instance) is highly circumscribed. This has the consequential effect of creating formidable barriers to the realization of consumer sovereignty, for as Hood (1986: 173) concludes, 'these pressures in practice get weaker the more practically indispensable the service is to the ordinary consumer'.

The centrality of water and energy services in the everyday lives of individual households is paralleled by the strategic position that the utility industries occupy in the economy as a whole. The 'lifeblood' products of electricity, gas and water run through the veins of the entire economy and form an integral part of the foundation for economic, physical and social development. Investment decisions in these primary areas of infrastructure have wide-ranging 'knock-on' effects across other sectors of the economy.

The provision of core physical services, in the form of water and energy infrastructure, is an essential precursor to, and catalyst for, residential and industrial development. Decisions about the timing and location of these services predetermines the pace and direction of urban growth. They also interact directly with the issues of territorial and intergenerational equity. Investment in the capital infrastructure required to supply water and energy to new or remote communities may be inordinately low, or alternatively, may result in the setting of disproportionately high access charges for individual consumers, if left to market forces alone. An additional complication of releasing the levers of public control over infrastructure planning and development is that private water services companies could potentially exploit the strategic power of the industry, in respect to land use and development, for their own commercial advantage.

The fundamental place that water and energy services occupy in the structure of daily life – on an individual and societal level – has been expressed using the concept of merit goods. Merit goods as defined by Musgrave and Musgrave (1984: 78), who originally enunciated the term, are those goods 'the provision of which, society (as distinct from the preferences of the individual consumer) wishes to encourage or, in the case of demerit goods, to deter'. Beckerman (1986: 17) adds that they 'are goods that, on basically ethical grounds, society believes should be supplied to – and where appropriate actually consumed by – everybody, perhaps only to certain minimum levels, whether they like it or not and whether they can pay for it or not'.

Describing certain areas of individual and household consumption as merit goods is more than simply an exercise in economic taxonomy. For the attribution of merit goods status connotes a sense of public priority, and brings with it an overlay of public policy attention and intervention, in particular, the need for action to overcome information failure, imperfect knowledge and underconsumption. Beckerman (1986) captures the policy dimension of merit goods when he states:

> Once 'merit' goods are admitted into the proper sphere of public policy it is obviously easy to show that most of them will not be consumed to socially optimal levels unless they are provided or financed or subsidised by the public authorities in one way or another, or made the subject of mandatory legislation.
>
> Beckerman (1986: 17)

In addition, some areas of the utility industry activity fall within the realm of public goods in the classical economic sense. Examples of public goods would include, the provision of water for public fire protection and the recreational use of water authority reservoirs and open space. As with public goods generally, conventional market principles – and in particular the price mechanism – cannot be applied to these activities as a means of limiting entry and charging for service use.

Inelasticity of demand for utility services

The theory of the market, as a mechanism for commodity production and exchange, is predicated on two central operating principles. The first principle maintains that there is a strong and continuous nexus between the demand for a particular good and its price. Therefore if price moves, in either an upwards or downwards direction, demand will respond in an obverse manner (price elasticity of demand). The second principle holds that the demand for a particular good changes in line with income. Hence the higher a household's income the more a particular good will be consumed. Or alternatively, the higher the income the more consumption of basic goods will be supplemented by the consumption of luxury goods (income elasticity of demand). If, however, for particular classes of goods and services, the interaction between demand and price, or demand and income, is low or ambiguous, then the capacity of the self-adjusting *deus ex machina* of the market system to achieve equilibrium (or the matching of supply and demand), will be seriously retarded.

The essential and relatively non-substitutable nature of water and energy services suggests *a priori* that the association between level of demand and price or income, in the domestic sector at least, will be weak. For, irrespective of how low a household's income may be, or regardless of price increases, a reasonably constant level of demand for water and energy services is likely to exist, as this is necessary for physical and social well-being. Similarly, although the level of demand may rise with an increase in income or a decrease in price, it is unlikely to do so in direct proportion to changes in income or price, nor is it likely to continue to rise indefinitely beyond the point where the need for these basic services is satisfied. In these respects then, water and energy exhibit the properties of inelastic demand.

The income inelasticity of demand for energy has been well documented by researchers such as, Bradshaw and Harris (1983), Dilnot and Helm (1987), Micklewright (1988), Johnson et al. (1990), Boardman (1991a), Hutton and Hardman (1992) and Brechling and Smith (1992). In contrast, the income and price inelasticity of water services has received much less research attention. An explanation for this lack of research interest might lie in the fact that until recent years, water tariffs represented an almost insignificant element in the budgets of most households. Also the absence historically of volume-related charging systems in the domestic water sector in Britain has complicated the task of calculating water elasticity of demand.

Consumption and expenditure studies have consistently underlined two central themes in the structure of domestic fuel demand: (i) that fuel expenditure represents a far greater proportion of low-income household budgets than it does in the budgets of higher income groups, and (ii) that although household expenditure on fuel generally rises with income, it does so at a proportionately lower rate than for most other commodities, and for expenditure generally:

> The elasticities confirm the results of other studies of household energy demand that domestic fuel has the demand characteristics of a 'necessity' – in other words, a 1 per cent change in income will result in less than a 1 per cent change in domestic fuel use. The income elasticity is especially low for private renters and pensioner households.
>
> Brechling and Smith (1992: 38)

Expenditure data from the 1990 Family Expenditure Survey shows that the lowest income quintile spent an average of £8.62 per week on fuel, which represented 10.5 per cent of total household expenditure, whereas the highest income quintile spent £14.05 per week, which was 3.1 per cent of total household expenditure. Yet significantly, while fuel expenditure amongst the highest income group was 63 per cent higher than that of the lowest income group, expenditure across all commodity areas as a whole was 446 per cent higher. Figure 2.2 illustrates the way that fuel demand – as expressed through expenditure – differs from demand for other commodities generally, as household income increases.

The income inelasticity of demand for fuel can also be seen when a comparison is made between expenditure on fuel and expenditure on other goods and services. Table 2.1 based on data from the 1990 Family Expenditure Survey, juxtaposes the change (from the bottom to the top quintile) in fuel expenditure with changes in expenditure in other major commodity areas, excluding housing. It can be seen that, with the exception of tobacco, expenditure on fuel stands out as being by far the least responsive to changes in income.

Figure 2.2   Income elasticity of demand for fuel.

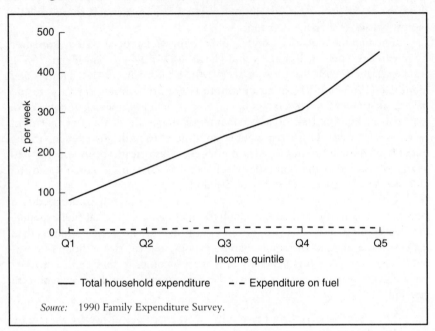

Source: 1990 Family Expenditure Survey.

The implications of the finding that fuel expenditure forms a dispropor-tionately high component of low-income household budgets, and that fuel demand is relatively inelastic, are at least twofold. First, it underlines the status of energy services as 'basic social primary goods' (Helm and Yarrow: 1988) – 'primary' in the sense that a discernible minima (or core level) of demand is apparent, irrespective of income or objective capacity to pay, and 'basic' in the sense that growth in demand for fuel rises at a far lower rate than virtually every other area of household consumption, as income increases. Second and most importantly, it highlights the distributionally sensitive nature of energy policy and practice. Helm et al. (1988a: 43–44) draw attention to this when they state that as 'energy comprises a substantial proportion of the household budgets of the poor, the pricing policy of the energy utilities is likely to have a consider-able impact on poverty'.

The primary place that energy consumption occupies in most households also effects the extent to which price elasticity of demand exists in this sector of the market. As a result of its physiological and ascribed importance to individual well-being, domestic consumers are, in effect, locked into particular patterns and levels of demand. The broad parameters of this demand are likely to fixed, regardless of movements in price. The generally fixed character of domestic energy consump-tion was illustrated in the Department of the Environment's qualitative study on *Attitudes to Energy Conservation in the Home* (DoE 1991a: 86):

Table 2.1 Differences in household expenditure on major commodities: Average weekly household expenditure increase in expenditure between 1st and 5th income quintile groups.

Commodity/service group	Percentage increase
Fuel	63%
Food	241%
Alcohol	666%
Tobacco	65%
Clothing and footwear	727%
Household goods	519%
Household services	432%
Personal goods and services	563%
Motoring expenditure	1692%
Fares and other travel costs	554%
Leisure goods	667%
Leisure services	1103%
Miscellaneous	674%
Total expenditure	446%

Source: Central Statistical Office (1991a) table 6.

Most saw the scope for making savings as fairly small, whether by cutting down what they use or by becoming more efficient. They felt that a more than marginal reduction in spending would eat into their comfort or change their lifestyle in unacceptable ways. Many would compensate for a fuel cost increase by cutting back on other areas of spending, rather than by cutting fuel use itself.

Nevertheless, there is likely to be some scope for reducing household demand in the face of extreme price pressure, through for instance, moderating appliance use and introducing more efficient heating systems. However, the margin for reducing demand will generally be far smaller amongst low-income households, either because the minima of energy demand has already been reached or because of an inability to access the capital required to institute appropriate energy efficiency measures (DoE 1991a,b).

The existence and influence of income and price inelasticities in water services is less well known in Britain in particular. However, as suggested earlier, because they share many of the properties of energy services – with an even more substantive claim to essentialness – a strong *a priori* argument could be made that similar inelasticities will apply.

The dominant system of charging for domestic water and sewerage use (i.e. standard charges based on rateable value of property) and the absence of data on household water consumption, have not provided the requisite preconditions for calculating elasticity of demand. However, in recent years, as a result of the introduction of domestic metering trials throughout selected areas

Figure 2.3   Relationship between water charges and demand.

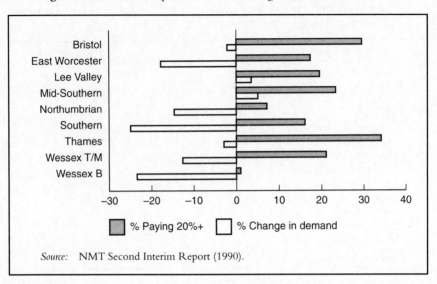

Source: NMT Second Interim Report (1990).

of England in 1989, some very rudimentary information on water elasticity is becoming available. Preliminary evidence from the metering trials indicates, that although domestic consumer demand for water may be influenced – at the margin – by price, the overall relationship between demand and price is generally an inelastic one. This is reflected in Figure 2.3 which is based on data from nine of the twelve trial areas where comparable figures were available. Figure 2.3 compares the proportion of domestic consumers paying over 20 per cent more for their water, with changes in demand. It shows, in the metering trials at least, that there is generally an indirect and imprecise relationship between price and demand, in water consumption, with the overall picture portraying a distinctly inelastic complexion.

The emerging data on elasticity of domestic water demand in Britain is broadly consistent with that from countries elsewhere (OECD 1987; Paterson 1987; Mann 1989; MMBW 1991), which shows that although there appears to be a relationship between prices and demand, the nature of this relationship is relatively weak and indirect compared to the 'price elasticity' of commodities generally. It also suggests that very considerable increases in tariffs (even to a greater extent than for energy) will be required, if reductions in domestic water consumption are to be sustained over the longer term.

The price inelasticity of demand characteristics of energy and water has potentially serious ramifications for domestic consumers generally, and low-income consumers in particular. Because many domestic consumers are effectively 'captive' to an established level of energy and water consumption (determined by factors such as condition of housing, type and efficiency of appliances, amount of reserve capital for undertaking modifications aimed at improving consumption efficiency, family size, and medical conditions), their ability to respond to price increases in conventional consumerist ways, by for example reducing consumption or finding substitute products, will inevitably be constrained. And as expenditure on these essential services is a more substantial part of the budgets of low-income households, price increases will have a regressive impact:

> . . . to the extent that demand elasticities are lower among lower income groups, the poor may end up paying higher prices and the resulting distributional consequences might be judged unsatisfactory. Generally, it is not obvious that charging more to precisely those customers who have the least opportunity to substitute out of the given good or service is a desirable outcome.
>
> Helm and Yarrow (1988: iv)

At a more general level, in a commercial environment where the capacity of domestic consumers to respond to price signals is limited, the utility industries – particularly when backed by the power of monopoly supply – will have formidable leverage. This could result in the introduction of tariffs for the domestic sector well in excess of those necessary to meet marginal cost requirements, with virtual impunity. There is also the danger that charges levied in the price inelastic sector of the market (i.e. domestic consumers) may be artificially inflated in order to enable lower prices to be set in more competitive, price elastic sectors (indeed this is given economic sanction under so-called *Ramsey pricing principles*). In many instances, commercial and industrial enterprises have considerably greater room for manoeuvre in terms of energy consumption (i.e. in aggregate level, form of energy used and time of use), particularly over the longer term, than is generally the case with domestic consumers. Hence the motivation exists for energy utilities to adopt a more 'creative' marketing strategy with the non-tariff sector, possibly at the direct expense of domestic consumers through some form of cost cross-subsidization.

Natural monopoly

The water and energy industries have been traditionally classified as natural monopolies. The natural monopoly features of energy and water services, with the corollaries of single firm dominance and an absence of competition, has often formed the substance for arguing that these public utilities should operate within a framework of public ownership. But the basis for classifying electricity, gas and water services as natural monopolies is neither clear-cut nor without its problems.

The case for defining utility services, like water and energy, as natural monopoly services has been predominately an economic one. Sharkey (1982: 54), in one of the most influential recent works on the subject, enunciates the core of the economic basis of natural monopoly, when he states:

> . . . there is natural monopoly in a particular market if and only if a single firm can produce the desired output at lower cost than any combination of two or more firms. Natural monopoly is defined in terms of a single firm's efficiency relative to the efficiency of other combinations of firms in the industry.

However, as the privatization programme of the British Government over the last decade has illustrated, the designation of areas of production and supply as natural monopolies and their reclassification, in a number of instances as 'less than natural monopolies', is not decided on economic factors alone. The conventional 'least cost' economic test as to what constitutes the appropriate structural arrangements for utility industry operation, like those indicated by Sharkey above, has been attenuated by political objectives, such as a desire to break up the monolithic structure of the industries, or to introduce an element of choice, however contrived, for domestic consumers of utility services.

In addition, the features that contribute to the creation of natural monopoly conditions in particular industries may change over time, for:

> [w]hether or not an industry is a natural monopoly is not an immutable fact. Technology and tastes (demand) are the fundamental influences, and as these change, optimal industry organization can change; industries which once were in this category may be removed from it, and new industries may become natural monopolies.
>
> Waterson (1988: 145)

Within these shifting boundaries of the concept of natural monopoly then, to what extent can the water and energy industries be described as natural monopolies? In assessing the natural monopoly characteristics of utility industries, a distinction needs to be made between the production and supply of utility services, although this distinction is sometimes less than clear in practice.

Generally it is argued that the production of electricity, gas and even water (via generation, procurement, and water and sewerage systems development and management, respectively) do not bear the theoretical hallmarks of natural monopoly, for it is possible to introduce competition and to reduce unit costs through the entry of new firms in these areas of production. While it may be possible to secure cost economies of scale through monopoly production, these are seen to be substantially outweighed by the efficiency and pricing gains that are derived from competitive pressures under a more heterogeneous model of industry organization (Littlechild 1988; Vickers and Yarrow 1988; Yarrow 1988; Veljanovski 1989b).

Whether utility production is theoretically amenable to efficiency improvements through the introduction of competition is, in a practical sense, beside the point. The more important issue, from an implementation perspective, is whether efficiency-enhancing competition is actually likely to emerge in the productive structure of the industries, theoretical possibilities notwithstanding. The character of the industries, in terms of their history, capital

requirements, technology and market structure may be such that new producers may be deterred from entering the field. Waterson (1988: 146) alludes
to this possible hiatus between theory and reality in the production and supply
of utility services:

> Of course, many natural monopoly industries are not in fact ones in
> which entry, even if allowed, is easy. Entry often involves very substantial
> expenditure, much of which would not be returnable if the project were
> to fail. For example, a potential supplier of water to a particular area
> would have to engage in earthworks whose alternative uses would be
> very meagre. In such cases entry may not be attracted into the industry
> even if the incumbent firm is grossly inefficient, as long as it has some
> hold either on customers or over the necessary resources for supply.

The requirement for major capital investment and the large 'sunk costs' involved, will act to deter new entrants into the field. In addition, predatory and
anti-competitive behaviour on the part of existing monopoly producers, with
the aim of preserving their privileged position in the market, will further
complicate the emergence of competition.

Concern about the restrictive practices of British Gas as the dominant
producer and supplier of gas to the contract market (i.e. large industrial and
commercial users) has been a residual theme in the regulation of the gas
industry since 1986:

> In spite of the strong economic factors acting in favour of a competitive
> contract market, in the late 1980s, the competition stayed away. It did so
> for two main reasons: first, British Gas' dominant market share enabled it
> to offer bargain-basement prices to selected (usually high load factor)
> customers who appeared likely targets for competition. Meanwhile, it
> could subsidise its revenues by charging more to customers where com-
> petitors did not wish to trade or could not afford the distance-related
> costs of transmission. Second, insufficient gas was available for any single
> competitor to take the risk of market entry.
>
> Powe (1992: 8)

The alleged anti-competitive posture of British Gas lead to the Office of
Fair Trading referring it to the Monopolies and Mergers Commission (MMC)
in 1987–88, and it formed the basis for the parallel reference to the MMC by
the President of the Board of Trade and the Office of Gas Supply in July 1992.

The initial years of the privatized electricity industry have been rife with
claims that the duopoly private generators have engaged in anti-competitive
practices, in order to preserve their market dominance. In an inquiry into the
operation of the electricity Pool in late 1991, the Director General of Electricity Supply found that there was some basis in the assertions of major
industrial customers and the RECs that PowerGen, and to a lesser extent,
National Power, had been manipulating the Pool to their own commercial
advantage.

In contrast to production, the supply, and certainly the distribution, of water and energy services have been viewed as being rather less amenable, theoretically and practically, to the introduction of competition. As such, they have often been referred to, until recent times at least, as classic exemplars of natural monopoly.

The arguments underlying the designation of water and energy supply as natural monopolies are essentially rooted in the fact that these services are distributed and supplied to consumers through an extensive *network* of pipes or power lines. Because the means for supplying consumers requires a complex and capital-intensive infrastructure, it would be inefficient, uneconomic and disruptive to duplicate these networks, in order to provide alternative avenues of supply. The operational consequence of the economic case for having a single network of water, or electricity, or gas supply, across a given geographical area, was seen inevitably to be the existence of monopoly provision.

In recent years, however, the seemingly immutable link between a single supply system and monopoly provision has been directly challenged, particularly in relation to energy services. Within a single system of distribution, under common carriage arrangements, the potential exists for the advent of multiple suppliers, each of whom would compete (in terms of price and service quality) for business from industrial, commercial and domestic consumers. With the introduction of appropriate metering technology, individual consumers would be able to switch instantaneously from one supplier to another on the basis of an assessment of which firm offers the best value for money at any given point in time. Alternatively, groups of utility consumers could band together and either directly, or through a third-party agent, negotiate a price/service agreement with an energy supplier.

It has been argued consistently by the Director General of Electricity Supply, that this scenario of multiple sources of supply, attuned to consumer demand, and providing domestic consumers with the opportunity to break free of geographically-bounded monopoly supply, will apply in the British electricity industry following the introduction of unrestricted competition in 1998 (Office of Electricity Regulation 1992b). Since October 1992, firms other than British Gas have been able to compete for the business of customers using 2500 therms and above, and under section 37 of the Competition and Service (Utilities) Act 1992, provision exists for the Secretary of State to lower, or to eliminate altogether, the competitive market threshold in the gas industry. This potentially opens up the domestic gas market to full entry by competitors of the current monopoly supplier, British Gas in the future. While under section 41 of the Competition and Service (Utilities) Act 1992 there is also the theoretical prospect of domestic consumers choosing their water supplier, it is generally accepted, not least by the water regulator himself, that water and sewerage services will retain their natural monopoly features for some time to come (Byatt 1991).

The extent to which the theoretical and policy dissolution of the natural monopoly basis to energy supply will radically alter the monopoly base of *domestic* electricity and gas supply in the future clearly remains to be seen. The same holds with even greater force in the water industry, which is the most naturally monopolistic of all public utilities. However, for the medium-term future, in electricity and gas supply, and for the foreseeable future in water supply, the domestic consumer will remain subject to a regime of geographical monopoly supply, with the consequential constraints that this places upon the exercise of consumer sovereignty.

Externalities

The existence of externalities, as part of the process of producing and supplying energy and water services, is an important and controversial dimension in public utility management. Externalities arise, as Helm et al. (1988a: 44) state 'when the private costs of production and consumption are not equal to those of society, because costs or benefits spill over to those not directly involved. These social costs are typically considered to be large in the energy sector'.

Externalities are the systemic by-products of the method of production and supply of energy and water services, which are effectively unaccounted for in the conventional pricing mechanisms of the market (Pearce et al. 1989). In this sense, the existence of externalities represents *market failure*, for the distribution of costs or benefits associated with providing a particular service is not confined to the parties directly involved in its production and consumption. The displacement of costs or benefits, under situations where externalities exist, is further complicated by the fact that future, as well as current generations of citizens, will experience their negative or positive outcomes.

Much of the discussion of externalities in the energy and water industries has focused understandably on their manifestation as negative costs, for instance, the release of large amounts of carbon dioxide into the atmosphere through fossil-fuel generation with its consequential effect on 'global warming', the ecological and social devastation caused by accidents in the nuclear power industry, and the environmental hazard of sewerage and effluent discharges into freshwater streams and coastal areas. Public concern about the environmental impact, or negative externalities, of the water and electricity industries was a powerful undercurrent during the privatization of both industries.

Utility externalities can also be of a positive kind and they can make a very significant contribution to economic and social welfare. The benefits to public health of reticulated water supplies and the macro-economic effects of a dynamic power industry, are two major instances of this. Because of their fundamental contribution to individual and collective social well-being, it could be argued that the paramount expression of positive externalities in the water and energy industries, could be found in the universal provision of adequate quantities of energy and water to all households in society.

The existence of utility industry externalities, coupled with the knowledge that conventional market mechanisms are unable to take account of the social costs or the social benefits involved, mandates government intervention in order to provide a corrective to the misallocation of costs and benefits. Stiglitz (1988: 76) outlines the central argument for government involvement:

> Whenever there are such externalities, the resource allocation provided by the market may not be efficient. Since individuals do not bear the full cost of the negative externalities they generate, they will engage in an excessive amount of such activities; conversely, since individuals do not enjoy the full benefits of activities generating positive externalities, they will engage in too little of these. Thus, for example, there is a widespread belief that without government intervention of some kind, the level of pollution would be too high. To put it another way, pollution control provides a positive externality, so without government intervention there would be an underprovision of pollution control.

While government intervention of some sort is usually seen as the natural corollary of externalities, there is less agreement about the shape that government action should take. The relative merits of using formal regulatory or market-based solutions are at the nub of the debate over what is the most appropriate way for governments to respond to environmental externalities.

The set of possible regulatory actions, designed to deal with the environmental by-products of the utility industries, lie on a continuum from direct ownership and control to the enforcement of minimal standards, in areas like pollution control, within a private utility industry structure. Recourse to ownership as a means of controlling negative externalities has fallen out of favour because of the apparent inability of governments to effectively manage their conjoint stewardship of the utility industries and the environment. The argument against ownership as a mechanism for effective environmental regulation is elaborated by Helm and Pearce (1990: 12):

> Is regulation likely to be tougher and easier to impose and monitor in the private or public sector? The intuitive and conventional answer that greater control is engendered through ownership is highly misleading. It may be better not to own the regulatee. The problem can be modelled through 'principal-agent' analysis. The incentives of government regulators needs first to be assessed. If they also own the polluter, they are likely to be susceptible to its financial performance. In the public sector, a politician is answerable for the performance of the firm, and will inevitably want to defend its record. In the UK water industry, Government Ministers frequently acted as *de facto* apologists for the low standards of water quality. Now that the industry is privatised, Ministers are still answerable for water quality, but have no financial responsibility to the shareholders of the water companies. There is an incentive gain through privatisation.

Even with the incentive gain that is seen to accrue from the separation of ownership from regulation, formidable difficulties still stand in the way of regulatory approaches to environmental management. No matter how pre-

cisely a government, or its regulatory agencies, set standards for the environmental management performance of utility industries, the practical difficulties
and the costs of effectively monitoring and enforcing these standards remains
acute. Along with the informational and financial costs associated with external
agency regulation of the complex energy and water industries, there is the
danger – based on the American experience – of regulatory capture, or co-
optation of the regulatory body, by the industries being regulated. Yet for all
this, governmental regulatory controls have constituted – and remain – the
primary device for managing environmental externalities in most countries.

Environmental economists like David Pearce, one-time adviser to the
Secretary of State for the Environment, argue that a superior alternative to
government environmental regulation can be found in the use of the market-
based and pricing measures. Although the specific elements of a market-based
approach to environmental management differ, they essentially revolve around
the introduction of new forms of *taxation*, designed both to offset the costs of
environmental damage and to act as a deterrent to the production and consumption of utility services with high negative externality effects. Among the
more commonly discussed types of market-based environmental measures are
carbon taxes (paid either at source by the industries or at the point of consumption by the consumer), a generic value-added tax on all domestic fuel, and
tradeable pollution permits.

Despite the fact that market-based environmental measures are formally
predicated on the *polluter pays principle*, it is likely to be consumers who will be
required, either directly or indirectly, to carry much of the burden of these
additional imposts. Pearce, explains the rationale for this:

> Making the consumer of the polluting product pay some of the clean-up
> cost may seem at odds with the PPP [Polluter Pays Principle] but in fact it
> is exactly what should happen. For the price mechanism now signals the
> 'true' costs of production to the consumer, comprising normal costs of
> production *and* the hitherto free environmental inputs. This is how the
> 'green power of market forces' works.
>
> Pearce et al. (1989: 158)

Thus far the introduction of environmental taxes, such as a carbon tax, has
been resisted by the British government – although Fells and Lucas (1991: 72)
describe the fossil fuel levy as 'a primitive carbon tax' – but taxes of this sort are
almost certain to become a prominent feature of the utility policy landscape
internationally over the next decade.

In September 1991 the European Commission announced plans for the
introduction of a carbon/energy tax throughout the member states of the
European Community. Under the European Commission's proposals, a
carbon/energy tax will be phased in over a period of eight years (from 1993),
with the effect of increasing the price of coal by 60 per cent and the price of gas
by one-third (Pearson and Smith 1991: 14). The additional revenue generated
by the tax – estimated at over 50 billion ECU – would be distributed back to

the member states to use as they wish, although, 'the Commission's proposals stress that the tax should be introduced on a revenue-neutral basis – in other words, the revenue should be used to reduce other taxes rather than to increase public spending' (Pearson and Smith 1991: 1). If revenues from the tax are used in this way, it will have the effect as Pearson and Smith point out of being doubly regressive since the application of a flat-rate carbon tax on energy consumption will hit the budgets of low-income households more severely, while tax cuts will largely be to the advantage of the better-off.

Whatever their possible merit as a means of identifying and allocating negative externality costs, therefore, environmental taxes raise significant social policy issues (Boardman 1990). Of particular importance is the distributional impact that value-added pollution and carbon taxes will have on domestic consumers. In a context where price inelasticity of demand is high, an increase in water and energy prices, to meet the costs of environmental externalities will *ceteris paribus* impinge more heavily upon low-income households.

An analysis of the distributional effects of the introduction of a 15 per cent value added tax on electricity and gas, carried out by the Institute for Fiscal Studies in 1990 (using Family Expenditure Survey data), highlighted the disproportionate impact that consumption-based taxes are likely to have on particular classes of domestic consumers:

> The distributional effects of the change are strongly adverse. The increase in tax paid by households in the lowest decile by income would be £1 per week, and that of the richest 10 per cent of households would be around £2, yet the richest decile are sixteen times richer before tax than the poorest. Worse still, the poorest decile cut their consumption of energy by 10 per cent, whereas the richest decile would hardly reduce their consumption at all.
>
> Pearson and Smith (1990: 12)

The more recent analysis of the distributional consequences of the proposed European carbon tax by the same authors confirms these findings.

A major implication of the regressive impact of environmental taxes is that compensatory mechanisms will need to be devised, if low income households are not to become the victims of the important policy objective of reducing global warming. This compensation would need to take several forms including the provision of additional social security benefits to offset tariff increases, and the extension of publicly-funded programmes aimed at providing low-income households with the means to substitute and conserve energy, without experiencing a decline in their overall quality of life.

In the area of water services, consumers already are subject to a form of 'water environment tax', arising from the £30 billion programme (1992 prices), introduced at the time of privatization, to clean up the water-related environment. Because of these environmental improvements, water charges are expected to rise on average around 5–6 per cent above inflation each year between 1990 to 2000, excluding the 'pass-through' costs of the water industry meeting *additional* European Commission environmental directives. The flat-rate nature of these increases in water charges, in tandem with the inelastic character of domestic water consumption, means that they will have a regressive effect similar to that of carbon taxes. The use of general taxation revenue would have provided a fiscally progressive alternative to the financing of necessary environmental improvements in the water industry. The need to increase social security benefits in order to offset the financially detrimental impact of substantially increased water charges on low income households was not formally recognized by the Government until October 1991.

Conclusion

In the first part of this chapter, the primary social and economic characteristics of the energy and water utilities have been outlined. In combination, these features of the utility services make them substantially different from most other commodities and services in the economy. While it is true that some other commodities share one or two of the characteristics of public utility services (e.g. food and housing in terms of 'essentialness'), no other area of human consumption manifests the array of complex attributes found in public utility services. Because of this, it is inappropriate to assert – as has been the case in Government and industry circles over recent years – that public utility services are essentially no different from other commodities and that as such, decision making on their production and distribution should be devolved to market forces alone.

The life-maintaining products, and potentially life-destroying by-products, of public utility services places them in the front line as determinants of contemporary quality of life, at both an individual household and societal level. This, in combination with the structural characteristics of the industries, which will be monopolistic for some time to come for ordinary consumers, invariably means that the random stewardship of the free market will be inadequate to the task of managing the major distributional and environmental issues implicit in the provision of public utility services.

Water and energy services provision are interwoven with major questions of public policy and as such the state is inevitably implicated in the management of public utilities, irrespective of where the locus of ownership lies. The function of the state is first and foremost a regulatory one, aimed at ensuring that the strategic contribution of the public utilities is directed at constructive economic and social ends. In addition, the state has a vital financing role to play, aimed at securing equity of access to utility services.

The next part of the chapter examines the regulatory function of the state and, in particular, the developing model of public utility regulation in Britain.

Public utility regulation

The social and economic dimensions of public utility services form the substantive case for arguing that the provision of water and energy services is subject to a form of market failure. The market is apparently incapable, left to its own devices, of efficiently and equitably supplying water and energy services to domestic and other consumers and therefore the intervention of the state, in some way, is required to counteract the endemic deficiencies of the free market system in the supply of essential water and energy services.

In the past, the existence of market failure in the production and provision of public utility services provided the rationale for a policy of state ownership and nationalization of the utility industries. However, the emergence of the *theory of government failure* (Helm and Yarrow 1988; Vining and Weimer 1990) as a form of conceptual and ideological counterpoint to the argument of market failure, has ostensibly weakened the credentials of *dirigiste* policy-making. The symptoms of government failure in the management of utility industries, in the eyes of its proponents, include an intrinsic inability to achieve productive and allocative efficiency outcomes, and to provide effective stewardship of both the public, and the consumer, interest (Demsetz 1989).

Yet despite the strong reservations shared by many orthodox welfare economists about the dynamics and impact of government intervention in the industrial economy, it is generally acknowledged that a government-led regulatory regime of some sort is required in the management of utility services. In large part, the qualified support for public utility regulation, has its origins in an empirically-based fear of the exploitation of market power by monopoly enterprises. Sherman (1989: 10–11) captures the essence of this anxiety about monopoly power:

> Without competition in the form of free entry, a single supplier must be expected to follow many understandable tendencies of monopolies. To raise revenues, prices may be adjusted so that markets with less elastic demands will have prices proportionately farther above marginal costs; and more subtle discrimination by price may be attempted, again because it allows more revenue to be raised. Unless quality is clearly defined and easily monitored, it may be altered. Reliability of service may suffer, for example, when there is no threat from alternative suppliers, and consumers may be forced to wait for service. Costs rise too as managers shirk or avoid difficult decisions. Innovation may not occur either, for the enterprise has no great incentive to make its own ways of doing things obsolete.

Regulation is usually viewed as an inevitable structural concomitant of industries containing elements of monopoly. Even on the outer reaches of economic liberalism, a form of regulatory oversight of natural monopoly utilities is seen as necessary, if only until such time as more functional competitive mechanisms can be introduced into these areas of the economy (Veljanovski 1989a,b). Much of the substance of the debate over regulation and the public utilities lies not around the question of whether regulation *per se* is required, but rather around 'second-order' issues such as, the most appropriate *form* that regulation should take, and the *scope* that should be given to regulatory intervention.

The disincentives to efficiency and the barriers to consumer sovereignty implicit in monopoly industries (particularly where demand elasticity is low), necessitates the introduction of a regulatory system that provides a set of proxy market conditions and 'disciplines', and affords a level of protection both to the public interest generally, and to the consumer interest specifically. Regulation in this context is '. . . a means of reaching those parts of industries which competition cannot reach' (Gibson and Price 1988: 42).

Public utility regulation consists of two primary strands: *economic* and *social regulation*. Economic regulation centres around the role of the utility industries in the economy (e.g. monopoly practices, competitive structure, contribution to economic growth) and the financial management of the utilities (e.g. rate of return, pricing and productive efficiency). Although social regulation is a less precise concept, it is generally seen to encompass areas of utility activity directly related to interactions with consumers (e.g. information provision, standards of service, consumer redress), and areas of utility practice which intersect with environmental and social policy (Swann 1988). The demarcation between economic and social regulation is not clear-cut, nor should it be, for in practice the two dimensions of regulation are intertwined. An example of this can be found in the way that utility prices and standards of service are invariably linked.

Discussion of regulation often tends to focus on the negative, restraining and rule-application function, of regulatory bodies. But whilst the 'power to constrain' is unequivocally a central element of regulation, the exercise of regulatory influence can also encompass more positive dimensions. Along with setting and enforcing the parameters for commercial behaviour, regulation can act, among other things, to provide financial stability for the utility industries, to create opportunities for industry development and innovation, to extend the scope of consumer power, to promote access and equity in the provision of utility services, and to stimulate industry-wide 'best practice'. All these serve the long-term interests of both the utilities and their consumers alike.

Regulation can additionally contribute to strategic management of vital infrastructural resources. Without some measure of policy overview and direction via the regulatory machinery, the operation of the utility industries is likely to be characterized by disparateness, conflicting objectives and insular commercial behaviour premised on short-term planning horizons. Under this latter scenario, public utilities are unlikely to be able to respond to the macroeconomic, social and environmental imperatives implicit in the contemporary and future management of water and energy resources.

The British model of regulation

The British model of utility regulation, involving the establishment of an independent regulator's office with government department status to supervise the operation of privately-owned utility industries, has been developed through the selective adaptation and, in a number of key respects, the substantial modification of traditional American systems of utility industry organization and regulation. The American experience of utility organization – with its private ownership/ public regulation configuration – patently influenced the British Conservative Government's thinking on the restructuring of the water and energy industries. Yet the development of the regulatory framework, in tandem with the denationalization of the utilities, has departed in a number of significant ways from American practice. These departures represent, to borrow a phrase from Sir Geoffrey Howe's influential critique of the dying days of the Thatcher Government, differences of both 'substance and style'.

The promotion of competition and the control of monopoly profits are the building blocks of economic regulation of the public utilities, and one of the more fundamental differences between the British and American systems is the way in which the financial and pricing structure of the industries is regulated. In Britain, a price-based formula tied to the retail price index and making provision for efficiency savings (RPI – X) is employed as the principal device for ensuring that the utilities are not exploiting their monopoly pricing power, while at the same time providing an incentive for productive efficiency. American regulators, on the other hand, have conventionally used a rate of return approach, involving the setting of tariffs on the basis of operating costs and an allowed rate of return on capital.

A variant of the rate of return approach had formed part of the financial management of the nationalized industries by successive British governments and for this reason alone rate of return may have been rejected by the Thatcher Government as an appropriate regulatory device for the privatized utilities. Of even greater significance probably was the widely acknowledged limitations of rate of return (or 'cost plus') regulation. In particular, rate of return regulation is seen to provide no in-built incentive for efficiency, or the reduction of costs and because it is directly based on return on capital, it is said to encourage profligate capital expenditure (described as the *Averch–Johnson effect*).

In contrast, the strengths of the price cap formulation were seen to reside in its ability to act as a stimulus to productive efficiency both through the operation of the X factor (where the utilities are required to reduce prices at a rate normally below the level of inflation) and because the regulated companies are allowed to retain as profits any efficiency savings made in addition to the designated X target. It was also held to be neutral on the question of capital expenditure.

In practice, however, the distinction between these two approaches to economic regulation has been nowhere as clear-cut as it appears in theory, and over time the British regulators appear to have increasingly applied rate of return calculations in their analysis of the financial and pricing structure of the utility industries. The methodologies used by OFGAS in the 1990–91 review of the Gas Tariff Formula and OFWAT in the Periodic Review, illustrate the importance that the regulators attach to the question of what constitutes an appropriate rate of return for the regulated utilities (see Chapter 4). This serves to reinforce the scepticism of a number of commentators about the extent to

Table 2.2 A schema of British public utility regulation.

Regulatory domains	Regulatory instruments	Source of powers
Economic regulation		
• Competition	Policing, promoting restructuring and market entry, 'Yardstick competition'	Legislation (primary and CSUA)/licence
• Financial viability of companies	Price controls/tariff review	Licence
• Efficiency	Price controls/tariff review	Licence
• Capital investment	Monitoring regulatory accounts	Licence
• Price protection (monopoly sectors)	Price controls/tariff review	Licence
• Diversification – protection of core business	Monitoring regulatory accounts	Licence/legislation (CSUA)
Social regulation		
• Obligation to supply	Determinations	Legislation
• Service quality	Performance standards/complaint handling/ tariff reviews	Legislation (primary and CSUA)/licence
• Protection of 'vulnerable consumers', e.g. elderly, disabled	Codes of practice	Legislation/licence
• Tariff protection for rural consumers	Price controls	Legislation/licence
• Debt and disconnection	Codes of practice	Legislation/licence
• Consumer representation	Consumer committees	Legislation
• Occupational health and safety		Legislation
• Quasi-environmental protection, e.g. energy efficiency	Codes of practice/performance standards	Legislation (primary and CSUA)/licence

Note: A few of these provisions are not applicable to all three regulatory bodies.

which the British price-control instrument differs markedly from the much-denigrated American approach (e.g. Helm et al. 1988b; Weyman-Jones 1990; Stelzer 1991; Vickers 1991).

As was seen in Chapter 1, the attention given by the Government to the regulatory framework of the utility industries appeared to accelerate with each successive privatization. And indeed this 'filling in' of the detail of the regulatory regime continued after the completion of the privatization schedule for the three utilities, with the enactment of the Competition and Service (Utilities) Act.

A developmental approach to the building of a regulatory system more directly relevant to the monopoly conditions under which the utility industries operate (at least as it applies to captive domestic and other consumers), might be seen as a conscious expression of a pragmatic and incrementalist approach to policy-making, where the learning of the past informs the practice of the future. Alternatively, it could be viewed as a belated attempt to paper over the cracks of earlier policy-making. Vickers (1991) sees the supplementation of regulatory powers in the later privatizations and beyond as evidence of compensatory policy-making and argues that the Government underestimated in its earlier efforts, the problems of market failure in the utility industries.

In terms of their scope, the powers progressively ceded to the regulatory bodies in the privatization legislation and in the Competition and Service (Utilities) Act 1992 (CSUA), look *broadly* similar to those that are available to the regulatory commissions in America. The energy and water regulators in Britain have strong residual powers in relation to economic regulation and weaker, but still potentially quite potent, leverage in the area of social regulation. Table 2.2 sets out a schema of British public utility regulation, indicating the domains and instruments of the regulatory system in this country.

The emerging British model of utility regulation, however, deviates markedly from its American counterpart in six significant respects, namely:

- The importance attached to competition.
- The functions ceded to the regulators in respect to industry policy and capital investment.
- The primacy given to shareholder interests.
- The informal and discretionary nature of the regulatory system.
- The emphasis on personality.
- The closed structure of regulatory decision making.

Each of these is briefly considered below.

Competition

Rather ironically, the British approach directs greater attention to the pro-competition function of the regulatory agencies than appears to be the case in the bastion of capitalism. Despite their long history of public regulation of privately-owned utilities, and the claim of Stelzer (1991: 60) that the 'US favours competition', the Americans have only recently begun to examine how greater competition might be introduced into the gas and electricity industries. The ostensible heterogeneity of the public utility structure in America, with its mix of publicly- and privately-owned utilities, is deceptive; for to all intents and purposes, the utilities operate as geographical monopolies. The restructuring of the ESI in Britain and the explicit powers given to the Director General of Electricity Supply to facilitate the development of competition across the primary sectors of the industry – including the eventual dismantling of geographical monopoly provision for all consumers – have no extant equivalent in the American regulatory environment. The injunctions on the Director General of Water Services to extend competition where possible in the endemically monopolistic terrain of water services look positively radical by comparison with the situation in America.

Industry policy and capital investment

The planning and investment decisions of the public utilities impact not only on the quality of utility services provided directly to consumers, but they have substantial 'ripple effects' throughout the economy as a whole. The issues of continuity and security of supply of energy and water at a society-wide level involve important questions of national interest. In addition, decisions taken about current and future methods of producing and distributing electricity, gas and water often have major environmental implications. Although none of these macro-effects necessarily makes the effective development of utility policy incompatible with a structure of private ownership, they underscore, at a minimum, the need for a strong Government policy framework for the industries, coupled with vigorous and far-sighted public regulation.

The capacity of the existing regulatory framework in Britain to contribute to these broader policy issues, as opposed to narrow economic regulation based around prices and competition, is still to be fully determined, but by and large the industry regulators have been ceded extremely muted powers in this important domain of public policy. The Government's rejection of a substantive role for the regulatory agencies in utility industry policy and development was illustrated, at the outset, in their refusal to admit the North American device of 'least-cost planning' into the regulatory arena. Since the middle of the 1980s, least-cost planning has been adopted by the majority of American state regulatory commissions as a mechanism for encouraging a longer-term planning approach by the energy utilities. According to Berry (1992: 783):

> New economic institutions are currently evolving in the electric utility industry to expand the scope of long-range planning. Regulatory commissions have spurred this evolution through requirements for least cost planning that take into account improved load forecasting, conservation and other demand management measures, consideration of alternative technologies for supplying electricity such as solar power, and the environmental impacts of power production and consumption.

In Britain, the emphasis on competition and market forces as the drivers of energy policy, in combination with the operation of the price control formula (which unlike rate of return regulation, gives the regulatory bodies little formal scope for adjudicating on the capital structure of the industries) has meant that the electricity and gas regulators have only limited and indirect leverage over the investment and demand management practices of the energy utilities. While the water regulator has been given a more significant role to play in supervising the large capital works programme in the water industry, this role is primarily confined to a monitoring and auditing function (i.e. ensuring that the companies are meeting their specified capital investment targets), rather than involving an active role in the formulation of water services policy.

The limited policy function of the regulators, in tandem with the amorphous role of the executive and legislative branches of government following privatization (made more so by the abolition of the Department of Energy and the Select Committee on Energy) suggests that there is a very real danger of a deep and destructive policy vacuum being created in the field of utility services in Britain.

Priority to shareholders

It was shown in Chapter 1 that the model of regulation constructed in Britain gives clear and unambiguous priority – in statute at least – to the interests of utility company shareholders:

> . . . to secure that licence holders are able to finance the carrying on of the activities which they are authorised by their licences to carry on.
>
> Electricity Act 1989 s. 3(1)(b)

> . . . to secure that companies holding appointments . . . are able (in particular, by securing reasonable returns on their capital) to finance the proper carrying out of the functions of such undertakers.
>
> Water Industry Act 1991 s. 2(2)(b)

The regulators' duties with respect to the protection of consumers are secondary and subject to the fulfilment of primary duties such as those cited above. Under the American system, regulators are mandated to seek a balance between shareholder and consumer interests, 'to ensure reliable service at just and reasonable rates.' The thrust of the American approach is outlined by two Commissioners (O'Leary and Smith) on the New Mexico utility commission:

> Regulators understand their duty to balance the interests of rate-payers [i.e. utility consumers] and shareholders when making a decision. They understand they have an economic function to set price, but they act in an environment of inputs, constraints, and concerns that are not economic in nature . . . in performing the task of balancing the interests of the ratepayer and the investor, [the regulators] are responding to the

mandate given them by their state legislators. This mandate of 'balancing' implies that the criterion of fairness be considered. This objective may not make it possible for the economic criterion of efficiency to be achieved.

Nowotny et al. (1989: 224)

In contrast, the British model requires the regulators to give primacy to shareholders in the event of conflicts of interest arising between the stakeholders in the utility industries. In this sense, regulation for consumer protection has been treated very much as a secondary and contingent dimension in the structure of utility regulation in Britain.

While the 'just and reasonable' test used by American regulators is manifestly subjective and open to quite different interpretations (and hence has been criticized on the grounds that it gives rise to regulatory uncertainty), it does provide a means of building equity and distributional considerations into the framework of utility regulation, and it has apparently been used in this way by a number of utility commissions in America.

In addition to a requirement to give precedence to shareholder interests, the British regulators are bound by the stricture that no 'undue discrimination' or 'undue preference' be given to particular classes of consumers in the fixing of tariffs. This has the effect of circumscribing the scope for regulatory intervention aimed at assisting groups of consumers who experience specific problems in accessing, or maintaining access to, utility services and it effectively forecloses the option of pursuing equity objectives as a part of regulatory policy-making.

An attempt by one of the regulators to intervene in this way would be open to legal challenge, although the position of the courts in Britain on 'undue discrimination' is largely untested and ambiguous (Sharpe 1992). Certainly, the prospect of a legal challenge is likely to have the effect of deterring the regulatory bodies from taking action which positively discriminates in favour of low income consumers, regardless of the equity merits of doing so. This was evidenced in the Director General of Gas Supply's position on the use of funds generated through the 'E factor' in the British Gas tariff review (see Chapter 4).

It can be seen in Table 2.2 on the system of British regulation, that the regulators have a duty to give particular attention to the needs of certain sections of the population – namely elderly and disabled consumers, and in some instances, customers living in rural areas. Although action on behalf of elderly and disabled is also limited by the general sanction against discrimination in tariff-setting, this statutory mandate gives the regulators a formal point of leverage over the utility companies on their policies and practices *vis-à-vis* these two groups of consumers. If these provisions were introduced on the basis of 'vulnerability' and special needs, it could be argued, from an equity perspective, that low income customers generally should have been included under this protective net (Fitch 1992). Measures to include similar provisions for low income consumers in the Competition and Service (Utilities) Bill in 1991–92 were rejected by the Government.

Emphasis on informal processes and discretion
Despite the scope for the use of discretion in determining 'just and reasonable' rates, the American system of regulation is highly formalized, rule-bound and legalistic in its approach to regulatory decision making (Stelzer 1991). By comparison, the British model of regulation is seen to be rather more informal, fluid and discretionary in character. Indeed, in the view of one commentator at least, the British approach stands the danger of 'evolving into an informal system of rule-making which operates through negotiation and bargaining in the shadow of the law' (Veljanovski 1991: 9).

The distinguishing ambience of the British regulatory system arises firstly, from the largely non-statutory mechanisms used to regulate the privatized utilities and secondly, from the highly personalized style of regulation that has been employed.

Although the privatization legislation, and more latterly the Competition and Service (Utilities) Act, provide the structural outline of regulation, much of the working machinery is to be found in secondary legislation (regulations) and most importantly, in the licences issued to the utility companies. But even the licences do not provide the sort of operational detail needed to build a functioning regulatory system, and much of this has had to be established *in situ* by the regulators themselves. Following Swann (in Button and Swann 1989), the British approach might be defined as essentially *de facto*, as opposed to *de jure*, regulation, with its absence of a precise statutory framework and its attendant reliance on quasi-legal instruments and negotiation.

The fact that, under the British model, the regulators have considerable room for manoeuvre and scope to determine much of the shape of the regulatory regime is likely to be both a strength and a weakness. The substance of its strength resides in the ability of the regulators to shift the focus of regulatory attention into fields not originally envisaged, or overlooked, by the Government at the time of privatization, and to quickly adapt to changing circumstances and conditions. There is evidence that this has happened, to the benefit of domestic consumers, in the regulation of the gas industry, and some initial indications that this may happen in the water industry as well (see Chapters 4–6). The excursions of the regulators into domains beyond those originally included in their orbit has led to claims that the regulators have breached the terms of the 'regulatory bargain' struck between the government and shareholders at the time of privatization (Veljanovski 1991).

The primary weakness of the discretionary, evolutionary model of regulation lies in the fact that the rules and decision-making criteria can be opaque, elusive and ever-shifting, with a consequently negative effect on 'due process' and a denuding of the ability to externally monitor regulatory activity. Equally, it can give rise to arbitrary styles of regulatory policy-making. This interacts closely with the issue of style.

Personality-driven model

At the level of style, the British model of regulation differs most notably from its American progenitor in its reliance on, what could reasonably be described as, 'personality-led regulation'. In other words, much of the focus, and certainly the character, of the public bodies set up to regulate the privatized utilities in Britain, imitate the persona of their respective directors.

The general *modus operandi* of the Office of Gas Supply, Office of Water Services and Office of Electricity Regulation – which could be categorized in a short-hand way as, confrontation, suasion and *laissez-faire* respectively – mirrors the interventionist philosophies and personalities of their Directors General at least as much as it does the different structural arrangements and environmental conditions of the three utility industries concerned. This contrasts with the way that the state public utility commissions operate in America, where the legal and structural framework of regulatory practice, rather than the predilections of individuals, determines the shape and substance of regulatory control. In America, of course, the apex of the regulatory agency is usually occupied not by one individual but by a number of elected or appointed commissioners.

The emphasis on personality in the nascent British model of regulation may reflect the relatively recent advent of public regulatory bodies in this country and hence represent no more than a transitional phase. In line with a Weberian thesis of organizational development, the charismatic/individual leadership model of regulation may shift over time towards a more formal and institutionalized approach. Alternatively, as Walker (1990) speculates in his amusing article 'Enter the Regulators', the individualistic style of the regulatory bodies may have developed in response to the imprecise brief given to the first generation of utility regulators, as well as being somehow consistent with the slightly eccentric way things have been traditionally done in the British polity. 'Regulation as individual rather than system' might also have been seen as somehow more expressive and symbolic of the independence and autonomy of the regulatory regime. Whatever the reason, the individually-centred nature of the regulatory system is enshrined in the original legislation:

> The Acts of Parliament which carried out the privatisations and established the powers of the regulatory agencies lay the various duties upon the Directors of the various industries [*sic*] and not upon the regulatory agencies as corporate bodies. Each agency is there to assist the Director and not legally to share in the decision-making process.
>
> House of Commons Library Research Division (1991a: 1)

Clearly, to be effective, regulation needs to be a dynamic and adaptive process, with scope being given to the regulatory body to make changes in the regulatory regime in line with changing conditions and with tactical shifts in the behaviour of the regulated companies. Yet whether this should involve the centralization of regulatory decision-making power around individuals to the extent that has occurred in Britain is another matter. The highly personalized style of the utility regulatory structures is likely to mean that the system of controlling and monitoring the behaviour of the privatized utilities will be idiosyncratic, and even arbitrary. The individualistic style of the regulatory machinery will invariably lead to problems of succession, with possibly disruptive philosophical shifts in emphasis following a change in regulator. It could also act to constrain public access to, and understanding of, the arcane workings of the regulatory system and might create 'some worrying gaps in the lines of public accountability' (Walker 1990: 158). There is a particular danger of this happening in the relatively closed decision-making environment of British utility regulation.

Closed structures for regulatory decision making

In America, a quasi-judicial process, involving public hearings and formal opportunities for consumer input and advocacy, is used for determining pricing and other major regulatory decisions. Brown (1986: 10):

> In all cases the PUC [State Public Utility Commission] reaches a decision after a series of public hearings, in which the utility must present its case, and at which intervenors can present countervailing views, and indeed can cross examine the utility representatives. This process allows consumers, either directly, or more commonly through their representative bodies, to have a direct input into the decision making process.

The American system has been criticized on the grounds that it is expensive, litigious and leads to interminably protracted decision making. On the positive side, however, it has clear advantages in terms of transparency of decision making and potential openness to a plurality of views and interests.

The American 'rate hearing' approach to the setting of tariffs and performance standards was spurned by the Government as an appropriate way of regulating the privatized utilities. The quinquennial tariff review process, centring around closed negotiations between the regulator and the industry, with provision for public consultation at the discretion of the regulator, was instituted in its stead. The absence of a formal public arena for determining major regulatory issues might be off-set, to some degree, by the regulators adopting an inclusive information dissemination and decision-making approach.

On paper at least, the British model of regulation looks less substantial than that used in America. It could be argued, however, that the emphasis in the British model on informality, flexibility, discretion and expedition in decision making, might be to the ultimate advantage of utility consumers: in the hands of the 'right' regulator these attributes could be exercised to better effect than would be the case using the more belaboured and legally constricted American approach. But the fundamental dilemma is that in its strength lies its weakness, for the British model appears to be all-too-heavily reliant upon tapping a continuous supply of dominant regulatory personalities of capacity, openness and goodwill.

Conclusion: Accountability in the British regulatory system

Another difficulty for regulators is that their decisions are taken in secret with outsiders in no position to judge whether or not consumer interests have really been protected. That may be inevitable in view of the need for commercial confidentiality but it also places everybody in an awkward position. Regulators are largely protected from political interference by Statute. Parliament has not really exercised accountability over them. Occasionally Regulators appear before Select Committees to describe their work, but the appearances are neither frequent nor detailed enough to constitute effective control. Even the public hearings organised by American regulators are completely absent from the UK scene. Yet in the long run it is unsatisfactory for such major decisions over such a large part of the economy to be taken by a small number of individuals so completely free from outside interference or accountability.

House of Commons Library Research Division (1991a: 2)

Public utility regulation intersects directly and indirectly with major areas of public policy, for example, environmental policy and infrastructural planning. It also results in distributional outcomes which affect society as a whole and, in particular, impacts upon the quality of life of low income and other disadvantaged groups of consumers. Because of its importance and place in the polity, utility regulation should be firmly attached to the fabric of political and public accountability.

In America, the lines of regulator accountability appear to be rather more clear-cut than is the situation in Britain, i.e. via democratically elected regulators and through structures for open decision making. In Britain, more weight seems to have been placed on the need for individual leadership and independence than on clarity of accountability.

At first glance, the British regulatory model appears to provide an intricate and elaborate system of formal and informal accountability, as Figure 2.4, outlining the major players in the British regulatory environment, seems to suggest. But this merely serves to disguise a reality where at best, the utility regulators' accountability is confused, and where at worst, the regulators stand the danger of being accountable to everyone and no-one.

The accountability problem in the British system is best illustrated through looking more closely at the primary formal line of political accountability. Each of the Directors General is technically accountable to Parliament, but beyond the presentation of their annual reports to Westminster, no mechanisms have been established to ensure that this actually takes place in a systematic and regular way. The Select Committee system in the House of Commons is one obvious arena where the regulators might be made to account for their actions and the electricity regulator's encounters with the former Energy Committee (as part of its inquiry into the consequences of electricity privatization in 1991–92) and the Trade and Industry Committee (in its investigation into

Figure 2.4   Players in the regulatory environment.

1. LEGISLATURE:
   Parliament: to whom regulators are notionally accountable, expenditure is voted by
      Parliament, annual reports presented to Parliament
   Parliamentary Select Committees: ad hoc investigations of policy framework and
      regulatory machinery, e.g. House of Commons Trade and Industry Select
      Committee, Environment Select Committee, ex-Energy Committee

2. EXECUTIVE:
   Secretary of State: 'the directors are appointed by and are answerable in broad terms
      to the appropriate Secretary of State. If the director does not carry out his
      duties satisfactorily, he can be replaced'. Lord Reay, Lords debate on CSU Bill,
      9/3/92, col. 1193
   Treasury: approves expenditure of regulatory bodies (funds raised through licence fees)

3. JUDICIARY:
   High Court – Judicial Reviews: review of legality and validity of procedures used in
      regulatory decision-making (but not of substantive policy/decisions)

4. ECONOMIC REGULATION AND AUDITING QUANGOS:
   Monopolies and Mergers Commission: key institutional bulwark to utility regulators'
      powers – referral if actions of utility companies seen to be against 'the public
      interest', settle disputes over licence modifications
   Office of Fair Trading: enforcement of general competition law and consumer protection
   National Audit Office: 'The Comptroller and Auditor General has been given the financial
      audit of these bodies and the National Audit Office will soon need to investigate the
      efficiency and effectiveness of their operations'. Beauchamp (1990: 58)

5. OTHER GOVERNMENTAL AGENCIES:
   Environmental or 'Quality regulators'; Department of Social Security, European
      Commission, local authorities

6. MEDIA:
   Primary non-institutional vehicle for regulator public accountability

7. INTEREST GROUPS, including consumer interest groups:
   - source of external information and monitoring
   - source of specialist policy advice on consumer issues
   - point of additional leverage on the utility companies
   - prompter of regulatory vigilance and action (aids regulator's evaluation of own
     effectiveness, accountability and independence)
   - support in political arena regarding strengthening regulatory powers, resources, etc.
   Consumer councils/committees: responsible for following up individual complaints,
      monitoring company practice, input into consumer policy
   Public Utilities Access Forum: community sector-regulator forum on low-income
      consumer issues
   Independent consumer and advocacy organizations, e.g. National Consumer Council,
      Consumers' Association, National Right to Fuel Campaign, Age Concern
   Community services organizations: e.g. citizens' advice bureaux, welfare rights and
      money advice groups

British Coal and British energy policy in 1992–93) have achieved this in part. But compared to the Director General of Electricity Supply, the other two utility regulators have been almost immune from the scrutiny of Parliament.

In reality, the most powerful political influence on the activities of the regulators is not Parliament but the respective Secretaries of State. Under the legislation, the relevant Secretary of State has the power to appoint the regulator and has residual powers in key areas such as the issuing of licences and references to the Monopolies and Mergers Commission. The significance of the Secretary of State is clearly recognized by the Director General of Electricity Supply: 'in important respects the power that I have derives from or is constrained by the Secretary of State' (Littlechild, in Veljanovski 1991: 116). The apparent gap between the theory and practice of the regulators' political accountability may explain the hesitancy of the last Secretary of State for Energy when questioned on the matter during the Energy Committee's investigation into electricity privatization:

> Mr McAllion: Is the Director General accountable to yourself?
> Mr Wakeham: He is accountable, I think, to Parliament, if somebody can tell me if that is correct. He is accountable directly to Parliament, yes, but he publishes his reports and he certainly will—
> Mr McAllion: If he is directly accountable to Parliament, surely he will be directly accountable to Parliamentary Select Committees?
> House of Commons, Energy Committee (1992c: paras 352–3)

The evident danger in the rather confused lines of formal accountability is that it will result in an accountability vacuum, where the decisions of the regulators will slip through the net of political scrutiny entirely. On the other hand, the scope for intervention by the Secretary of State potentially threatens the very independence upon which the edifice of British utility regulation centrally rests.

Outside the political arena, the primary institutional device for examining the actions of the regulators lies in the process of judicial review. But this is essentially confined to questions of procedure, i.e. whether or not the regulator has exceeded his or her legal powers or remit (Emery and Smythe 1986). It does not generally encompass the review of instances of substantive decision making, unless some breach of statutory power has occurred. The judicial review process is likely to be constrained also, in the view of a number of commentators (e.g. Beesley 1991; Veljanovski 1991), by a reluctance on the part of the courts to intrude too deeply into the terrain of the regulatory agencies, and by 'the fact that, where discretion is so wide, there are few pegs on which to hang an application for review' (McHarg 1992: 392).

Ideally the regulators will be accountable ultimately to the consumers of utility services. Generally, however, this line of accountability is indirect and is refracted through intermediary bodies such as the consumer committees, interest groups and the media. As such, the strength of the accountability nexus between the regulatory agencies and utility consumers will be heavily dependent upon the capacity of these intermediary bodies to represent effectively the collective, and in some instances the divergent, interests of domestic consumers. The decision to establish consumer committees under the wing of the regulator, in the water and electricity industries, potentially weakens the extent to which these bodies can call the regulator to account; although the degree to which this has actually occurred is discussed in Chapter 6.

The most significant structural barrier to the regulatory agencies establishing a strong accountability relationship with ordinary consumers, however, lies in the fact, as shown earlier, that the regulators have what might be described as, an 'antecedent set of accountabilities' to the shareholders of the private energy and water companies.

During the passage of the Competition and Service (Utilities) Bill, the National Association of Citizens Advice Bureaux sought to include an amendment requiring the relevant Secretary of State to set standards of performance for each of the regulators. While this amendment would have consolidated further the 'residual' powers of the Secretary of State, it was viewed as a way of adding a layer of transparency and external accountability to the arcane and closed regulatory system. The amendment was opposed by the Government on the basis that:

> . . . to perform his duties effectively, the director must, in our view, retain his independence of the political process. For the Secretary of State to set performance standards for the regulator as the amendment envisages would involve him in second-guessing the director and would compromise that independence.
>
> Lord Reay, House of Lords, 5/3/92, col. 1097

If, ultimately, the effectiveness of a regulatory system is dependent upon the clarity and precision of the lines of accountability that exist between the regulators and the primary stakeholders in the regulatory process, then the British system looks fundamentally flawed. As much as anything else, the British model of regulation seems to be founded on trust. This may turn out to be an unsound principle around which to build a structure of economic and social regulation in an area as vital as the public utilities.

3

Objectives and outcomes of the privatization of the public utilities

The economic and political objectives of the privatization programme

Introduction

Before 1979 there was a general acceptance that what were then called public utilities – water, electricity, gas – are best provided for a society by one kind or another of public ownership. The New Right substituted and acted so far as it could on the ideal of shareholders, entrepreneurs, and in general what is called free enterprise.

Honderich (1991: 88)

The sale of the public utilities in Britain could be seen to represent the zenith or nadir, depending on one's point of view, of the privatization programme carried out under the leadership of Margaret Thatcher. The privatization of the utilities – particularly, water and to a lesser extent, gas and electricity – had been seen by many to take the Government, and in turn the public, into previously uncharted waters. The denationalization of the utilities overturned key dimensions of 'the 1940s settlement' (Gamble 1989: 2) and directly challenged beliefs, built up over 40 years, about the role of government in strategic areas of the economy and about the immutability of public control of the utility industries.

The privatization programme began fairly unambitiously, with the National Freight Corporation being the sole industry specifically identified for sale to the private sector in the Conservative Party manifesto in 1979 (Conservative Party Central Office 1979). It was only during the second term of the Thatcher government's period of office that attention began to be directed towards the privatization of the public utilities. The culmination of the privatization programme was achieved during Mrs Thatcher's third term, with the sales of the complex water and electricity supply industries.

The tenets of radical liberal political philosophy have provided much of the intellectual momentum of privatization. A desire to test and apply New Right theories of the state and the market to the British polity has been a residual objective over much of the history of the privatization programme. However, at the level of practical policy-making, the privatization programme has been motivated by a set of rather more concrete political and economic objectives. Paramount amongst these have been promoting wider share ownership, reducing the Public Sector Borrowing Requirement (PSBR) and improving the operational efficiency of public utility industries.

Despite having a clear ideological underpinning, there is little evidence that the sale of the public utilities was carried out according to some predetermined blueprint. Indeed, in the view of most commentators, the privatization policies of the Thatcher and Major Governments generally have been characterized less by ideological consistency and policy coherence than by heuristic and often pragmatic responses to political and financial exigencies (Kay et al. 1986; Gamble 1989; Marsh 1991). The privatization of the energy and water industries was characterized, however, by generally similar policy objectives, although the emphasis given to specific objectives varied in line with the different political and economic climate within which each sale was conducted.

In the first part of this chapter, the economic and political objectives explicit in the Conservative Government's utility privatization programme will be examined. The extent to which these objectives have been achieved is considered in the second part of the chapter, and in the chapters that follow.

Privatization – the economic arguments

The primary economic arguments used to justify the privatization of public utilities and other public enterprises take as their starting point a critique of the defects of public ownership, and revolve centrally around two major issues: (i) the constraints on economic freedom arising from the existence of government-run monopolies and the associated failure of these industries to give appropriate priority to the interests of consumers, and (ii) the seemingly endemic inefficiency of public enterprises. These arguments have been articulated in varying forms by representatives of the Government (e.g. John Moore, in a series of speeches to the City in 1983 and 1985, John Redwood, 1988, and the water and electricity privatization White Papers), as well as by academic economists such as Beesley and Littlechild (1986), Curwen (1986) and Veljanovski (1987, 1989b).

Economic freedom and consumer sovereignty

> The nationalised industries have . . . unfortunately not been very good at
> satisfying their customers . . . Services often did not seem to match needs
> or expectations.
>
> Moore (1986: 83)

In the view of advocates of privatization, the existence of large nationalized
industries with effective monopoly power over demand and supply, act as a
severe brake on the exercise of individual economic freedom. This constraint on
freedom is manifest in two major ways; firstly, it inhibits the ability of 'corporate
individuals' (i.e. private sector firms) to gain a market share of those parts of the
production and service economy controlled by the nationalized industries and
secondly, as a result of this absence of a free market (or even a marginally open
one), the individual consumer has no capacity to exercise choice in the purchase
of goods and services supplied by public sector enterprises.

Choice is reified as the passport to consumer sovereignty and ultimately,
service quality. Therefore, in the absence of choice the consumer is captive and
exposed to the vagaries of a producer-dominant service system. The level of
producer domination, characteristic of many nationalized industries, in turn
engenders an insensitivity towards, and a disinclination to respond to, the needs
and wishes of consumers. This caricature of complacent public monopoly providers is juxtaposed against the metaphor of the market and the inherently responsive and customer-friendly environment of the private sector: 'privately owned
companies have a greater incentive to produce goods and services in the quantity
and variety which consumers prefer' (Beesley and Littlechild 1986: 38). The
introduction of similar incentives – related to the existence of competing sources of
supply and the requirement of profit maximization in the interests of shareholders
– into the erstwhile nationalized industries would secure a framework of rights and
protections for consumers unattainable under public ownership.

As with the characterization of the free market economy generally, the
concept of consumer sovereignty has as much untruth to it as it has truth. In
order for consumer sovereignty to have practical, and not just rhetorical,
meaning a set of preconditions are necessary. These include the existence of a
range of product choice, conditioned by the actual preferences and needs of
consumers (rather than, as is often the case, both preference and product being
'manufactured' by the producers themselves), the absence of significant levels
of information asymmetry between producers and consumers, the sensitivity of
price to consumer demand (i.e. producers as 'price takers' rather than 'price
makers') and the ability for consumers to exit without financial or other loss.
Only rarely, in most commodity markets, do these preconditions apply.

Improving efficiency

> Public enterprises perform relatively poorly in terms of their competitive
> position, use labour and capital inefficiently and are less profitable.
>
> Moore (1986: 83)

What hampers the [electricity] industry is its structure and its position in
the public sector.

'Electricity Privatisation', White Paper Cm. 9734

The function of the market as creator and protector of consumer sovereignty
has carried considerable symbolic potency in the economic case for privatization – as reflected in the way that it has been frequently invoked by the
Government in support of privatization policy – but the substantive case for
denationalization is built not around consumer sovereignty, but around the
argument of economic efficiency.

Opponents of public ownership start from the premise that the efficiency
performance of public enterprises is invariably overshadowed by that of their
private sector counterparts, or in the absence of counterparts (as in the case of
monopolies), by the prospective private businesses that should displace them.
The superiority of the private sector is seen as absolute, despite the failure of a
quarter of a century of research into the comparative performance of the public
and private sectors to lend clear support to this belief.

The endemic inefficiency of public enterprise – particularly as manifested
in low rates of return on capital investment relative to that obtained within the
market generally – is said to be the result of two factors. Firstly, their monopoly
or quasi-monopoly position within the public sector affords them protection
and insulation from the economic rigour of market forces. Hence poor management practices, bad investment decisions and low levels of worker productivity escape the sanctions for failure that ostensibly apply to firms in the private
sector (i.e. takeover and bankruptcy). Secondly, the location of the industries
within the province of government is seen as intrinsically detrimental to their
economic performance. Much of the failure of the nationalized industries had
been attributed by partisan and non-partisan commentators alike to the defects
of government management (Curwen 1986; Levacic 1987; Veljanovski 1987;
Seldon 1990; Ashworth 1991). Criticisms of the management track record of
successive British governments include, the subordination of long-term capital
planning and investment to short-term political and fiscal priorities, the imposition of unnecessary constraints and controls on the commercial prerogatives of the nationalized industries and the sheer inability of government
ministers to make good business decisions.

The economic viability of the nationalized industries has been also affected, it is often asserted, by the burden of non-commercial objectives conventionally imposed upon them by government. Pryke (1986: 117) makes this
point when he argues that the 'most likely explanation for the poor performance of the public enterprise activities is that they are in public ownership. It
could have had a harmful effect by inducing the belief that the activities should
act as social services and take the national interest into account'.

Generally it is held by all but the most partisan of privatization proponents, that the mere transfer of monopoly industries from the public to private
sectors is insufficient in itself to achieve either the consumerist or efficiency

outcomes attributed to the market, for ownership is not the key variable (Dunsire et al. 1988; Helm et al. 1988b; Cullis and Jones 1989; Parry 1990; Parker and Hartley 1991; Bibby 1992). In order for these outcomes to be realized, privatization needs to be accompanied by a restructuring of public monopolies, with the aim of stimulating competition.

Competition is the engine by which the force of change, in the structure and output of one-time public sector activities, is to be driven. The advent of competition in hitherto closed and insulated enterprises, it is asserted, will lead to a veritable chain reaction of positive effects, like increased productivity and efficiency, greater public accountability and enhanced consumer power. For Moore (1986: 92) the efficacy of privatization is intertwined with competition: '[t]he long-term success of the privatisation programme will stand or fall by the extent to which it maximises competition. If competition cannot be achieved, a historic opportunity will have been lost'.

The political objectives of the privatization programme

> . . . the government's aims in relation to privatization have changed substantially over time. As they have changed, and the political aims have become more important, so the government has offered incentives to ensure successful asset sales and broader share ownership.
>
> Marsh (1991: 461)

The political agenda of privatization, as Marsh suggests, appeared to take on more importance for the Thatcher Government as the privatization programme progressed. The essentially political issue of fiscal management occupied a significant place in the rationale for privatization from the outset. Over time, however, it was supplemented with the explicitly political objectives of reducing trade union power, permanently overturning *dirigisme* and socialism in British public policy, and popular capitalism.

The ascendancy of the political purposes of the programme reflected the increased confidence and parliamentary dominance of the Thatcher Government after successive electoral victories. In addition, the economic objectives of privatization – competition, efficiency, choice and lower prices – which seemed tenable in the earlier privatizations, became (until ESI privatization at least) more and more difficult to sustain and to justify as the framework and mechanics of utility privatization evolved.

Fiscal management

As elsewhere in the world the difficulties in reconciling revenue with expenditure in the government accounts provided considerable impetus to those of us arguing for a large [privatization] programme and helped by enabling it to be built into the framework of the national budget. It became something all wings of the Conservative Party could agree on, left and right, as it made available more money both for spending

Figure 3.1 Privatization proceeds 1979–1992.

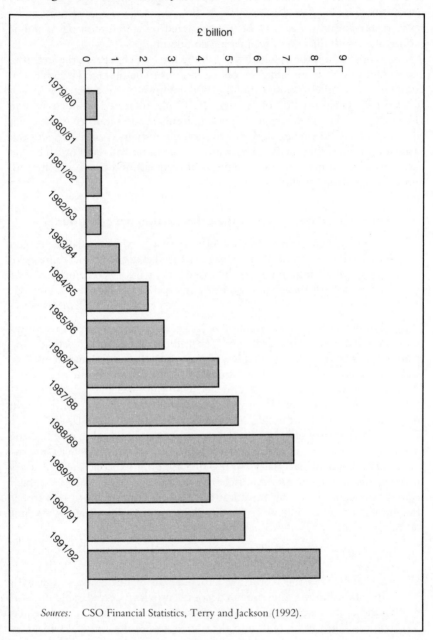

Sources: CSO Financial Statistics, Terry and Jackson (1992).

Figure 3.2 Public Sector Borrowing Requirement 1979–1992

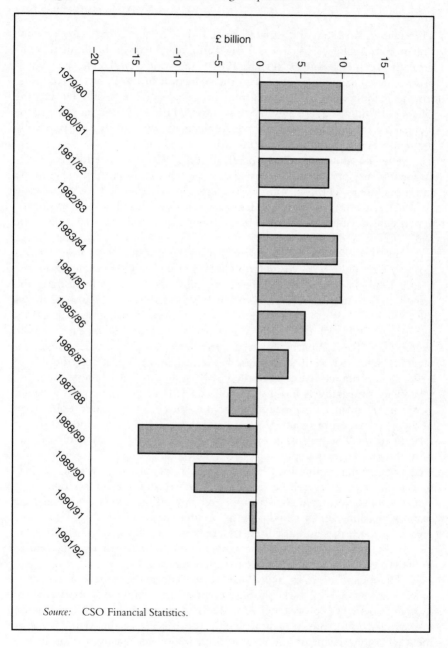

Source: CSO Financial Statistics.

programmes, and for the tax cuts dear to the hearts of both sections of the party.

Redwood (1988: 147)

Throughout the 1980s and early 1990s, the development of a secure revenue stream from public asset sales has formed an integral part of the Government's fiscal management strategy (Heald 1984; Hogwood 1992). The growth in privatization receipts contributed to the reduction in the Public Sector Borrowing Requirement (PSBR) during the decade of the 1980s. During the Chancellorship of Nigel Lawson, it also afforded the Government some scope for making tax cuts, without the concomitant necessity of making politically unpopular cuts in public expenditure (Johnson 1992).

The 'accounting conventions' (Kay et al. 1986) employed by the Government to use privatization proceeds as an offset against current expenditure and the failure to set this income against future loss of revenue (that would have been derived from the industries had they remained in public ownership) has drawn considerable criticism (Curwen 1986; Heald and Steel 1986; Levacic 1987; Vickers and Yarrow, 1988).

By 1991–92, proceeds from the privatization of state enterprises totalled almost £42 billion, with around £39 billion of this being generated from the period 1984–85 (sale of British Telecom) onwards. Figure 3.1 illustrates the growth in privatization receipts between 1979 and 1991–92. Figure 3.2 shows the annual level of the PSBR over the same period. It can be seen that from 1987–88 to 1990–91 the PSBR was a negative figure (effectively a Public Sector Debt Repayment), which is attributable, in part, to the substantial revenues obtained from asset sales. For example, privatization proceeds in 1988–89 contributed over half of the PSBR of minus £14.7 billion.

The comparatively healthy state of the PSBR during these years gave the Government financial manoeuvring room to further other political objectives of the privatization programme. Helm and Powell (1992: 91) allude to this in relation to the ESI privatization in 1990–91: 'The maximisation of revenue from the sale was less important than in Telecoms [*sic*] and gas, as the public sector borrowing requirement became a public sector debt payment.' In particular, the temporary release from the PSBR-related concerns would have enabled the Government to focus more directly on the objective of widening share ownership, which could only be progressed at some financial cost (e.g. providing incentives and discounts to attract new entrants to the equity market). It also took the pressure off the Government to maximize revenue returns in the sale of the water and electricity supply industries.

The recent return to high PSBR levels reflects the impact of the economic recession, as well as the abandonment of strict monetarist approaches to fiscal management (a process started under the Chancellorship of Nigel Lawson in the mid-1980s). But in common with its predecessors, the Major Government is heavily reliant on the level of privatization receipts remaining high – £5.5 billion in both 1993–94 and 1994–95 (HM Treasury 1992: table 1.1) – to notionally reduce public expenditure. As the supply of saleable industries and the Government's shareholdings in privatized companies like British Telecom dry up, these revenue targets will become increasingly harder to achieve (Hogwood 1992).

Beyond the short-term expedient of raising revenue, it was argued by the Government, that eliminating the ex-nationalized industries' call on government loan finance for capital works, through changing ownership and facilitating the industries' access to private capital, would reduce the 'crowding out' of private sector investment by the public sector. As a process of shifting the source of demand for investment capital, privatization of the utility industries has indeed achieved this end. However, the overall impact of this change in the locus of demand on the capital market generally is rather more suspect, for as Kay et al. (1986: 29) argue, '[t]raditional crowding-out arguments are clearly not applicable here and to the extent that there is an effect it is to change the composition, rather than the total, of private sector borrowing'.

A more tangible benefit of shifting the source of investment demand is derived from the fact that it removes the capital debt of the newly-privatized companies from the Government's fiscal balance sheet. This was particularly important to the Government in the case of the water industry and was, arguably, at the heart of its motivation for selling the industry. In the absence of privatization, the projected ten-year capital investment requirement (£26 billion at 1989 prices) would have been added to public sector debt and would need to have been financed through increases in charges, or out of taxation revenue, or both. Through privatizing the water industry, the Government has been able to relieve itself of a sector with a high future debt profile. At the same time it has been able to distance itself from the inevitably adverse popular reaction to annual real-term increases in water charges arising from the capital investment programme.

Creating a share-owning democracy

The British Telecom issue did more than just enable Britain to establish the world's first large scale privatisation programme. It also led by chance to the invention of part of popular capitalism . . . The idea of seeking a large new generation of small savers came out of the exigencies of a marketing campaign to sell the world's largest ever equity offering . . . At last the prospect opened up, not merely of individuals owning a direct stake in the country through the ownership of their own land and houses, but also through direct ownership of a part of industry itself.

Redwood (1988: 147)

The use of the privatization programme as a means of extending share ownership within the workforce of the ex-nationalized industries and amongst the public at large, has become more explicit as the programme has progressed. The 'Tell Sid' marketing of British Gas shares confirmed the new agenda in the privatization process and a desire to widen share ownership was given as part of the rationale for water and electricity privatization in the relevant White Papers. More recently, the National Audit Office (1992a,b) reports on the sale of the water and electricity industries and cites share ownership as a primary objective in both cases.

The emphasis given by the Government to stimulating public interest in the sale of the nationalized industries began in relative indifference and concluded, in the case of the later public utility sales, in high fervour. Amongst the measures used by the Government to stimulate public interest in the sale of the public utilities were the substantial discounting of shares at flotation, the use of customer incentives such as bill vouchers and bonus shares, and the orchestration of slick and expensive publicity campaigns.

The political benefits for a Conservative Government in broadening the individual shareholder base of the equity market are reasonably self-evident. In establishing 'a rentier interest in the market' (Clarke 1987: 71), it is probable that members of the electorate who hold shares would be more receptive to the pro-market policies of the Conservative Party as Veljanovski (1987: 68) explains:

> The political dimension of this [privatization] has not escaped Conservative Party Central Office. TSB created about 1.5 million shareholders; 1.2 million retain shares in BT and another 5 million in BG . . . This suggests that the average constituency electorate will have about 20,000 shareholder voters, which could make a difference in marginal seats.

McAllister and Studlar (1989), in an analysis of voting patterns in the 1987 General Election, provide empirical support for the thesis that the Conservative Party is likely to be the electoral beneficiary of share ownership in the privatized industries. In this study (1989: 172), the researchers concluded that the Conservative Party 'gained 10 per cent more of the vote among new share owners, compared to those who had never owned shares, while Labour lost 9 per cent of the vote, net of other things'. Although the aggregate net gain for the Tories from the privatization shareholder vote was relatively small – i.e. 1.6 per cent – it would constitute a useful and possibly decisive contribution in a tight election campaign.

The political advantage accruing to the Conservatives from dispersed share ownership would also be manifested in a situation where the Labour Party (or any other party with a prospect of winning government) sought to renationalize privatized industries where the equity participation of individual investors is high, as this would '[threaten] not only the gentleman in the pin stripes but the voter in the bus queue' (Redwood 1988: 39). So, even if the direct political pay-off for the Conservative Party is relatively small in terms of additional votes, dispersed share ownership has the effect of applying a brake on the range of alternative policy options available to future governments and effectively places renationalization and public ownership in the 'no-go area' of British politics.

Short-term electoral advantage aside, broadening share ownership might also be viewed, along with the sale of council housing (under the rubric of 'popular capitalism') as a project aimed at longer-term ideological objectives. The inculcation of an anti-state, pro-market and entrepreneurial culture was manifestly part of the agenda of Thatcherism (Keat 1991) and the extension of property relations through equity and home ownership was seen as a primary mode of achieving this. Empirical studies into the values and attitudes of the British population suggest, however, that the impact of this ideological project has been limited (Jowell et al. 1990, 1991; ICM 'State of the Nation' polls, *The Guardian* 17/9/90, 14/9/92) and that 'the hold of this ideology on the population at large seems no better assured now than it did ten or more years ago' (Hill 1990: 32).

The Government's share-owning agenda also intersected with the objective of consumer sovereignty. The consumer is most 'sovereign', it was asserted when she/he can influence the policies and practices of producer firms as a shareholder and 'owner'. The powerlessness of small shareholders *vis-à-vis* management in monolithic corporations has been used, on occasions, as a metaphor for the failings of the contemporary democratic state, by a number of radical liberal public choice theorists. But the impotence of the individual shareholder with small equity holdings, in the face of institutional control of the modern corporation was, not surprisingly, never acknowledged by the Government.

Reducing trade union power

The [nationalized] industries' performance on both productivity and manpower costs has also been disappointing. Public sector trade unions have been extraordinarily successful in gaining advantage for themselves in the pay hierarchy by exploiting their monopoly collective bargaining position.

Moore (1986: 82)

The weakening of the power of the trade union movement had been a major policy goal of the Thatcher Government over the decade of the 1980s (King 1987; Gamble 1988; Hill 1990; Metcalf 1991). The policy instruments which the Thatcher Government used to debilitate the industrial and political strength of trade unions included, the use of state power to suppress strike action (reaching its apotheosis in the miners' strike of 1984–85), the introduction of a range of legislative measures to control the power of union leadership, the termination of the corporatist relationship between government and the Trades Union Congress which had existed over much of the post-war period, and the privatization of the nationalized industries.

Historically, the nationalized industries had been a stronghold for the trade union movement, with a proportionally high membership relative to employees in the private sector and a capacity, due to their strategic location in key industrial sectors of the economy, to negotiate substantial improvements in wages and working conditions. Most importantly, the conditions achieved by workers in the nationalized industries often had a vanguarding effect, where the

benefits they achieved ultimately flowed on to employees in other sectors of
the economy. This nexus between monopoly union negotiating power, with a
concomitant ability to win award changes without necessarily any increase in
productivity, and the general escalation of worker demands throughout the
economy, was one that the Thatcher Government was keen to sever. Privatization of the major strategic industries potentially provided a platform from
which to achieve this.

The Thatcher Government was, arguably, at its strongest and most assertive in the industrial relations field and the ability of successive administrations
under the leadership of Mrs Thatcher to moderate the claims of the trade
unions constituted one of its most noteworthy achievements (Gamble 1988;
Vane 1992). The union movement was placed very much on the defensive
throughout the 1980s and its failure to marshal significant public support in the
face of a sustained assault upon its traditional prerogatives, was paralleled by a
decline in its own membership base. In 1979, union members made up around
55 per cent of the eligible population, whereas in 1984, this had fallen to less
than 46 per cent. Even accounting for unemployment, union membership as a
proportion of the working population had dropped by around 5 per cent over
this period (Halsey 1988: 188–189). The membership of unions affiliated with
the TUC fell by almost one-third between 1979 and 1989 (Metcalf 1991).

While trade union power in Britain has patently declined since 1979, the
part that the privatization programme has played in this is by no means clear. A
number of commentators have argued that the effect of privatization on the
trade union movement has been relatively minor (Thomas 1986; Marsh 1991).
Yet there are a number of areas where privatization could be seen to have had
some impact.

The process leading up to privatization – the 'liberalization' stage –
where nationalized industries have been obliged to introduce more efficient,
commercial regimes has led to the rationalization of work practices and the
shedding of labour (Pint 1990). In the water industry, for instance, the number
of workers employed across England and Wales between 1985 and 1989 fell by
around 11 per cent, over three-quarters of whom were employed in craft and
manual jobs (Water Prospectus 1989). The 'down-sizing' process in a number
of the nationalized industries has also been used as a form of role model to
encourage other parts of the public sector to adopt a more streamlined and
productivity-conscious approach.

Evidence suggests that some sectors of the workforce in the privatized
industries, particularly the low skilled, have been negatively affected by privatization (Thomas 1986), and this has certainly been the case in the different, but
associated arena of contracting out (PSPRU 1992). If as Thomas claims, the
nationalized industries tended to equalize the working conditions of skilled and
low-skilled workers in this sector (through collective bargaining), then it is
probably not surprising that the eradication of what might be seen as a form of
'wage cross-subsidization' would become an early target of a profit-conscious
management in the newly privatized industries.

The emphasis that successive governments have given to the equity participation of employees in the privatization of their own industries, through free and discounted shares, suggests that the promotion of a form of worker capitalism has become an important dimension in the battle to eradicate trade union militancy. Workers, it could be argued, would be less likely to make 'irresponsible' demands for improved wages and working conditions and would be less receptive to the idea of industrial action, or even union membership, when they have a direct investment in the profitability of their company. The way that the Thatcher Government promoted the National Freight Consortium as the new wave worker-management concept lends support to the hypothesis that the shop floor itself formed part of the battleground in the fight against collectivism.

The provision of 'transfer payments to the employees of the privatised firms' (Pint 1990: 283) via employee share ownership schemes, has also been an effective strategy for weakening trade union resistance to the privatization programme. In addition to the shareholdings of individual trade unionists, the trade union movement at a central level is substantially implicated in the privatization programme as large corporate equity holders, as Veljanovski (1987: 69) points out:

> Trade unions are also major institutional investors. The control of pension funds ensures that the trade unions themselves have a vested interest in the performance of the stock market. Since BT and British Gas now make up significant sections of the quoted stock, prudent portfolio management requires that trade union pension funds hold a number of BT and British Gas shares.

Defeating socialism and collectivism

> Thatcher made no secret of her wish to see socialism destroyed as an effective political force in Britain, and a two-party system organised in which both parties fully accepted the legitimacy of capitalism and markets.
>
> Gamble (1988: 221)

More than any other British government in living memory, the Thatcher Government made a concerted and conscious attempt, not only to undermine the electoral base of the major opposition party (which is presumably the object of all governments), but to demolish the moral and philosophical edifice of the Left in Britain.

The privatization programme occupies a critical place in the challenge to the legitimacy of collectivist solutions to economic and social problems in contemporary British society. The development of a pro-market constituency through the policy agenda of popular capitalism is aimed explicitly at this end.

Of equal importance is the fact that the denationalization of public enterprises strikes – both symbolically and literally – at the very heart of 'the socialist objective', expressed through the original Clause 4 of the Labour Party Constitution (i.e. public ownership of the means of production, distribution and exchange). The intellectual and physical momentum of the privatization programme over the past decade or so, not only served to reinforce the belief that governments should not be entrusted with a direct role in industrial production, it has helped to elevate this belief to the status of a political truism. The Labour Party's rather anxious attempts to redefine its position on nationalization and the public utilities, initially via the muted concept of 'social ownership' and later, by its proposals to strengthen the public regulation of privatized industries (*Looking to the Future* 1990; *Labour Opportunity Britain* 1991), underlines the extent to which the anti-collectivist idea has become the monolith on the political landscape in Britain.

Apart from the problem of confronting the hegemony of anti-collectivism, future governments with a socialist programme are likely to encounter significant practical problems if they attempt to renationalize the privatized industries. The options, for a hypothetical radical socialist government of the future, in returning the privatized industries to the public sector would be (i) to renationalize *without* compensation, (ii) to renationalize with the payment of compensation on the basis of *original* price paid for shares, or (iii) to renationalize with compensation based on *current* share value. The first option would probably be politically suicidal; the second would, in the light of the windfall increase in the value of most privatized company shares, be only marginally less so; and the third would be extremely expensive. The difficult economics of renationalization was not lost on the Labour Party in the 1992 General Election campaign, as evidenced by the ever-receding time frame for fulfilling the party's manifesto commitment to bring the water industry back into public ownership. In effect, through discounting the share price of most of the privatized enterprises, the Thatcher Government effectively stymied the ability of future governments to renationalize without huge financial, and probably political, costs. This dimension of the politics of privatization, is highlighted by Vickers and Yarrow (1988: 181):

> . . . renationalisation on less than fair terms would be a process in which the losers would know that they had lost but the gainers would not know that they had gained in relative terms. The Chairman of the Conservative Party, Mr Norman Tebbit, probably had these considerations in mind when writing to BT shareholders in 1986 asking them to think how much a Labour Government would cost them. This suggests that a side effect of the privatisation program has been to make more visible some consequences of various electoral outcomes for the distribution of wealth in the UK.

In the next part of this chapter, the broader distributional outcomes of the privatization programme will be evaluated against the Government's political and economic objectives. Primary emphasis will be given to an appraisal of the public utility asset sales (relevant to the issue of fiscal management), share ownership and the financial performance of the private utility companies. The substantive issue of the direct outcomes of energy and water privatization for domestic consumers forms the basis of Chapters 4, 5 and 6.

Matching performance with rhetoric: the outcomes

Introduction

The character of the political and economic objectives of the privatization programme, representing as they do, a set of diffuse and shifting policy priorities, would suggest in itself that the Government's success in meeting these objectives would be likely to be mixed. If for no other reason, the privatization programme will give rise to variable outcomes because a number of its primary objectives are incongruent, or even in conflict. An example of this, which has drawn most attention, is the inherent conflict between the objective of obtaining the best price for the industries at the point of sale and the objective of creating a competitive framework for the operation of the privatized utilities:

> The aim of selling public enterprises to raise revenue and that of privatising them in order to maximize efficiency, by placing the firms in a competitive environment, are in conflict. The greater the market power of a newly privatised firm, the higher are likely to be its profits and so the greater its stock market valuation. If a public enterprise has its market power reduced by being broken up into several parts and has its protective regulations dismantled, it will be unable to earn monopoly profits. As its share value on the Stock Exchange will be lower it will fetch less for the state coffers.
>
> Levacic (1987: 266–267)

Other examples of tension between the disparate policy objectives in the programme include trying to encourage wider share ownership, inevitably involving a degree of discounting, at the same time as attempting to maximize the returns to the Treasury, and seeking to release essential service industries from public intervention and control while also promising consumers new protections and rights.

Another factor complicating the attainment of the Government's preferred outcomes is that in some instances – notably in the natural monopoly sectors of the public utilities – the predominant economic objective (i.e. the creation of a vigorous competitive environment) is simply incompatible with the existing, and over the medium-term at least, future structure of the industries themselves.

The outcomes of the privatization of the public utilities will be assessed in relation to the three core objectives of (i) maximizing revenue from the sale of the three utilities, (ii) extending share ownership and (iii) improving the economic performance of the utility industries. This account of the outcomes to date gives some indication of the macro-distributional effects of utility privatization and begins to provide an answer to the overriding question of who has won and who has lost as a result of public utility privatization?

Revenue from the sale of the public utilities

The extent to which maximum proceeds were generated from the sale of the utilities is an issue of considerable importance, not only for the limited evaluative reference point of whether the Government's stated objectives were achieved, but for the broader public interest perspective of how historically accumulated and publicly-funded assets have been valued and sold.

In the earlier utility privatizations – British Telecom and British Gas – the Government was heavily criticized for selling these industries for substantially less than their actual worth (Buckland 1987; Bishop and Kay 1988; Vickers and Yarrow 1988; Chapman 1990; Whitfield 1992). The aggregate loss, including flotation costs, in these two sales has been estimated, conservatively, to be in the order of £2.5 billion (Vickers and Yarrow 1988). Bishop and Kay (1988: 35) concluded that:

> The flotation process is the subject of much self-congratulation between Government and its financial advisers. We are less impressed. The fact that there is excess demand for a product which can be sold tomorrow at a substantial premium on today's price is not a measure of the product's popularity. Still less is it a testimony to the skill of the retailer. The fixed price issues have been sold at substantial – in some cases absurd – discounts . . .

While being less explicit in its criticisms of the sale process, the official Parliamentary auditors, the National Audit Office (1987: 15), concluded in relation to British Gas that 'it is difficult to say whether the Department [of Energy] maximised the sale proceeds'. In particular, it raised queries about the Government's expenditure on underwriting costs and shareholder incentives, and questioned whether the Government had managed to strike the best bargain with the directors of British Gas, on behalf of British taxpayers.

Against this background of concern about the undervaluation of the privatized industries (which was regularly replayed in the media), it might be expected that the Government and its City advisers would seek to strike a discernibly better bargain in the water and electricity privatizations. But if anything, evidence from these sales indicates that the reverse occurred.

The question of what is the 'true value' of utility assets is a vexed one. The Labour Party has consistently argued that the utilities should be valued according to the actual costs of replacing their assets (e.g. in House of Commons debates on the 16 January 1991 and 2 July 1991). On this calculation, the water companies would have been valued at £34503 million on a current cost basis and £8665 million on a historical cost basis (National Audit Office 1992a: table 6). The Government, supported by the National Audit Office, has dismissed this as a hypothetical and massively unrealistic valuation and the latter has argued

Table 3.1 Effective market capitalization of the public utilities.

Capitalization	Water companies	Regional electricity companies	Generating companies	British Gas	Total
Offer market capitalization	£5239	£5181.6	£3597.9	£5603	£19621
Premium day 1	19%	21%	21%	10%	
Premium £ equivalent	995.41	1088.14	755.56	560.30	3399
End day 1	£6234	£6270	£4353	£6163	£23021

that the 'accounting value of assets is not . . . a reflection of the underlying value of the company to investors, particularly in an industry like water where capital assets are highly specialised. Investors assessment of the value of a company is based on the expected stream of future dividends' (1992a: 25).

A simple measure conventionally used by economists to assess the extent to which the privatized industries have been valued correctly, entails comparing the effective market capitalization of the industries at sale, as expressed in the offer price of shares, with their market capitalization at the end of the first day of trading on the Stock Exchange. This will invariably produce a valuation much lower than that based on asset replacement at current cost, but it provides an indication of how the market values the industries immediately they come up for sale. Table 3.1 shows the effective market value of the energy and water utilities at the end of trading on the first day of sale. It can be seen that the market value of all of the utilities appreciated considerably over the course of the first day's trading on the Stock Exchange and that the accumulated undervaluation of the energy and water utilities, according to this measure, was in the region of £3.4 billion.

The first day's trading indicates the market's immediate response to the privatization sales, but a more accurate measure of the industries' valuation might be obtained over a longer time-frame, when the market has had an opportunity to settle down. The initial response of the market may artificially inflate the value of the industry, or conversely it may not capture the full value of the industry being sold. In both the water and ESI sales, the Department of the Environment and the Department of Energy respectively, used a three-week 'aftermarket' period to determine whether the objectives of the sales had been achieved (National Audit Office 1992a,b). The movement in utility share prices over the first full three weeks of trading on the Stock Exchange is outlined in Table 3.2. Using a three-week period, then, to estimate the market value of the utilities, reveals that the utilities were effectively worth a total of £23389 million, which is around £3.8 billion, or 19 per cent, more than the *gross* proceeds the Government obtained from their sale. By mid–December

Table 3.2   Increase in public utility share prices over first three weeks.

Utility	Percentage		
	End day 1	*End 1 week*	*End 3 weeks*
British Gas (£1.35)	10 (27)	11 (29)	11 (31)
Water companies (£2.40)	19 (46)	21 (50)	28 (68)
RECs (£2.40)	21 (51)	22 (53)	20 (48)
Generators (£1.75)	21 (37)	21 (38)	18 (31)

⋆ Premium on fully-paid basis and premium on part-paid basis (in parentheses). Payment for privatization shares made through instalments; the part-paid premium is the percentage change in value of the first instalment after trading commenced.

1992 (the anniversary of the sale of three of the four utility sectors), the total market capitalization of these companies was £37.2 billion, an aggregate valuation almost 90 per cent higher than that set by the Government when the industries were sold.

The Government justified the apparent undervaluation of the public utilities on the grounds (i) that they were selling into an untested market, (ii) that the utilities – particularly the water industry – represented an 'investment risk' (National Audit Office 1992a: 9), and (iii) that a small premium on the shares (around 10 per cent) was necessary in order 'to promote wider share ownership' and 'to ensure a healthy aftermarket in the shares of each company' (House of Commons Committee of Public Accounts 1992: vii).

The untested market argument would seem to lack plausibility after the highly successful, and heavily oversubscribed, flotation of British Telecom, where the market acceptability of a modestly-priced utility became immediately apparent. The dimensions of the risk factor appear, in retrospect, to have been grossly overrated by the Government and its advisers. This is underlined by the extremely high level of investor interest in the water industry at flotation and subsequently, to the point where almost three years after the sale, water shares were described as having 'been an outstanding investment to date' and '1992's top performing sector' (*Investors Chronicle*, 4/9/92, p. 58). The Director General of Water Services, in his analyses of the capital structure of the water companies has also consistently characterized the water industry as 'low risk' (OFWAT 1991l; 1992o). The third argument about the need to guarantee a share premium, in order to stimulate individual investor interest, underlines the improbability of reconciling the task of maximizing returns to taxpayers from the sale of public assets with the tendentious objective of broadening share ownership.

The direct beneficiaries of the discounted sale of the utility industries have been the institutions and individuals who invested in privatization shares. Substantial profits were made by those investors who sold their shares within the first few weeks after the sale. For investors who have retained shares in the privatized utilities, the discounts built into the sales have provided the platform

Figure 3.3 Movement in the value of private utility shares.

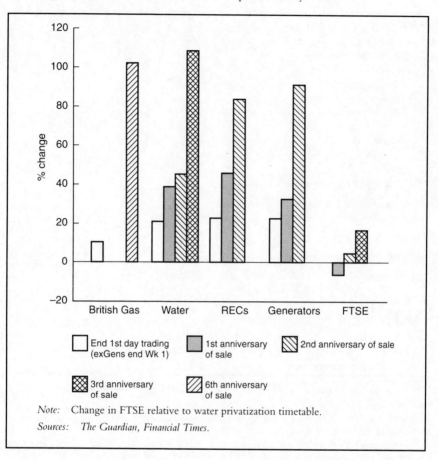

Note: Change in FTSE relative to water privatization timetable.
Sources: *The Guardian, Financial Times.*

for a sustained growth in the value of these equities, as illustrated in Figure 3.3. On the other side of the ledger, the loss of substantial sums of public revenue in the sales has been to the immediate and longer-term detriment of taxpayers in general. Gross proceeds do not represent, however, the actual gain to public revenue as a result of the sales, as costs such as underwriting and banking fees, advertising and marketing, and shareholder incentives have to be deducted. In addition, debt write-offs, taxation relief and incidental payments to the privatized industries have to be taken into account. Once this is done the amount obtained from the sale (i.e. net proceeds) looks even less satisfactory than that cited earlier. This is most noticeably the case with water privatization, where the net proceeds of the sale change from £3594.4 million (the official figure) to *minus* £1578 million. Tables 3.3 and 3.4 set out the balance sheets of the sale of the water and regional electricity companies. It would seem difficult to

Table 3.3   Sale of the water authorities ($£$ million).

Direct costs:	
(1) Cash injections	1572
(2) Shareholder incentives	85
(3) DoE costs	
Underwriting	33.2
Selling and broking	6.7
Marketing	36.3
Advisers fees	25.8
Bank costs	26.1
Overseas costs	15.4
Minus interest	(12.6)
Sub-total (a)	130.9
(4) Minus debt introduced	(72.9)
(5) Restructuring costs (b)	74
Sub-total (c)	1789
Indirect costs:	
Debt write-off	5028
Total costs:	6817
Proceeds:	
Gross proceeds	5239
Official net sale proceeds	3594.4
Actual net sale proceeds	−1578

The water companies were also given tax allowances valued at $£7700$ million.

Notes:
(a) In addition, the Water Authorities spent $£176$ million on marketing, advisers and associated privatization costs.
(b) Restructuring costs includes cost of creating National Rivers Authority and new regulatory arrangements, and expenditure connected with preparation of legislation.
(c) DoE aggregate (1), (3), (4) and $£15$ million of (2) only in calculating costs.

Sources: National Audit Office (1992a); House of Commons Committee of Public Accounts (1992).

conclude, on the basis of an examination of the balance sheets of these privatiz-ations, that the objective of maximizing the returns to the public purse from the sale of the utilities was actually achieved. Yet surprisingly, this has been, on the face of it, the conclusion drawn by the National Audit Office (1992a,b) in its reviews of the water and ESI sales. The findings of the National Audit Office have to be treated, however, with a measure of caution as it is con-strained by the fact that it has no remit to examine the broader policy context of the sales ('the Office cannot question matters of policy'; Beauchamp 1990: 55) and that its frame of reference in evaluating the sales is confined to the objectives set – in some cases retrospectively – by the initiating department.

Table 3.4 Sale of the regional electricity companies (£ million).

Gross proceeds:	
Sale of shares	5181.6
Direct costs:	
Shareholder incentives	112
Department of Energy costs	
Underwriting	36.6
Selling/broking commission	10.5
Marketing	15.2
Advisers fees	28.8
Banks fees	92.3
Overseas costs	18.5
Minus interest	(33.6)
Sub-total	168.3
Total	168.3
Total costs:	280.3
Proceeds:	
Net sale proceeds	4901.3

Note: In addition the RECs were injected with debt totalling £2.8 billion, repayable over 18 years.
Source: National Audit Office (1992b).

The National Audit Office reports on the sales do, however, contain occasional coded criticisms, for example on the sale of the RECs, 'the valuation of the companies' assets was reasonable *in the circumstances of this sale'* (National Audit Office 1992b: 2; author's emphasis) and less frequently, explicit condemnation of the Government's actions, as in its criticism of the Government for not making provision in the sale of the ESI for the 'clawback' of excessive profits in the first year of privatization.

The House of Commons Committee of Public Accounts (1992: xvi) seemed to get closer to the fundamental public interest question of whether the British taxpayer got value for money in the sales, when it stated in relation to water privatization that '[w]e note that the water companies' shares maintained a premium of some 20 per cent on a fully paid basis during the first six months of trading and performed above the general stock market trend. These factors indicate that the Department achieved their objective of a full take-up of shares *with something to spare'* (author's emphasis).

Extending share ownership

The extension of share ownership has been one of this Government's central aims – and privatisation makes a major contribution to its achievement. The ownership of shares gives individuals a direct stake in the success of British industry.

Conservative Party Research Department (1991: 97)

The Government's popular capitalism agenda became increasingly important over the life of the utility privatization programme. This has been evidenced subsequently in the fact that official *ex post facto* accounts of the privatization process, such as those produced by the National Audit Office, have elevated widening share ownership above fiscal management and other objectives. The success of the share ownership campaign, which has been instituted at substantial direct and indirect costs to the Exchequer, constitutes therefore an important test of the efficacy of the privatization programme. In conjunction with providing an answer the question, 'Has the Government extended the participation of individual investors in the stock market?', an analysis of the pattern of share ownership created by the public utility sales, adds another piece to the distributional jig-saw puzzle on the winners and losers in the privatization programme.

At a superficial glance, the campaign appears to have been an outstanding achievement for the Government. The number of adults owning shares has increased from less than 5 per cent in 1979 (Grout 1987) to around 22 per cent in 1992 (NOP 1992), with much of this growth being attributable to the sale of privatized industries. The level of over-subscription in the share offers at each successive flotation attests to the success of the Government in stimulating public interest in the equity market.

On closer examination, the achievement of popular capitalism is something of a mirage. The following data illustrate this:

● The majority of people (57 per cent) who owned shares in privatized companies held only one privatization issue (NOP 1992: table 10A).
● The bulk of shareholders have only a small tranche of equities – both by volume and value (NOP 1992: table 30A).
● Substantial numbers of individual investors sold their privatization stocks in the period immediately following the flotation of the privatized companies and continually thereafter, e.g. the number of shareholders in the water industry had halved within seven months of the sale (House of Commons Committee of Public Accounts 1992).
● The long-term decline in the level of individual ownership of the stock market has not been arrested by the share ownership campaign, i.e. 54 per cent in 1963, 28 per cent in 1981, 21 per cent in 1989 (Central Statistical Office 1991c: table 2).

Beyond general rhetorical injunctions to the British public 'to go forth and buy', the Government has never been particularly explicit about what it is actually trying to achieve in the quest for universal share ownership (a fact which drew criticism from the National Audit Office in the REC sale). But, if the Government was seeking to use the privatization sales as a device for either

(i) stimulating interest in the share market generally (i.e. people would move on to buy tranches of stocks in addition to their privatization holdings), (ii) prompting investor/customer engagement in the ongoing management of the privatized companies, or (iii) countering the domination of institutional players in the stock market (i.e. pension funds and insurance companies) – all of which would seem to be constituent elements of the share-owning democracy scenario – then the data above show anything but success. The view of the chairman of the London Stock Exchange underscores this, when he concluded that '[w]ider share ownership is a delusion – what we have is a lot of investors owning a few shares, basically in privatisation stocks' (*The Observer*, 2/8/92).

Table 3.5 Share ownership in the utility industries.

Total shareholders		Equity held by individuals (%)	Equity held by small shareholders* (%)	Equity held by large shareholders** (%)
British Gas [1]				
1987	3 111 872	35	27	59
1988	2 903 416	32	25	66
1989	2 695 450	30	22	68
1990	2 480 564	28	20	69
1991	2 178 855	25	18	73
1992	2 036 826	23	16	74
Thames Water [2]				
1990	391 896	26	23	54
1991	331 844	23	19	65
1992	306 165	20	17	71
South West Water [3]				
1990	57 249	19	16	75
1991	43 166	14	13	77
1992	39 876	13	11	73
Norweb				
1991	286 340	N/R	19	75
1992	228 263	N/R	15	79
Midlands Electricity				
1991	353 809	26	20	31
1992	284 629	17	17	50

[1] At privatization, 4.55 million shareholders.
[2] At privatization, 680 816 shareholders.
[3] At privatization, 129 064 shareholders.
N/R = Not reported.
Different definitions used due to different company reporting practices:
* Defined as less than 1000 shares (with exception of Thames and Norweb, less than 501 shares).
** Defined as minimum of 100 000 shares (with exception of Norweb, 50 001 shares).
Source: Company annual reports.

An analysis of the pattern of individual shareholdings in the utility industries, over time, does little to support the late Ian Gow's claim during the
Second Reading Debate on the Water Bill that privatization will lead to
'genuine public ownership' (House of Commons, 8/12/88, col. 511). Not all
of the privatized utilities provide details on the shareholder composition in
their Annual Reports, so it is difficult to assemble an aggregate picture. But
amongst those that do, there is evidence of a clear trend away from individual
small investor equity in the companies; which was relatively limited even at the
outset. Table 3.5 illustrates this. The withdrawal of the small investor has been
complemented in most cases by an increased concentration of ownership
amongst large investors. In reality, the small individual investor and the 'customer shareholder' occupy very peripheral places in the ownership structure of
the privatized utilities. Rather than changing the composition of equity holdings in Britain, the sale of the utility industries appears to have simply mirrored,
as well as entrenched, the domination of the institutional sector in the stock
market generally.

The distribution of individual share ownership follows, not surprisingly,
the major contours of inequality in British society, 'shareholders were drawn
disproportionately from men, from people in the middle age-groups, from
those in the professional and managerial socio-economic groups, and from
those with higher income levels' (*1988 General Household Survey*, 1990: 165).'

The 1987 and 1988 *General Household Surveys* on share ownership found
inter alia that people with a gross weekly income of £50 or lower were almost
six times less likely to own shares than people in the highest income group, and
that the level of share ownership was twice as high in the South East of England
than in the North of England. Both surveys found that the proportion of
people in manual socio-economic groups and with lower incomes holding
shares, was marginally greater in the case of privatization stocks than for shares
generally. But this was hardly of a sufficient order to suggest that privatization
has acted as significant egalitarian influence on the stock market.

A more recent survey carried out by NOP Omnibus Services for the
Treasury (January and February 1992) largely confirms the earlier *GHS* findings; although it did not collect income data, and hence is not comparable
along this dimension. Along the key axes of class, gender, age and regionality,
the NOP survey reveals a similar degree of inequality of participation in the
equity market as that identified in the *GHS*. Interestingly, the results of the
NOP study do not appear to support the earlier finding that privatization issues
engendered marginally greater involvement amongst manual socio-economic
groups. Social class AB was five and three times more likely to hold privatization shares than social classes DE and C2 respectively, whereas they were four
and two and a half times more likely to hold shares generally. One explanation
for this could be that more people in the manual socio-economic group (compared to other groups) cashed in their shares between 1988 and early 1992,
possibly as a result of the impact of the recession and rising unemployment.
The pattern of share ownership according to social class, in the NOP survey is

Figure 3.4 UK share ownership by social class (1992).

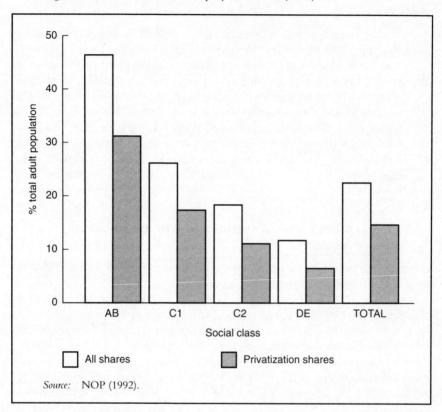

illustrated in the bar chart (Figure 3.4). Irrespective of the minor differences between the results of the three surveys on share ownership, it would seem obvious that the benefits of privatization shareholding (and as Figure 3.3 earlier indicated, these have been considerable) have not been equally shared amongst the population. Overall, the share ownership campaign has acted to simply re-trace, rather than re-draw, the extant dividing line of property ownership and property rights in British society.

It has been seen from the above that British taxpayers incurred a considerable financial loss through the sale of the utility industries. Here it is apparent that the prospect for recovering some of this loss, at an individual level, through ownership of discounted privatization shares has been disproportionately distributed across the population. So whatever else the privatization programme has achieved, or might achieve in the future, it could hardly be said to have advanced the cause of social justice in Britain. In his account of the Thatcher years, Lord Gilmour (1992: 101–102) suggests that the

Government could have adopted an alternative approach to popular capitalism, which would have resulted in a far less regressive outcome:

> The best and fairest way of carrying out privatization would have been that suggested by Samuel Brittan . . . his scheme was that, instead of state assets being sold to investors, shares in them would be given to all adult citizens in equal numbers . . . it would have helped to mitigate probably the worst feature of Thatcherism: the treatment of the poor. It would also have been far the most ethical method. After all, in theory, the nationalized industries belonged to the nation. Therefore privatization on the Brittan plan would merely have given to the people in one form what they already owned in another. By contrast privatization by sale deprived those not rich enough to subscribe of part of their property.

Aspects of the economic performance of the privatized utility companies

The drive for improved efficiency lay at the heart of the Government's economic case for privatization of the public utilities. But in the view of most commentators, change in ownership, in itself, is not a sufficient condition for achieving greater efficiency, and that in order for this to be realized, competitive forces need to be introduced into the operating environments of the utilities. Studies of the utilities privatized in the 'first wave' – i.e. British Telecom and British Gas – generally confirm the hypothesis that privatization minus substantive competition results in few, if any, efficiency gains (Bishop and Kay 1988; Vickers and Yarrow 1988; Dunsire et al. 1991). Indeed, the research by Dunsire and his colleagues (1991: 38), involving an examination of the economic performance of a wide range of both privatized and (still) nationalized enterprises concluded suggestively that even the advent of competition does not guarantee improved performance:

> . . . neither investigation supports the simple assertion that change in ownership necessarily changes enterprise performance, even in its sophisticated form, where capital market change is assumed to be accompanied by increased competition and improved managerial incentives. Sometimes it does, sometimes it doesn't.

The retention, at privatization, of the geographical monopoly structure of the public utilities (with the exception of electricity generation, and electricity supply to large users), would suggest then that the signs were not particularly propitious for a significant lift in the efficiency performance of the industries. In fact this seems to be a conclusion that the Government itself formed, at least in the case of the water industry, for the 'efficiency targets set by the Secretary of State [in the setting of the K factor] implied a reduction of around 3 per cent per year in the base level of operating costs. This target was broadly in line with the performance aims set for the former water authorities' (Office of Water Services 1992o: 22).

It is still much too early in the case of the later utility privatizations to properly assess efficiency outcomes subsequent to the change in ownership. Very few analyses of the economic performance of the water and electricity supply industry, based on empirical research, have emerged thus far, and the few studies that have been published focus primarily on the performance of the industries immediately preceding, or around the time of, privatization (e.g. United Research 1990; Thompson et al. 1991).

Here, three selected aspects of the economic performance of the three utilities will be briefly considered – profitability, executive salaries (relevant to the question of management incentives) and employment. These are all elements which contribute to the mosaic of economic performance, but just as importantly, they interact with the issue of the distributional consequences of the privatization programme. They also form significant parts of the landscape of the privatized utilities which should be kept in mind in the analysis of the consumer-related effects of privatization in the chapters that follow.

Profitability

In most studies into the comparative performance of public and private enterprises the levels of profit achieved by the industries is used as an indicator of economic performance and efficiency. However, it is highly debatable whether profitability – particularly for industries operating in monopoly or quasi-monopoly conditions – is a relevant measure of efficiency. According to Vickers and Yarrow (1988: 39), '[g]iven some degree of market power, it might be expected that private firms will tend to be more profitable, but this in itself has no direct bearing on the question of economic efficiency'.

Irrespective of whether profitability occupies a legitimate place amongst the indices of efficiency in the utility sector, it is clearly a matter of importance to the direct stakeholders of utility industries – management, shareholders and consumers. Managers and shareholders benefit directly from rises in company profit and conversely, in theory at least, suffer from poor profit performance. Whereas, for consumers the flow of benefits tend to run the other way with, for example, the achievement of a high level of profitability possibly suggesting that the utility provider is gaining 'monopoly rents' through excessively high charges.

By any standard the profit performance of the public utilities since privatization, as indicated in Table 3.6, has been remarkable. British Gas' profit performance has deteriorated, however, over recent times, which is related in part to the loss of around half of the highly-profitable contract gas market to competitors (British Gas 1993a: 3).

For each of the utility companies, with the exception of British Gas, the short time-frame between privatization and the release of the 1991–92 profit results, would seem to render as highly implausible the argument that vigorous profit growth is directly attributable to the 'efficiency-related effects of

Table 3.6   Privatized utility company profits since privatization.

Utility	Years	Percentage increase
British Gas	1985/86–1992	49%
	[1985/86–1990/91	99%]
Water companies	1988/89–1991/92	137%
RECs	1989/90–1991/92	47%
Generators	1990/91–1991/92	24%

Source: Company annual reports.

privatization'. In any case, a major acceleration in profits has tended to occur during the early stages of privatization. For example, water industry profits grew by over 90 per cent in the first full year of privatization (1989–90 to 1990–91), and the RECs performed some 22 per cent above the projected profit level set out in the prospectus at the time of privatization. This would seem to add further weight to the view that these two industries were significantly underpriced at sale.

Figure 3.5   British Gas profits before taxation.

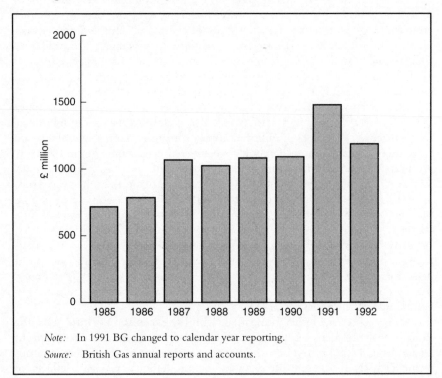

Note: In 1991 BG changed to calendar year reporting.

Source: British Gas annual reports and accounts.

Figure 3.6 Water company pre-tax profits (1989–92).

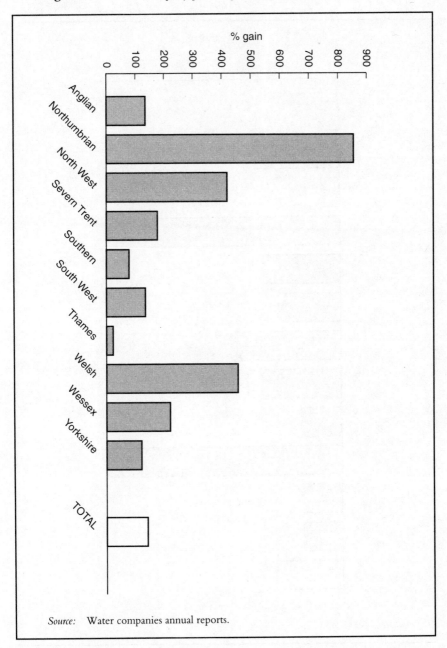

Source: Water companies annual reports.

Figure 3.7   Regional Electricity Company pre-tax profits (1989/90–1991/92).

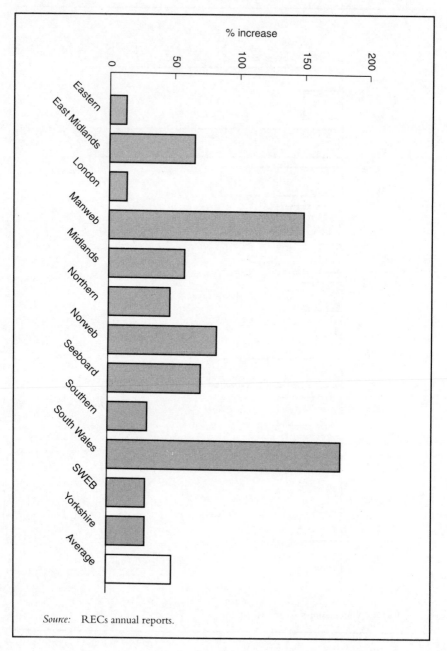

Source: RECs annual reports.

Equally, this may indicate that the efficiency strictures, set for the companies (the K and X factors) as part of the privatization settlement, were particularly unchallenging. In the case of the RECs, it has been suggested that the ability of these companies to exceed the prospectus profit forecasts by some margin is the result of 'their success in conning the Department of Energy in the pre-privatization negotiations' (interview with OFFER staff, July 1992). The National Audit Office (1992b) report on the sale of the RECs also implied that this was the case. In his explorations into the capital structure of the water industry, the Director General of Water Services has regularly reminded the water companies that the privatization settlement has been very much in their favour (Office of Water Services 1991l; 1992o,z).

Figures based on average increases in profits in the water and electricity supply industries disguise individual company profits out-turns well in excess of the norm, such as those achieved by companies like Northumbrian Water, Welsh Water, South Wales Electricity and Manweb. Figures 3.5–3.7 illustrate the year-by-year performance of British Gas and the individual profit performance of the water and regional electricity companies over the first period of privatization. The privatized companies have responded to negative media and public reaction to these profit figures by arguing that sustained profit growth is necessary if the industries are to secure the level of capital investment required to accommodate future demand and to upgrade the existing infrastructure, and in order to be able to deal more effectively with environmental externalities (for example, Carney 1991). Because of the scale of the capital works programme, this argument has rather greater validity in the water industry than in the other utility sectors. But even in the water industry, just on 38 per cent of the water companies' profit, £450 million (on a current cost basis), was reinvested in the business in 1991–92; although this represented a substantial

Table 3.7 Privatized utility taxation (£ millions).

Utility	1990/91	1991/92
Water services companies	128	143
Proportion of pre-tax profit (%)	9.4%	9.5%
RECs	332	409
Proportion of pre-tax profit (%)	29%	28%
Generating companies	241	266
Proportion of pre-tax profit (%)	34%	30%
National Grid	126	163
Proportion of pre-tax profit (%)	33%	33%

Note: Includes all forms of taxation, including overseas taxation. The latter is likely to represent only a very small proportion of the total taxation paid, for example, it represented just over 2 per cent in the case of Severn Trent Water in 1991–92.

Source: Company annual reports.

Figure 3.8   Increase in REC chairmen's salaries (1990/91–1991/92).

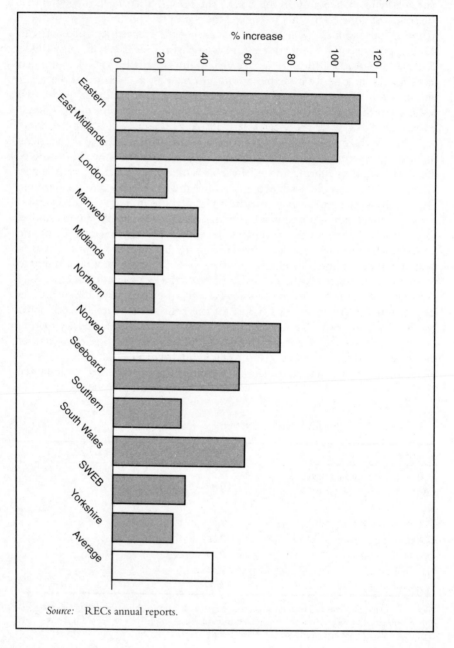

Source: RECs annual reports.

increase from 1990–91, when only 25 per cent of profits was retained in the business (Office of Water Services 1992z: 10).

In addition to enlarging the pool of finance available for investment in capital and plant (and increasing the size of dividends paid to shareholders), profit growth also potentially adds to public revenue receipts, through larger payments of corporation taxation and the like. But artificially low rates of taxation can also have the effect of increasing company profitability. The taxation paid by the water and electricity companies in England and Wales is shown in Table 3.7. It can be seen that the water industry has fared particularly well, with a relatively light taxation impost compared to the electricity industry. This would seem to partly explain the water industry's strong profit performance since privatization. The lower rate of taxation paid by the water companies is the result of the tax allowances agreed to by the Government at the time of privatization. The total amount of taxation paid by the ten water and sewerage companies in 1991–92 was £143 million. By comparison, the water industry generated some £636 million in dividends and other payments to the Exchequer in its last year under public ownership in 1988–89.

Executive salaries

A very tangible measure of the rewards for management in the privatization process is obtained by examining the movement in executive salaries over the period leading up to, and following, privatization. Most reviews of the privatization programme have considered this issue (e.g. Bishop and Kay 1988; Chapman 1990; Whitfield 1992) as have copious media reports. A dramatic change in the level of salaries paid to top executives has invariably formed part of the immediate fall-out of privatization.

In the water industries in 1990, for instance, the highest paid director in the Southern, Welsh and Yorkshire water companies received salary increases in the order of 209 per cent, 74 per cent and 59 per cent, respectively (Company Annual Reports 1991). The chairmen of the regional electricity companies similarly made major salary gains in the year immediately following privatization. This is illustrated in Figure 3.8. It is important to note that these figures do not include other elements of the executive remuneration package, such as pension contributions and executive share options. Executive salary increases have usually been justified on the grounds that firstly, senior managers in the nationalized industries were notoriously underpaid relative to their private sector counterparts and therefore changes have been required in order to achieve some form of parity. Secondly, the industries will be constrained in their ability to attract talented management expertise unless high salaries are awarded. Thirdly, salaries need to reflect the greater responsibilities of senior executives in the more commercially exposed and higher-risk environment of the privatized utilities. The last argument, in particular, has been contested by commentators, and even *The Times* (24/9/91) fulminated on the subject in an editorial in the following terms:

High private sector remuneration is only justified by a high level of personal risk-taking and a significant personal contribution to increased profitability by the executive concerned. It is the reward for enterprise and wealth creation. That is why it is so objectionable to see heads of privatised near-monopolies being rewarded as if they were buccaneering captains of industry, when many of the industries they run are not performing well, and their prices were being manipulated by the regulators to make sure they were profitable.

In the water industry, at least, there are indications that after the initial remunerative haemorrhage the level of executive salary increases has abated. The average increase in salary for the highest paid directors in the water companies in 1991 was 14 per cent, with the highest rise in South West Water of 39 per cent (Company Annual Reports 1992). In the light of media and public hostility to the earlier round of salary rises, this relative degree of moderation may reflect the power of public opinion. The average increase in 1991 was still, however, well in excess of the movement of salaries and wages in the British economy generally over the same period.

Employment
Data on aggregate changes to employment in the privatized utilities is easy enough to gather, but how to interpret it is another matter. One person's 'over-manning' is another's 'service quality', just as one person's 'productivity and efficiency gains' is another's 'personal and social dislocation'. The extent to which job losses or increases have been caused by privatization *per se* and not by general economic growth or decline, shifts in demand and changes in technology, is also uncertain. A further compounding factor is that in virtually all cases the nationalized public utilities experienced a sustained level of labour shedding over the decade leading into privatization (Whitfield 1992; Hogwood 1992). The same is true also for the industries, like British Coal and British Rail, that remain tenuously in the public sector.

The picture portrayed in Figure 3.9 is one of an overall reduction in employment in the public utility sector since privatization. But taken individually, the trend in the water industry runs counter to this, with a net increase in employment of 13 per cent since 1989. The aggregate figure for the RECs masks variations across the companies, with the range being represented by East Midlands with a net increase of 10 per cent in its labour force and Manweb with a net decrease of 17 per cent. Overall though the predominate pattern is one of labour shedding, with 10 out of the 12 companies having reduced their workforce since privatization (Company Annual Reports 1992). The utility sectors experiencing the largest job losses since privatization have been British Gas (minus 15 per cent) and the electricity generating companies (minus 23 per cent), and the unequivocal message given by management in both these sectors is that the reductions in personnel will continue apace over the next several years at least.

Figure 3.9 Changes in employment in the privatized utilities (UK-based employees).

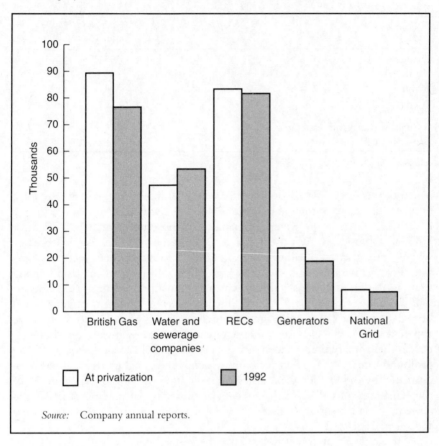

Source: Company annual reports.

Most of the water and sewerage companies have embarked upon extensive diversification programmes since privatization, most notably in areas like waste management, process engineering and leisure management. These extensions to the 'non-core' area of the water companies' business have been made largely through taking over and purchasing existing enterprises. The apparent against-the-trend employment record of the privatized water industry can be explained after taking a closer look at the distribution of employment across the 'core' and 'non-core' activities of the companies. Table 3.8 provides illustrative data on three water companies and it is unlikely that this pattern would be much different in the other water companies that have diversified their operations. The table shows that over the period 1990–92, employment in the 'core' water and sewerage activities of the three companies declined marginally overall, while employment in the 'non-core' areas rose dramatically.

Table 3.8   Employment change in the water industry.

	1990		1992	
	Water and sewerage	Other	Water and sewerage	Other
Thames	7688	61	7562	1786
North West	7100	0	7035	1166
Welsh	3397	314	3547	1149
Total	18185	375	18144	4101
Growth in water and sewerage			−41	−0.2%
Growth in other activities			3726	993.6%

Source: Company annual reports.

Much of this ostensible employment growth is unlikely to represent new jobs, however, as many of these jobs would have already existed and would simply have been added to the water companies' staffing establishment as a result of business acquisitions. Whitfield (1992: 268) argues this has happened else-where, 'privatised companies have increased their workforce since privatisa-tion, but this is almost entirely due to takeovers and mergers. The underlying trend in the core business is still downwards'. In some instances, privatization will have an employment-related impact well beyond the organizational boundaries of the utility companies themselves. This is probably nowhere more apparent than in the electricity industry, where the move away from domestic coal as the primary fuel in electricity generation, will have a consequential and profound impact on the level of employment in the coal industry. It has been estimated by the Henley Centre, for example, that the proposal to close 31 of the remaining pits in Britain would have the effect of making 31000 mine workers – and possibly as many as 63000 other workers – redundant (*The Guardian*, 21/10/92).

It would be incorrect to attribute the general decline in employment in the public utility sector simply to 'the privatization effect', for obviously factors such as technological change have played a pivotal part. Yet, in acknowledging this it is clear that labour-shedding has become a common means of securing 'efficiency gains' for many of the privatized utility companies. Whatever the commercial justification for this – and arguably cutting jobs is an all-too-easy and not particularly effective way of improving economic efficiency – those workers in the public utilities, and in associated industries like coal, who have been made redundant over recent years could hardly be included amongst the beneficiaries of the privatization programme.

Conclusion

Nearly all the industries were sold off for much less than they were worth . . . Thus the government was a negligent guardian of public assets, failing to look after the interests of the collective public. Yet individual members of the public profited mightily from the government's lax generosity.

Gilmour (1992: 103)

This chapter has shown that a fair measure of disharmony exists between the outcomes of privatization and the objectives of the programme as enunciated by the Government. In general, the Government failed to realize, in the sale of the industries, an appropriate return on the decades of accumulated public investment in the utility industries. A significant part of the financial benefit accruing from utility privatization has been appropriated by the shareholders of the privatized companies, in the form either of windfall gains on the value of shares or inflated dividends. This, in combination with the flawed implementation of the Government's wider share-ownership programme, has meant that the majority of the British population have been net losers through the sale of the three industries. Importantly, through the exclusion, by and large, of poor households from the share-ownership programme, the sale of the utilities has merely served to deepen the level of material inequality in British society.

It is still too early to draw firm conclusions about the financial performance of the newly privatized water and energy companies, but certainly their profit performance looks impressive. Arguably, however, this rapid rise in profitability following privatization has had more to do with the generous terms of the privatization settlement negotiated between the industries and the Government, than with the efficiency initiatives introduced by the companies themselves. The way in which these substantially increased profits have been distributed is a microcosm of intrinsic inequity within the privatization process generally, with the direction of benefits appearing heavily to favour shareholders and company executives.

As a number of commentators have argued (Dunleavy and O'Leary 1987; Sherman 1989; Vickers and Yarrow 1988; Pint 1990) the privatization sales could be viewed as a classic expression of the policy-making art of 'concentrating benefits and diffusing costs'. To this extent, the Government's approach was extremely successful, as its patently regressive method of relinquishing public assets encountered little effective political resistance.

It is now time to consider whether the Government's promise of new consumer rights and prerogatives has had more substance than much of the rest of its explicit rationale for privatization.

4

Prices and tariff structures

Introduction

. . . a system of economic regulation will be designed to ensure that the benefits of greater efficiency are systematically passed on to customers in the form of lower prices and better service than would otherwise have occurred.

Secretary of State for the Environment et al. (1986: 1)

Greater competition will create downward pressures on costs and prices, and ensure that the customer, not the producer or distributor, comes first.

Secretary of State for Energy (1988: 16)

In attempting to answer the question of how domestic consumers have fared under the privatized utility industry framework in Britain, one must necessarily begin with a caveat. As the privatization of two of these industries is a relatively recent phenomenon, it would be injudicious to be too definitive about the impact of ownership change. Clearly many of the ground rules – particularly in respect to the role of the regulatory bodies – are still evolving. The influence of the regulatory regime on the operation of the industries is still being tested, not least of all by the regulators themselves. Developing practice experience may strengthen the ability of the regulatory bodies to act as catalysts for consumer-oriented reform of the industries; conversely, under the theory of 'regulatory capture', the regulators' effectiveness may recede over time, in line with their growing connections and familiarity with the utility industries. At an industry level, the structural, policy and practice changes effected by the new companies in the wake of privatization may weaken in impact over time. Alternatively, it may take several years to achieve the kind of 'customer conscious' culture change that is seen to characterize the private sector.

Given the highly-charged political environment in which these owner-ship changes have been affected, it is manifestly in the interests of both the Government and the privatized industries to project a strong image of 'cus-tomer care' during the formative phase of the restructuring process. This would serve to allay public anxiety about the possible impact of the private control and provision of utility services, as well as win belated popular support for the privatization programme. On the other hand, the interests of opponents of the Government's privatization programme lie in applying the most negative gloss possible to the behaviour of the privatized industries and to the actions of the regulatory agencies. This oppositional instinct to 'damn outright' has been frequently in evidence in House of Commons debates on the consequences of privatization.

Clearly, it will be a number of years before an evaluation of privatization along any dimension – be it in regard to efficiency, or competition, or con-sumer outcomes – will be able to be completed with confidence. The evalua-tive task is rendered all the more difficult through the absence of comparable 'before' and 'after' data in a number of areas. It is also impossible to predict what might have happened had the utility industries remained in public ownership, although some commentators like Yarrow (1992) have attempted to do so. However, in recognizing the limits to definitive analysis, it is possible – even at this reasonably early stage – to identify a number of impacts and trends arising from privatization and the advent of independent regulation, in the key domestic consumer domains of prices and tariff structures, debt and disconnection practice, consumer protection and standards of service, and con-sumer representation. This chapter and the two that follow examine the evi-dence on outcomes, to date, in each of these areas.

Price is probably the domain of public utility practice of most immediate importance to consumers. The question of price is significant in any instance of producer–consumer interaction, but this is particularly so in areas of natural monopoly, where there is an ability to charge monopoly prices – either directly through raising tariffs or indirectly through attenuating service quality – *independent* of consumer demand and conventional market forces. Not sur-prisingly, there appears to be a direct correlation between the importance attached by domestic consumers to the question of utility prices and socio-economic status (DoE 1991a; MORI 1992). The structure and level of energy and water tariffs has a critical bearing on the extent to which these essential services can be accessed by, and are affordable to, low income households in Britain.

In the public marketing of the utility privatization programme, the Gov-ernment regularly drew attention to the way that domestic consumers would benefit through lower prices for utility services (as reflected in the quotations from the White Papers above). In this chapter, the pricing outcomes for domestic consumers in the three utility areas will be reviewed. As each of the utilities has had a somewhat different recent history in respect to pricing, they will be considered individually in order of privatization.

Gas

Tariffs over the first five years of privatization

The regulation of prices for domestic gas consumers, as with the other utilities, is built upon the RPI − X formula first developed by Professor Stephen Littlechild for British Telecom. Over the first five years of its privatized existence, British Gas was allowed to raise its prices for tariff consumers, i.e. consumers purchasing less than 25 000 therms (in 1991, the average annual consumption for domestic consumers was 651 therms; British Gas 1992c: 35) by the retail price index *minus 2%*, under the formula regulated by the Office of Gas Supply. The standing charge was exempt, notably, from this constraint and could be raised by the level of the retail price index each year.

In the view of many commentators, the initial price cap set for British Gas represented a rather modest efficiency target for a national monopoly provider:

> Taken as a whole, the pricing constraints imposed on British Gas can hardly be described as stringent. The implicit target of a 2 per cent per annum reduction in nongas costs should not prove to be onerous. Some demand growth over the five-year period was predicted in the prospectus for the share issue and, given the existence of scale economies, this should lead to reductions in real unit costs even in the event that internal efficiency is not improved. Moreover, the nationalized BGC was set a target of reducing its real net trading costs per therm by 12 per cent between financial years 1982–1983 and 1986–1987 and managed to meet this target within the first three years of the four-year period.
>
> Vickers and Yarrow (1988: 265)

The formula was seen to be particularly generous in light of the provision enabling British Gas to automatically pass-through to tariff consumers any increases in the purchase price it paid for gas from off-shore suppliers.

Between 1987 (the first full year of privatization) and 1991, British Gas prices for domestic consumers rose by 19.5 per cent. As the cost of living increased between these years by 31.6 per cent (Department of Trade and Industry 1992c: table 54), domestic gas tariffs effectively *decreased* in real terms by just over 12 per cent. At the same time, British Gas moved progressively towards the development of uniform standing charges across the country, involving above average increases in standing charges for consumers in the North of England and the Midlands between 1987 and 1991 (25 and 24 per cent, respectively, compared to 13 per cent for the rest of Britain), although

Figure 4.1   Changes in domestic gas tariffs 1986–92.

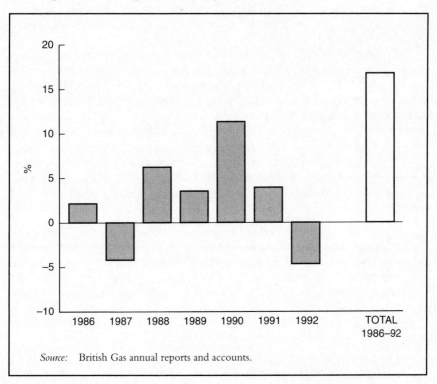

Source: British Gas annual reports and accounts.

these were still below the actual level of inflation for the period. Figure 4.1 illustrates the year-on-year movement in prices for gas tariff customers between 1986 and 1992.

The real terms' decrease in gas tariffs over the first five-year period had more to do with 'the fall in gas purchase costs that had occurred as a result of the fall in world oil prices' (Vickers and Yarrow 1988: 279) than with efficiency improvements effected by British Gas itself. Commenting on the only occasion where British Gas actually cut tariffs over the period (the 4.5 per cent reduction in tariffs in 1987), Sir Denis Rooke, the then chairman of British Gas stated that '[l]ast year we felt the full benefit of the 1986 oil price falls which, in line with the price formula under our authorization to act as a public gas supplier, produced a reduction in the price of gas to tariff customers' (British Gas 1988: Chairman's Statement).

In fact it could be argued that British Gas had even greater scope for reducing tariffs (on the basis of cheaper gas purchasing costs) than those actually achieved over the 1987–91 period. Between 1987 and 1991 the average price of natural gas (inclusive of the gas levy) purchased by British Gas increased by 5 per cent, from 17.85 pence per therm to 18.79 pence per therm (Department of Trade and Industry 1992c: table 63). Once inflation is taken into account, the average price of natural gas was 27 per cent cheaper in 1991 compared to 1987.

Translating this fall in gas costs to the tariff market (gas costs represent around 40 per cent of British Gas' costs in supplying this sector; Office of Gas Supply, 1991d: 6) reveals that the 'full equivalent price' in 1991 of £100 worth of gas (at 1987 prices) was £108.32, whereas the actual price charged by British Gas was £112.10. In other words, tariff prices between 1987 and 1991 increased by over 3 per cent more than would have been necessary had the full saving on gas purchase costs been passed through to tariff consumers.

The validity of the assertion that the efficiency target set for British Gas at the time of privatization was not particularly onerous, was effectively acknowledged by the Director General of OFGAS in his review of the gas tariff formula:

> . . . the judgement of OFGAS and its consultants was that British Gas achieved this [efficiency gains under the old formula] without showing any signs of being an organisation under serious cost pressures. Nor, on examination, did OFGAS find any reason to believe that these cost savings were one off in nature or a simple squeezing out of pre-privatisation 'fat'.
>
> Office of Gas Supply (1991d: 12)

This, in conjunction with the consistently high levels of profit generated by British Gas between 1986 and 1991, gives credence to the view that, while domestic consumers have benefited from decreases in tariffs during the first quinquennium of privatization, the fall in tariffs could well have been greater had British Gas been subjected to a more testing price cap. In relative terms, tariff consumers have not experienced anything like the price gains that have been made by large users in the contract market, who have been subjected to a marginally more competitive gas supply environment. This is illustrated in Table 4.1 for the period 1988 to 1991.

Table 4.1   Changes in gas tariffs for all sectors 1988–91.

Sector	Change
Domestic	+24%
Industrial:	
small (less than 50 000 therms)	+14%
medium (50 000–300 000 therms)	−4%
large (greater than 300 000 therms)	−4%
RPI	+27%

Source: Derived from Department of Trade and Industry (1992c: tables 54 and 61).

The review of the gas tariff formula

During 1990–91, the Office of Gas Supply carried out a major review of the formula regulating British Gas' charges to tariff customers. Although the process of consultation used in the review has drawn some criticism from consumer and community sector organizations, it is generally acknowledged that the package of measures announced by OFGAS in April 1991, should result in substantive gains for domestic gas consumers over the second five years of privatization from April 1992. There is, however, the prospect that the settlement agreed between OFGAS and British Gas during the review could be subject to renegotiation, following the referral of British Gas to the Monopolies and Mergers Commission (see below).

Under the revised tariff formula, the regulator has set a more demanding efficiency target for British Gas. The new price cap (X) on charges to tariff customers has been raised from the original minus 2 per cent to minus 5 per cent (i.e. the retail price index minus 5 per cent). This should result, according to the Director General, in gas prices being '15 per cent or more lower than they would otherwise have been at the end of five years' (Office of Gas Supply, 1991h). The resetting of the level of X has been complemented by three other changes in the regulatory regime which will impact directly on domestic consumers, i.e. a change in the way that gas purchasing costs can be passed through to consumers in the future, provision for the pass-through of energy efficiency costs (described as the 'E factor'), and the modification of British Gas' Authorization incorporating standards of performance (Condition 13A). The first two of these will be discussed below, the third is considered in Chapter 6.

In the first of these measures, the regulator has removed British Gas' ability to pass-through in full increases in gas purchase costs to tariff consumers. The free hand of British Gas in dealing with gas purchase costs under the previous formula was identified as a significant issue requiring action, by a number of organizations including the Gas Consumers Council, during the tariff review consultation:

> Of particular concern is the pass-through of costs of new gas as this automatic cover reduces the incentive for BG to negotiate the cheapest price for new contracts. There may even be an opportunity for British Gas to pay over the odds for gas to keep out competitors as the higher price can be passed on automatically to tariff customers.
>
> Gas Consumers Council (1990: 3)

From April 1992, the allowable pass-through of wholesale gas costs has been indexed (using a 'gas price index') and is subject to a 1 per cent reduction each year. This provides a hitherto absent efficiency incentive for British Gas:

> The advantages of a gas cost price cap are essentially the same as those of the RPI price cap – that is, the arrangement gives British Gas a clear

incentive to improve its purchasing efficiency because lower costs will lead to higher profits.

Office of Gas Supply (1991d: 7)

This will become increasingly important as the cheaper sources of gas supply from the Southern Basin gas fields in the North Sea become exhausted and as existing long-term contracts between British Gas and gas producers are renewed.

Measures to stimulate energy efficiency serve two different, and potentially conflicting, policy agendas. Firstly, they meet a set of environmental imperatives aimed at protecting the global environment, through reducing energy consumption. Secondly, they occupy an important place in the strategy to address fuel poverty, for when targeted effectively, energy efficiency programmes raise the end-use quality of energy services to low income households. This may not necessarily result, however, in a net reduction in energy consumption (Owen 1990; Boardman 1991a; Neighbourhood Energy Action, 1991).

As a corporate sponsor, British Gas has a history of involvement in community-based energy efficiency and energy-conservation programmes, exemplified by its financial support for the major energy efficiency charity, Neighbourhood Energy Action. However, up until the 1991 review of the gas tariff formula there was neither the regulatory framework, nor the economic incentive for energy efficiency to be treated as a core operational activity of British Gas. Indeed, the thrust of economic regulation worked in the reverse direction, with the structure of economic rewards weighted in favour of inefficient, and at times the profligate, use of gas (Office of Gas Supply 1991e). Under the revised tariff formula, British Gas is able to designate areas of energy efficiency expenditure and, with the approval of the regulator:

> the cost of these energy efficiency measures [can] be passed through to consumers in the same way as gas purchasing costs. This, in theory at least, will enable British Gas to view expanded gas sales and greater energy efficiency in the same commercial light.

Office of Gas Supply (1992d: 4)

The administration of 'E factor' funds and projects will be the responsibility, following the announcement by the Government in May 1992, of the Energy Savings Trust. In the first year of operation, British Gas will contribute £6 million for three pilot projects, one of which is explicitly directed at low income households. In addition to British Gas, the regional electricity companies in England and Wales and the two Scottish electricity companies, have been signed up as participants in the Trust.

The 'E factor' initiative has been warmly welcomed by both the energy conservation and fuel poverty lobbies and the Office of Electricity Regulation has been urged to introduce a similar device in the electricity industry (Boardman and Houghton 1991). Yet, as an effective measure aimed at reducing either carbon dioxide emissions or fuel poverty (or a combination of both) the 'E factor' and its Energy Trust corollary are likely to constitute an inadequate policy response.

The 'E factor' methodology, with its emphasis on market incentives rather than regulatory controls, falls well short of the *least-cost planning* approach to energy investment and resource management employed in many parts of North America (Brown 1990; Berry 1992). But even as a mechanism for stimulating market-led decisions in favour of energy efficiency, its structure of incentives is flawed, for although explicitly identified expenditure on energy efficiency is compensated through the price formula, any loss of income associated with reduced energy demand is not. As revenue foregone through lost sales of energy will form the major potential cost of energy efficiency programmes for gas and electricity companies, the inability to pass these losses on through the pricing formula is likely to act as a significant deterrent to expansive and imaginative energy efficiency activity on the part of companies concerned. The 'E factor' in other words, only tinkers at the margins of the incentive structure of the price formula, and it does little to modify the dominating tenor of the reward and profit structure of the privatized energy industries, which is fundamentally predicated on a capacity to sell more energy rather than less.

From a fuel poverty perspective, the use of the 'E factor' to generate large sums of money for projects directed specifically at low-income households, is constrained by the requirement that both the regulators and the utility companies avoid being seen to give 'undue discrimination' and 'undue preference' to particular classes of consumers (Sharpe 1992). While the creation of an independent trust to administer 'E factor' funds may obviate some of these problems, trust funds (which are effectively being provided by all consumers) will need to be distributed in a multi-targeted way, in order to avoid the charge that the generality of consumers is being taxed to fund services for the benefit of one sub-set of consumers only.

The levying of an 'E factor' surcharge on the tariffs of low-income households, along with domestic consumers generally, to finance measures to promote energy efficiency in affluent households, raises important equity considerations. The 'E factor' has the potential to become a form of disguised carbon tax − one directed only at domestic consumers (for it excludes the franchise sector of the energy market not subject to price regulation) and without any off-setting compensation for low-income households via the income security system.

The extent to which the 'E factor' will form no more than 'a marginal consideration in the marketing strategy of BG or the first step on the road to regulation for energy services' (Roberts 1992: 13), and the nature of its impact on low-income households is unclear at this point, as the development of the concept is still at a formative stage.

What is clearer, however, is that the package of measures developed by the regulator in the gas tariff review, constitute in aggregate a far superior settlement for the domestic consumer than that achieved at privatization. The achievement of the Director General of Gas Supply is rendered all the more noteworthy by the fact that the revised tariff formula was introduced in the face of considerable opposition from British Gas, particularly after the announcement of the Office of Fair Trading's proposals for the separation of the distribution and supply businesses of the company in October 1991.

The positive outcomes for domestic consumers have been obtained only after assertive – some would say belligerent – action on the part of the regulator. An example of this was the attempt by British Gas in March 1992 to meet the new price formula conditions by freezing, rather than reducing, tariff charges and it was only after OFGAS threatened enforcement action (Office of Gas Supply 1992c) that the company agreed to reduce its tariff by 1.7p or 3 per cent from the beginning of July 1992. Reflecting on these events, the Director of the Gas Consumers Council concluded that a 'reduction of this size can only mean that British Gas either got its sums wrong or decided to hoodwink its customers. Either way, British Gas has boosted the regulator's reputation and has dented its own credibility' (Gas Consumers Council 1992b).

At the time of writing, the story of the torturous negotiations and attempted renegotiations of the new tariff formula continues to unfold. British Gas' reluctance to make concessions, appeared to turn to recalcitrance as the implications of the OFGAS tariff and Office of Fair Trading (OFT) competition review began to sink in. The company expressed concern, in particular, about the simultaneous loss of dominance of the contract gas market (demanded by the OFT) and the reduced profitability of the increasingly important tariff sector of its business (through the RPI minus 5 per cent revision to the formula). It argued that the ground rules had changed substantially between the drafting of the conditions of the tariff review and their implementation, that is, in April 1991 it was an integrated entity, whereas by April 1992 (when the new formula came into effect) it was facing (a) the imminent separation of its transmission division, (b) a reduction in its share of the contract gas market to 40 per cent (by 1996) and (c) the loss of its supply monopoly to users above 2500 therms per year under the Competition and Service (Utilities) Act 1992. Because of this, it proposed that OFGAS reconsider the terms of the tariff review agreement.

The MMC reference

The impasse between British Gas and the regulatory bodies resulted, at the end of July 1992, in the Director General of Gas Supply using his powers under the Competition and Service (Utilities) Act to refer British Gas to the Monopolies and Mergers Commission (MMC). Initially the scope of the reference covered only the question of determining an appropriate set of financial arrangements for the operation of the gas transmission network. But the terms of the MMC inquiry were subsequently widened to encompass a full review of the gas market, following the issuing of parallel references by the President of the Board of Trade and the Director General of Gas Supply (Department of Trade and Industry 1992a,b; Office of Gas Supply 1992g, h). The reference by the President of the Board of Trade was made at the behest of British Gas itself – but apparently, only after failing to get the Department of Trade and Industry to intervene to prevent the OFGAS reference on the transmission network going forward to the MMC (OFGAS policy officer, Public Utilities Access Forum meeting, 22/9/92). In the view of the Director General of Gas Supply, the action of British Gas to widen the scope of the enquiry, represented a strategic move aimed at putting the results of the tariff formula review 'back into the melting pot in the hope that an outcome would emerge which was more favourable than the one the company had already signed up to' (*PUAF Newsletter* October 1992: 5).

Partly in order to meet the terms of the new formula, but also, possibly with a view to strengthening its position leading into the MMC investigation, British Gas announced in August 1992 a further reduction in tariff prices by 2 per cent from October. The two 1992 pricing changes represent an effective reduction in gas tariffs, over a full year, of 3.25 per cent.

Whether the pricing and standards of service reforms obtained through the tariff review will be sustained over the longer term is now effectively in the hands of the MMC. Certainly it is possible that some of the elements of the package could be revised, in light of the quite different gas market that may emerge after the release of the results of the MMC review in 1993. It is almost certain that the MMC will recommend major changes to the competitive framework of the gas industry. In the opinion of some observers, it is by no means self-evident that domestic consumers will be amongst those sectors who stand to gain from the more competitive gas market that is likely to emerge post the MMC review. The Gas Consumers Council, in particular, has cautioned that the breakup of British Gas and the introduction of competition in the tariff sector could result in higher tariffs, regional pricing and declining service quality for domestic consumers.

Water

Domestic water tariffs since privatization

Amongst the three utilities, the water industry has probably attracted the greatest amount of public and media attention since privatization. The sharp increase in water charges since 1989 has been a significant stimulus to this new interest in the activities of the water companies. In contrast to the energy utilities, above inflation price increases were explicitly structured into the economic framework of the privatized water industry at the outset. In setting the *K* factor in the price formula, the Government made provision for water and sewerage charges to increase by some 4–5 per cent each year in real terms (on average) until the end of the century. Price increases of this order were required, it was argued, to underwrite the costs of the £26 billion (1989 prices) ten-year capital investment programme of the water industry.

Table 4.2   Average household water and sewerage bills 1989–92 (unmeasured).

Year	£	Annual increase (%)	RPI increase (%)	Increase above RPI (%)
1989–90	118.80			
1990–91	134.27	13.02	7.7	5.32
1991–92	154.57	15.12	9.7	5.42
1992–93	169.56	9.70	4.3	5.40

Note: The average water and sewerage bill for the 3 per cent of households on *metered* supply in 1992–93 was £205, i.e. 21 per cent higher than for unmeasured households.

Sources: Derived from Centre for the Study of Regulated Industries (1992a); Office of Water Services (1992a).

Table 4.2 and Figure 4.2 show the movement of water charges over recent years. It can be seen in the table that average household bills for water and sewerage have risen at a consistent rate above the retail price index, despite the fact the Director General of Water Services negotiated a voluntary abatement by all but one of the water companies of a sixth of their K factor increase in 1992–93. This action on the part of the Director General followed widely-expressed concern about the level of profits generated by the industry in 1990–91:

> . . . in a situation where bills are rising rapidly, customers will not expect companies to make unnecessarily high profits and in particular to pay out excessive dividends . . . It is up to management to decide on dividends, but if companies were to use the present position to pay out dividends above those anticipated when the K factors were set they would need to be ready to answer pointed questions from customers and from the regulator . . .
>
> Office of Water Services (1991e)

Substantial political capital was made out of the Director General's successful negotiation of the abatement of K. The actual effect of this on the profits of the water companies would have been minimal, however, as it was more than offset by the real terms decline in construction costs – '15 per cent below the level assumed in 1989' (Office of Water Services 1992z: 4). As construction costs represent a major component of the companies' capital expenditure, the fall in these costs would have provided substantial savings. The impact of reduced construction costs on company profits was illustrated in the Director General's determination on South West Water's application for an interim adjustment to their price cap in December 1991, where it was estimated that the company was likely to save some £27 million over a three-year period because of lower costs (Office of Water Services 1991x).

Figure 4.2 provides a longitudinal picture of water charges and shows that the increases in recent years are part of a longer-term trend that has been in

Figure 4.2   Domestic water tariffs 1982–92 (average annual bill).

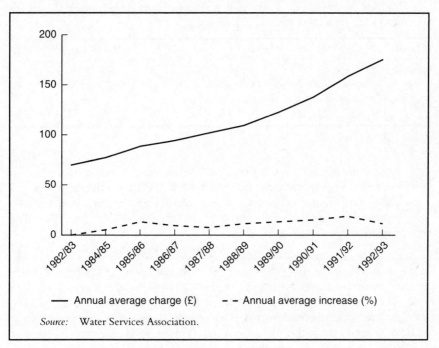

Source: Water Services Association.

evidence since the water industry entered its 'commercialized' course in the early 1980s. The figures before and after privatization are not strictly comparable because (i) current charges exclude the environmental service charge, which since 1989 has been funded out of general taxation revenue to partly finance the National River Authority (see Macrory 1989: 13) and (ii) previously, additional capacity/infrastructure costs were spread across all consumers (with a component for this in each consumer's bill), whereas it is now paid directly by new consumers through Infrastructure Charges. The exclusion of these elements would make the shift in the curve after 1988–89 somewhat sharper.

Contrasting explanations for rising water charges

The increases in water charges since privatization have been largely attributed by the Government, industry sources and OFWAT, to the costs associated with upgrading the infrastructure and environmental standards of the water services industry. This official explanation for the sustained water price increases experienced since 1989, and into the future, was reiterated by the Under-Secretary for State for the Environment in a House of Commons debate on the water industry in June 1991:

Table 4.3 Consumers' views on the 'privatization effect' and water bills: 'What do you think will be the main reasons for the water bills going up by more than the rate of inflation?'

Reason	Percentage
Because of privatization	28%
To pay shareholders/make money and profits	20%
Increased directors'/managers' salaries	9%
Total 'privatization effect'	57%

Source: MORI (1992: 81).

Privatisation has not of itself caused an increase in water charges. Privatisation has involved identifying all the requirements to ensure that the water industry meets agreed domestic and European Community standards, and costing those requirements and agreeing a capital programme to put them right.

House of Commons, 18/6/91, col. 157

While it is undeniable that the cost of the capital programme has been a major contributor to the rise in water charges, there have been other forces at work as well. The higher rate of return required by the private water companies – compared to their publicly-owned predecessors – and other factors associated with privatization has had an influence on the current level of charges in England and Wales. Certainly this appears to be the view of water consumers themselves. In the OFWAT-commissioned MORI survey carried out between November 1991 and January 1992, the primary explanation for future price increases was seen as being related directly or indirectly to privatization (Table 4.3).

Although the Director General of Water Services has been at pains to point out that this survey finding reflects the fact that 'customers have a poor understanding of the reasons for the real increases in bills' (Office of Water Services Annual Report, 1992), his own analyses of the capital structure of the water industry tends to belie the view that the 'privatization effect' has been insignificant. In his two major excursions into this area – the Cost of Capital (Office of Water Services 1991l) and The Cost of Quality (Office of Water Services 1992o) consultation papers – the Director General has emphasized that the return on capital obtained by the water companies need not necessarily be as high as that set at the time of privatization.

In 1989, the Government set a rate of return for the water industry at between 7 and 8.5 per cent, depending on the size of the company. After extensive investigation of the capital structure of the industry, however, the water regulator concluded that this appeared somewhat excessive, 'these returns on debt and equity would suggest a weighted average cost of capital of perhaps 5 per cent to 6 per cent in the longer term for a water and sewerage company. The rates could be a little higher for the small independent water only companies' (Office of Water Services 1991l: 27).

A reduction in the rate of return on capital is justified, in the Director General's view, because the water industry is a low risk area of commercial activity and it has a highly stable revenue-raising capacity. A future rate of return at the level envisaged by the Director General above would be similar to that applied by OFGAS in its review of British Gas' tariffs. Predictably, the water industry has vigorously contested the assumptions underlying the Director General's calculation of an appropriate rate of return and has countered that a 'level of at least 9.5 per cent is justified given the risks to which the water companies are exposed' (*Water Bulletin*, 6/12/91).

In his more recent Cost of Quality paper, published as part of the consultative process leading into the 1994 Periodic Review of the price formula, the Director General identified three future water charging scenarios based on different assumptions about the standards of environmental quality expected of the water industry. In the paper, the Director General concentrates primarily on the impact that environmental improvements will have on household bills in the future, representing the latest stage in his long-standing campaign to make the cost of environmental policy, as it affects the water industry, more transparent and to give customers 'the material on which they can make informed judgements about the quality of the service they want and the price they are prepared to pay' (Office of Water Services 1992o: 6). However, the paper also contains data on the financial structure of the water industry of more immediate relevance to the issues being considered here. If a sterner efficiency target (i.e. up from 3 per cent to 5 per cent) and a lower rate of return (weighted average of 6 per cent) were set for the industry, this would have a significant moderating effect on average household bills in the future. This is shown in Table 4.4.

Under this set of financial adjustments, household bills would continue to increase, but at a substantially reduced rate relative to alternative economic regulation scenarios. The calculations contained in Table 4.4 also have another implication, for they suggest that because of the generous terms of the privatization settlement, consumers have been paying more for their water than has been strictly required under the capital programme. Consumers in England and Wales appear to have been paying, in effect, a 'privatization premium' in their water bills since 1989.

In releasing the review of capital investment and financial performance of the water companies at the beginning of October 1992, the Director General of Water Supply declared his intention to make a 'formal reduction' of 2 per cent in the level of K for the majority of water companies in 1993–94. This is likely to have the effect in most cases of moderating the rise in water tariffs in 1993–94 by a broadly similar amount (Office of Water Services 1992z). This action – essentially involving an incremental revision of the economic and financial assumptions made at the time of privatization, to the advantage of consumers – possibly presages the sort of changes that could be introduced, following the completion of the Periodic Review of the price cap in 1994.

Table 4.4 The impact of future financial changes on water charges.

Projected increase in average household bill (real terms)

	1992/93–1999/2000
Environmental target:	
Progress maintained – lower	£215 (+27%)
Progress maintained – upper	£230 (+36%)
Pure and green	£255 (+51%)
(Average household bill in 1992–93: £169)	

Projected increase in average household bill minus *existing efficiency target*

	1992/93–1999/2000
Environmental target:	
Progress maintained – lower	£202 (+20%)
Progress maintained – upper	£217 (+28%)
Pure and green	£242 (+43%)

Higher efficiency target and lower rate of return measures: impact upon projected water charges

	% Saving on bill	Revised
Progress maintained – lower	8.8	£183
Progress maintained – upper	8.3	£198
Pure and green	7.5	£223

Percentage increase in average bill under higher efficiency target and lower rate of return (real terms)

	1992/93–1999/2000
Progress maintained – lower	8
Progress maintained – upper	17
Pure and green	32

Source: Calculated from data in Office of Water Services (1992o) *The Cost of Quality* (Figs 5, 8 and 9).

Variations in domestic water tariffs

An examination of average annual household bills across the country provides only part of the picture of tariff change since privatization. Two of the most significant changes, from the perspective of domestic consumers, have been the moves towards full cost apportionment, or what OFWAT describes as 'de-averaging' and the shifting relationship between standing and variable charges.

Ever since the demise of the Water Charges Equalisation Act 1977, differential water and sewerage charges have been levied across different parts of England and Wales. The case for differential tariffs, based on the variable costs of supplying different localities, is argued on the ground of economic efficiency and on 'the benefit principle' test of equity (i.e. apportioning costs in line with the benefits received). Full cost recovery reflecting the marginal costs imposed on the water and sewerage systems is fairer, under this view, as people pay the actual cost of supplying water services to their homes, and it removes cross-subsidization and promotes allocative efficiency. Similar arguments underpin the economic case for universal water metering.

Figure 4.3   Variations in domestic water charges (average household bill).

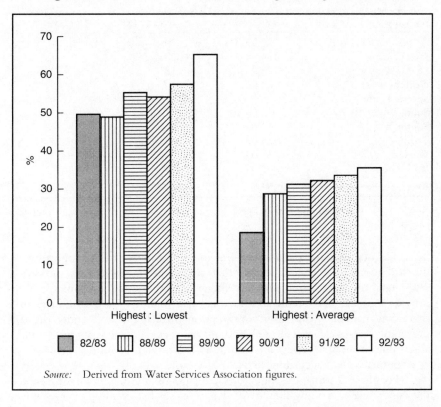

Source: Derived from Water Services Association figures.

The Office of Water Services is actively encouraging the water and sewerage companies to move towards 'de-averaged' charging systems, such as differential tariffs based on geographical location (zonal charges), seasonal tariffs and tariffs for different classes of consumers (Office of Water Services 1990c; interview with OFWAT charges control staff, July 1992). Severn Trent and Thames Water have introduced zonal tariffs and South West Water is considering introducing seasonal tariffs.

The gradual move towards more differentiated tariff systems across the country is reflected, at an aggregate level, in Figure 4.3. As can be seen from the chart, which shows the relationship between (a) highest and lowest and (b) highest and mean average household bills across companies, variations in the level of average household bills between companies have become greater over recent years.

Whatever the merit of the economic arguments, extensions to the use of cost-based pricing systems will result in much higher water and sewerage tariffs for some sectors of the domestic and non-domestic consumer population. They will also corrode further the nexus between water charges and capacity to pay.

Table 4.5   Domestic standing charges (water and sewerage) unmeasured.

Authority	1992–93 (£)	Increase 1990/91–1992/93 (%)
Anglian	57.93	20%
Dwr Cymru	134.16	27%
North West	25.00	18%
Northumbrian	64.00	60%
Severn Trent	–	–
South West	55.00	22%
Southern	41.50	26%
Thames	35.00	17%
Wessex	38.00	46%
Yorkshire	42.00	40%
Average	54.70	30%

Sources: Water Services Association (1992); Centre for the Study of Regulated Industries (1992a).

The standing, or fixed charge, element has always been proportionally much higher in the water industry than is the case in the energy industries. High standing charges are manifestly attractive to the water companies, as they provide a secure and predictable income stream. But they discriminate in a regressive manner against low consumption households, and under the still prevailing rate-based system of charging, against consumers living in low rate-able value properties. They also confound the driving economic principle of cost apportionment according to use of the system.

For these reasons, the Director General of Water Services has prompted the companies to review their tariff structures so that standing charges cover only billing and associated costs and he has argued that 'broadly similar standing charges [should be levied] across all companies' (Office of Water Services 1991u). In particular, the Director General has been anxious to see the disparity between measured (i.e. metered) and unmeasured standing charges removed, as higher standing charges for measured supplies acts as a disincentive to customers to take up the metering option (Office of Water Services 1992j). Tables 4.5 and 4.6 list the standing charges for the ten water and sewerage companies and indicate the percentage change in standing charges between 1990–91 and 1992–93. The figures illustrate marked variations in the levying of standing charges across the ten companies and show that practice is still a long way short of the uniformity desired by the Director General. Significantly, unmeasured standing charges – which in 1992, applied to all but 3 per cent of domestic consumers – have risen ahead of the rate of water price increases generally, i.e. 30 per cent compared to overall price rises of 26 per cent over the period. Although the average standing charge for metered households has increased at a rate well below the movement in water tariffs generally (possibly because of the regulator's advocacy), it remains substantially higher than the average standing charge for unmetered households.

Table 4.6 Domestic standing charges (water and sewerage) – measured.

Authority	1992–93 (£)	Increase 1990/91–1992/93 (%)
Anglian	69.93	−16%
Dwr Cymru	96.00	−19%
North West	99.00	9%
Northumbrian	96.00	26%
Severn Trent	28.32	25%
South West	91.40	16%
Southern	74.00	28%
Thames	50.00	19%
Wessex	70.30	23%
Yorkshire	54.00	−23%
Average	72.90	5%

Sources: Water Services Association (1992); Centre for the Study of Regulated Industries (1992a).

Water metering

Under section 145 of the Water Industry Act 1991, water companies have been prohibited from using rateable value-based charges after 31 March 2000. This legal constraint, stemming from the introduction of the ill-fated community charge, in conjunction with the new commercial orientation of the privatized water companies, has given rise to a search for charging alternatives. The most frequently cited substitute mechanisms are metering, flat rate charge or licence (effectively a 100 per cent standing charge) and a new generation property-related charge.

Metering is the option most favoured on economic pricing grounds (OECD 1987; Paterson 1987; Gadbury 1991; Rees 1992), but the ability to adopt consumption-based charging systems is constrained, in the short and medium term, by the absence of metering technology in most domestic properties. Only 3 per cent of households in England and Wales were metered in May 1992 (*OFWAT Information* Note No. 13). The proportion of metered domestic households in England and Wales will rise very gradually over time – independent of future regulatory or other policy actions – as water and sewerage companies are generally installing meters in new domestic properties. It has risen from 1 per cent of all households to its current level since privatization.

The impact that the introduction of *universal* metering would have on household water and sewerage bills is obviously impossible to determine precisely at this stage, although clearly there would be a substantial one-off direct or indirect increase in charges arising from the cost of installing meters in domestic premises (estimated on average to be around £200 per household). Households currently metered are already, on average, paying 21 per cent more than unmetered consumers, although the higher standing charge accounts for much of this. The overall distributional impact of universal metering in all likelihood would be uneven, with smaller households in high rateable value properties experiencing a net decrease in their water bills, and with the reverse applying to larger households in low rateable value properties.

The final results of the metering trials conducted in 12 areas throughout England will be available in 1993. Preliminary results of the metering trials indicated that 'about 65 per cent of households in the small trial areas are paying less than or the same as their previous RV bill . . . [with] about 20 per cent of households paying more than 20 per cent over their previous RV bill' (National Metering Trials Co-ordinating Group 1990: iv). Data from the metering trials will not be a reliable guide to the impact of volumetric charging on domestic consumers generally though, as the composition of the households in the 12 trial areas is not representative of the population as a whole (see below), and the tariff structure used in the trials has not reflected the full costs of metering:

> It should be remembered that the trial tariffs didn't attempt to recover the full costs of the meter installation (or allow for any savings). In a full scale meter installation the tariffs might look somewhat different.
>
> National Metering Trials Group (1992: 2–3)

It is most unlikely that a nationwide metering installation programme – akin to the programme to connect British households to natural gas in the 1960s – would be embarked upon because of the huge capital costs involved (estimated at around £4 billion). However, domestic metering of a more incremental kind has attracted a number of powerful sponsors in recent years – not the least of whom are the Department of the Environment (DoE/Welsh Office 1992) and the Director General of Water Services – and it will almost certainly become increasingly prominent as a method of water charging.

The Office of Water Services initiated a major national debate on water metering in November 1990, which at the time of writing still has some way to run. The consultation process on Paying for Water had a number of strands, of which only three will be considered at length here, i.e. consumer attitudes to metering, the position of the water companies on the metering issue, and the views of the community sector.

OFWAT used two approaches to gather the views of consumers on metering: through opinion polling and through the use of its ten customer services committees. In combination, the outcomes of this information search provided less than conclusive evidence that metering is the charging method preferred by the majority of consumers.

In the OPCS Omnibus survey, 46 per cent of consumers supported metering, compared to 25 per cent rates, 21 per cent banding and 9 per cent licence fee (Office of Water Services 1991f). A result which showed, as OFWAT itself pointed out, that 'at least as many people favoured one of the other choices' (Office of Water Services 1991u: 16). The fragility of consumer support for the metering option was emphasized in the survey finding that 59 per cent of those expressing a preference for metering, changed their view when it was suggested that metering could be accompanied by an additional charge of up to £30 on top of the current average bill. Indeed the reliability and interpretation of the survey results generally is clouded by OFWAT's warning that the survey results 'need to be treated with caution. It would appear that many respondents had not thought through the issues before the interview; and modified their views as the interview progressed' (Office of Water Services 1991u: 15).

A second OFWAT survey, which involved inviting customers to return a postal questionnaire included with domestic (unmeasured) water bills in February and March 1991, is an even more suspect guide to consumer preferences for different charging methods. Although 64 per cent of the nearly 290 000 people responding to the survey supported metering (Office of Water Services 1991u), the self-selected nature of the exercise makes any interpretation of the results perilous. Yet, as in the OPCS survey, there was little support for metering at anything other than the most minimal of additional cost, and only 15 per cent of respondents favouring metering indicated that they would be willing to pay up to £29 for metering costs (Office of Water Services 1991u).

A third survey, not formally conducted as part of the Paying for Water consultation, and directed primarily at gathering consumer views on more general water services matters, indicated that whether or not metering is the charging system most favoured by consumers *in abstract*, few had actually seriously considered having a meter installed:

> All customers who were aware of the meter option [40% of the sample] were asked the likelihood of their installing one in the next year or two. Very few (7%) seem likely, 20% say they are not very likely to and 69% say they are not at all likely to install a meter (75% of those in the DE social grade say they are not at all likely to install, compared with 59% of those in the AB social grade).
>
> MORI (1992: 67)

Submissions to OFWAT in the Paying for Water consultation by each of the ten regional Customer Service Committees (CSCs), based on local public consultations, also failed to offer clear support for one charging method over another. Altogether five CSCs favoured metering, while four CSCs supported a form of property banding and the remaining CSC expressed no overall preference. The CSCs in favour of metering were Anglian, Wessex, Wales, Southern and Thames, while the CSCs in support of property banding were Central, North West, Yorkshire and South West. Northumbria CSC indicated that it was firmly opposed to both metering and flat-rate charges.

Within the water industry itself, there appears to be only a small number of water services companies who favour metering as the *sole* device for levying water charges. In submissions to OFWAT, most companies expressed a preference for charges based on the new council tax, along with selected metering.

Only two companies – Dwr Cymru and Northumbrian – supported the use of flat rate charges. Perhaps not coincidentally, these two companies presently levy the highest standing charges for unmeasured supply.

The industry's general reluctance to introduce widespread metering stems from a number of concerns including the capital costs involved, the possibility that metering will result in widely fluctuating and depressed revenues through reduced demand (e.g. in a wet summer) and consumer hostility. But measures by the water companies to move away from the commitment to meter new properties have drawn a sharp response from the regulator. This was exemplified in June 1991 when, following representations from the Yorkshire Customer Service Committee and Sheffield City Council, the board of directors of Yorkshire Water decided to amend the company's policy on the compulsorily metering of new housing estates, in favour of offering consumers a choice about charging methods. Following intervention by the Director General of Water Services, however, the company quickly rescinded this decision.

The regressive impact of volumetric charging on low-income households has been, and will continue to be, at the nub of community and consumer sector concerns about metering. Metering could particularly affect large families and households containing a disabled member or members, but its impact is likely to be more generalized than this. Potentially, all households presently living in low rateable properties would face steep increases in their water and sewerage bills if they became metered. Because of these equity implications, metering has been opposed by most of the major consumer and welfare organizations, such as the National Consumer Council, the National Association of Citizens Advice Bureaux, Age Concern and the Child Poverty Action Group.

The opposition of community services and consumer groups to metering is in contrast to the position adopted by some sections of the environmental movement, with organizations, like CPRE declaring strong support for water metering on conservation grounds. Friends of the Earth, in contrast though, has indicated that it does not support a national programme of domestic water metering. The Department of the Environment/Welsh Office discussion paper 'Using Water Wisely', released in the summer of 1992, advocated water metering on environmental grounds.

In the view of two commentators, at least, 'the introduction of environmental issues into the metering debate is a red herring. Domestic household metering as a method of charging for water is unlikely to tackle this environmental problem effectively but metering will have impacts on poverty and equity which carry major implications for social policy' (Childs and Huby 1992: 2). As Chapter 2 illustrated, empirical evidence on the relationship between pricing and water consumption is ambiguous and often difficult to interpret. But the overall trend of the data seems to suggests that 'water demand is highly price inelastic' (Mann 1989: 166) and that very substantial price increases are required before consumption is reduced to any significant extent (MMBW 1991; Martin and Wilder 1992). This is particularly the case with water used inside the home, as opposed to more discretionary outside use.

In its submission to the OFWAT consultation, the National Consumer Council (1991b: 18) favoured the use of flat rate charges, despite its explicitly regressive impact, because the 'ease of administration makes the licence fee far more likely to be integrated into the social security system than any other. That being so, then whatever regressive effects it may have in theory would be heavily offset by the fact of its being rebated for those on low incomes'. Neither the NCC's position on water charging, nor its remarkable expression of faith in the capacity of the social security system, and more particularly the Government, to respond to changes in water tariffs, has drawn much support from other consumer and community sector organizations.

The National Association of Citizens Advice Bureaux concluded that while it was opposed to water metering, it was unable clearly to support either of the alternatives to metering being proposed by the Director General. In addition, it argued somewhat cryptically that the Director General's powers 'need to be strengthened in order to ensure a stable base on which to place public policy for help with water charges for those on low incomes or high levels of water dependency' (covering letter to submission Paying for Water, 1991a).

The fears expressed by community sector groups about the impact of metering on low income households appear to have been corroborated in the DoE/OFWAT-commissioned study on The Social Impact of Water Metering published in three volumes in September 1992. Despite the fact that the study was conducted in the socio-demographically unrepresentative metering trial areas, it clearly revealed that a small, but by no means insignificant, proportion of households experienced acute deprivation and/or financial hardship as a result of the advent of metering.

At first glance, the study showed, as expected, that there were winners and losers under metering, and that there is a strong correlation between higher bills and household size. However, it was obvious from the in-depth interviewing phase of the study (Second Report) that some of the putative winners under metering were only so because they had sharply reduced their water consumption, in some cases at a considerable cost to quality of life. Also, it was found 'that with the exception of retirement pension recipients (many of whom are one-person households), those receiving social security benefits, were more likely to report that they were paying much more' (Office of Water Services 1992t, First Report: 4–18).

Overall, the correlation between 'financial hardship', as defined in the study (i.e. problems paying water bill, large increases in charges relative to rateable value equivalent, difficulty paying water bill and difficulty meeting household expenses) and income was found to be less direct than the association between financial hardship and family size and medical conditions. This could well be attributed the significant underrepresentation of low income households in the sample group; for example, only 6 per cent were in receipt of income support, which is one-third of the national figure and only 9 per cent of the sample group were local authority housing tenants, compared to 24 per cent nationally. But in the other category of 'social hardship' as defined in the study (i.e. reductions in personal hygiene-related water use, worry about using water, perceived reduction in hygiene levels), low-income households were markedly overrepresented. This suggests that often low-income consumers made heroic (if possibly misguided) efforts to reduce their bill by reducing their water consumption, at times involving a severe curtailment in their use of water with potentially serious personal hygiene and public health consequences.

In essence, the study underlines a fundamental problem with volumetric charging, in that for all its apparent commercial logic and the arresting appeal of its use of 'the simple fairness test' (i.e. you pay for what you use), and for all its laudable environmental aims, it will be poor households who disproportionately bear the costs – if not in extra charges, then in reduced quality of life. More affluent consumers have an inherent capacity to absorb the additional costs of metering, either by paying more in water charges, buying water efficient appliances, or by reducing discretionary use (particularly outside the home). Most low-income households do not have a similar capacity. Interestingly, most of the equity implications of the data contained in the Second Report were either down-played or ignored by the authors in their Summary report and recommendations.

Electricity

> We are still unable to answer the question we posed in 1988 – 'whether or not the privatised electricity supply industry is likely in aggregate to have lower costs, and hence be able to offer its consumers lower prices, than would be the case if the industry remained in public ownership'.
>
> House of Commons Energy Committee (1992a: para 167)

> The estimates suggest that, on average, prices were up to 25% higher for domestic customers and up to 19% higher for industrial customers than would have been predicted on the basis of a continuation of pre-privatization trends.
>
> Yarrow (1992: 32)

Electricity tariffs since privatization

Changes in the movement of electricity prices since privatization are inordinately difficult to track. This is partly the result of the complex structure of price controls in the ESI, which the Director General of Electricity Supply himself has described as 'not easy to understand, nor is it straightforward to check whether or not a licensee is complying with them . . .' (Office of Electricity Regulation, Annual Report, 1992). But it is also because, in contrast to his counterpart in the water industry, the electricity regulator – until the recent Supply Price Control Review, at least – has shown little inclination to make the pricing systems transparent. Nor has he been prepared to publish, on a regular basis, comparative data on electricity tariffs across the country.

The journey towards answers about electricity prices is rather less direct than in the case of water, and far more circuitous than it should have to be.

For much of the 1980s, electricity prices for domestic consumers declined in real terms, largely as a result of the fall in coal purchase costs. In the period immediately preceding privatization, however, domestic electricity prices rose in excess of the rate of inflation. These Government-initiated increases in tariffs leading into privatization had two purposes. The first related directly to the sale of the industry, with the Government seeking to enhance the commercial attractiveness of the ESI to potential investors. John Wakeham, Secretary of State for Energy, explained this in his evidence to the Select Committee on Energy:

> . . . there was a rise in the price of electricity at the time when electricity was privatised because we had to strike the right balance between the interests of the consumer, the interests of the taxpayer and the interests of the shareholders and we set the prices at the time of vesting to give a return on the assets employed of 5 per cent.
>
> (House of Commons Energy Committee 1992c: para 336)

The second purpose was to 'factor in' a degree of pricing surplus so that electricity tariffs could be maintained at a politically acceptable level in the years immediately following privatization. This was outlined by Dr Dieter Helm, also in evidence to the Select Committee on Energy, 'the Government raised the price level in advance of privatisation, in a series of steps, in order to fossilise-in a price level which then would not rise by more than inflation'.

The subsidiary price cap (Licence Condition 3C) was introduced with the explicit purpose of keeping electricity prices for domestic and small business users to the level of inflation for the first three years of privatization. The three-year life of the price cap was based on the duration of the contracts drawn up between the generating companies and British Coal (and the 'back-to-back' contracts between the generating companies and the RECs) in April 1990. It may not be accidental that this three-year period was also sufficient to cover the time up to and beyond the next General Election. Figure 4.4 shows the movement of electricity prices between 1979 and 1992.

Despite the intent of the subsidiary price cap, electricity prices for domestic and small business consumers rose by an average of 10.5 per cent in 1991–92, which was well above the prevailing rate of inflation. The excessive price rise in April 1991 was an artefact of the method used for calculating the rate of inflation, where regional electricity companies based their price increases on a forecast level of inflation for the year to October. Thus through a combination of underestimating inflation in the preceding year (with provision being made in the licence for the 'catching up' of lost revenue through low inflation forecasts) and overestimating inflation for the forthcoming year, tariffs rose by some 6.8 per cent above inflation in 1991.

The above inflation rise in tariffs in 1991 made something of a nonsense of the subsidiary price cap and caused acute embarrassment to both the

Figure 4.4   Domestic electricity prices 1979–92 (average annual increase).

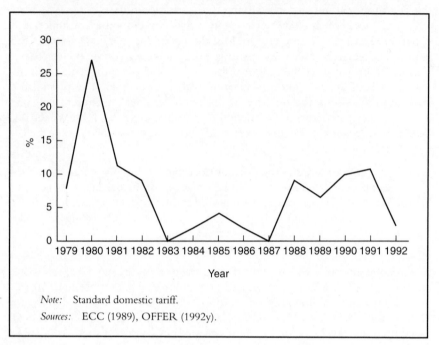

Note: Standard domestic tariff.
Sources: ECC (1989), OFFER (1992y).

Government and the regulator. In October 1991, the Director General wrote to the majority of the regional electricity companies 'pointing out that the rate of inflation was turning out to be significantly lower than the rates which they had assumed in setting prices for 1991–92 . . . [and] that, on the basis of the information that they had previously provided, it seemed likely that they might breach one of their price controls (the 3C subsidiary price cap)' (Office of Electricity Regulation 1992d). The Director General was asking, in effect, for some of the excess to be returned to electricity consumers. In the event, eight RECs exceeded the subsidiary price cap and while four of the companies agreed to return the full amount in reduced charges in 1992–93, the other four demurred. Ultimately, the four dissenting companies, who argued that they were not under any legal or moral obligation to respond to the Director General's request, agreed to return a proportion of the excess revenue raised in the form of reduced tariffs the following year (the level 're-paid' ranged from Eastern Electricity's 20 per cent to Northern Electric's 80 per cent). The effect of the clawback, in conjunction with a reduced level of inflation, resulted in domestic electricity tariffs rising on average by 2 per cent (in absolute terms) in 1992–93.

Over the period from April 1989, average domestic electricity tariffs have increased by 28 per cent, while inflation has risen by 24 per cent. This above inflation increase in domestic tariffs is particularly perplexing when it is

Table 4.7   Changes in electricity prices 1989–91: major sectors.

Sector	Change (%)
Domestic	+26%
Industrial:	
Small	+23%
medium	+1%
moderately large	−6%
extra large	+13%
RPI	+18%

Sources: Derived from Department of Trade and Industry (1992c: tables 54 and 61); Electricity Consumers Council (1989), Office of Electricity Regulation (1992).

considered that in 1991, the price of coal was 27 per cent cheaper in real terms than it was in 1988 (Department of Trade and Industry 1992c: table 63). As the cost of coal represents around 22 per cent of the cost of a unit of electricity to domestic consumers, it might be expected that the unit cost to domestic consumers would have fallen by around 8 per cent (in real terms) on the basis of coal costs alone. But rather than decline, domestic tariffs actually rose by 7.8 per cent in real terms over the period 1988 to 1991. This conundrum suggests that either the generating companies did not pass on coal purchase savings to the RECs and retained the savings as additional profit, or that the RECs themselves failed to pass on electricity savings to domestic consumers, with similar profit gains (or indeed some combination of both these factors).

One other possible explanation for the inverse relationship between coal prices and domestic consumer tariffs might lie in the way that the generation and supply companies have differentially distributed the benefits of savings in purchasing costs between classes of consumers. It could be hypothesized that the supply companies (which includes the generating companies, for they supply a significant proportion of electricity direct to industrial customers) are more likely to direct these benefits to the 'over 1 MW' sector where competition prevails, than to the captive franchise sector of the market. This hypothesis seems to be supported in part by the data in Table 4.7.

The recent rise in electricity tariffs for major industrial electricity users, like ICI, primarily as a result of the termination of a number of Government subsidy schemes, has prompted the Major Energy Users Council to call for the abolition of the 'fossil fuel levy'. In 1992 the levy, aimed primarily at providing financial support for the nuclear power industry, added 11 per cent to all electricity bills. The deleterious impact of this surcharge on electricity bills is likely to be felt just as keenly by low income households, as it is by industrial and commercial users of electricity in Britain.

As in the case of the water industry, there is evidence that variations in domestic tariffs across the country have widened since privatization. This is particularly evident in standard rate tariffs, as shown in Table 4.8.

Table 4.8   Variations in domestic electricity tariffs.

Standard rate	Price per therm (pence)		
	Lowest tariff	Highest tariff	Difference (%)
December 1989	Birmingham (MEB) 6.358	Liverpool (Manweb) 7.276	14%
December 1991	Birmingham (MEB) 7.536	Cardiff (S. Wales) 8.96	19%
Economy 7			
December 1989	Nottingham (E. Mid.) 4.428	Plymouth (SWEB) 4.85	10%
December 1991	Nottingham (E. Mid.) 5.282	Plymouth (SWEB) 5.927	12%

Notes: Based on 5000 kWh per annum – the average electricity consumption for all households in the 1986 English House Conditions Survey was 4435 kWh per annum (DoE 1991b); tariffs include unit rate and standing charge.

Source: Derived from Department of Trade and Industry (1992c: table 57).

Domestic tariffs post the subsidiary price cap

From the above account, it can be seen that the subsidiary price cap has not brought much benefit to domestic consumers. But with the expiry of the subsidiary price cap period in April 1993, domestic consumers face the full force of the RPI − X + Y price formula (Licence Condition 3B). This potentially will enable the RECs to increase tariffs above the level of inflation as most have plus X factors (average + 1.3 per cent) for distribution charges, and more importantly, to pass-through the full cost of purchasing electricity. The general supply price control (3B), though, is due for revision by April 1994 and a number of its existing elements are likely to change.

Theoretically, in a market where purchase costs are falling (e.g. arising from the decline in coal prices) domestic consumers stand to benefit from lower tariffs. However, it is by no means certain that electricity purchasing costs will continue to fall, firstly, because of the increased use of what is likely to be more expensive forms of electricity generation (i.e. nuclear, coal-fired power plant fitted with expensive flue gas desulphurization equipment and arguably, gas-fired power plants) and secondly, because full cost-pass-through (Y) provides no incentive for the RECs to purchase economically. Nor does it encourage the companies to adopt energy efficiency-oriented models of electricity supply. As Helm and Powell (1992: 103) conclude the 'introduction of a Y element assigns considerable risk away from the regional electricity companies towards their customers'.

It was for these reasons that the now-defunct House of Commons Select Committee on Energy in its examination of the Consequences of Electricity

Privatisation recommended that the subsidiary price cap be retained until full competition is introduced into the ESI:

> Controls on supply revenue from franchise customers ought however to continue beyond 1993, since these customers are dealing with a monopoly supplier for an essential service, and in our view such controls should remain in existence after each reduction of the franchise until the Director General is satisfied that there is fair and effective competition in supply to customers who have ceased to be part of the franchise. This could mean price controls of some sort continuing *beyond 1998* [author's emphasis].
>
> House of Commons Energy Committee (1992a: para 86)

Future decisions taken by the Director General on the Y cost-pass-through element of tariff formulae will have a major bearing on future electricity prices, as the costs covered by Y represent a substantial proportion of the cost of supplying electricity to consumers.

Competition and metering in the domestic sector

The Director General of Electricity Supply has set tremendous store on the advent of competition in the ESI. The efficacy of competition, as a mechanism for creating the sovereign domestic consumer, was a dominant theme in his consultation paper on 'Metering' published in January 1992. In this paper (Office of Electricity Regulation: 1992b), Professor Littlechild sketched a post-1998 world of advanced metering technology, opening up an ever-expanding horizon of consumer choice and lower prices, which has been described colourfully by the *Investors Chronicle* (19/6/92), 'OFFER's literally millennial vision is of a Britain where, by the year 2000, even domestic consumers can shop around RECs for current, measuring their juice use with portable radio meters'.

New metering technology potentially offers a number of significant advantages to domestic consumers – not the least of which could be the elimination of the specific-purpose and arguably stigmatizing pre-payment meter, along with an ability to externally monitor self-disconnection. But the Director General's paper substantially ignored two critical questions relevant to the introduction of a technology-led competitive regime in electricity supply, namely, who will pay for the installation of advanced metering technology in domestic households, and will the RECs be particularly interested in competing for domestic customer business in any event? Even if OFFER's optimistic estimate of £50–60 per meter were to hold true (the most advanced meters currently available cost between £110 and £130), this additional cost would still present a formidable entry barrier to many low-income households, particularly if consumers were expected to pay the cost up-front. The technology itself is likely to be complex and could be difficult for certain groups – such as the elderly, people with disabilities and people from non-English-speaking backgrounds – to use. The Consumers' Association (1992e: 2) underlined this issue in their response to the 'metering' consultation paper:

> Not all domestic consumers are able to use highly technical appliances. It is important, therefore, that the trial test the ease of use among different groups of consumers, for example, the elderly and disabled, to ensure the needs of all consumers are taken into consideration.

A danger clearly exists, under the advanced metering scenario, that two classes of domestic consumers will be created: those with the means and ability to make use of the technology and hence take the competition (and tariff) gains, and those without, who will be locked into monopoly supply and possibly higher electricity tariffs.

It is possible, however, that these concerns will remain little more than academic ones, for the vision of restless competition amongst the RECs and second-tier suppliers for domestic consumer business may turn out to be fanciful. The supply of domestic electricity is the least profitable part of the RECs commercial activity, and in the financial year ending 31 March 1992, six of the twelve RECs in England and Wales actually incurred losses in their supply businesses (Office of Electricity Regulation 1992y: figure 1). For this reason a number of observers have expressed the view that the prospect of a domestic electricity 'free market' in 1998 is hardly likely to cause enormous excitement amongst the supply companies:

> While technical advances in metering may, in fact, enable this [competition post 1998], it is unlikely that suppliers will pursue the very small electricity user in the same way that Mercury is now extending its domestic telephony market share. The price to the consumer of a unit of electricity is roughly the same as a unit telephone call, but, proportionately, the marginal costs of supply are much greater for the electricity company . . . Medium sized commercial consumers may eventually gain the benefits of choice, but these are unlikely to be extended to domestic consumers, who will remain customers of the monopolistic RECs.
>
> Roberts et al. (1991: 92)

It could also transpire that domestic consumers themselves might find little merit or cost-benefit in constantly monitoring their fuel costs and shopping around in the market place for their electricity supply. This issue of competition and choice in the utility industries is taken up in Chapter 7.

Conclusion

> No benefits of any kind can be seen for [water] consumers who are forced to pay monopoly supplier prices escalating above inflation.
>
> National Utility Services (1992: 1)

. . . whatever the merits of such a policy it cannot reasonably be claimed – as so often *is* claimed in political debate – that privatization was an exercise whose principal purpose was promotion of the interests of electricity consumers. Indeed, thus far, consumers have fared poorly from the venture.

Yarrow (1992: 33)

During the first period of privatization, each of the three utility industries experienced a fall in a number of their core underlying costs, i.e. gas and coal purchasing costs in the fuel utilities and construction costs in the water industry. This, in combination with the frequently-asserted efficiency gains from privatization, should have resulted in lower domestic utility tariffs over this period than was actually the case. The fact that domestic consumers did not benefit as directly as they should have suggests that either the original privatization settlement was deficient, or that its implementation has been flawed. Either way, it could be asserted with justification that, over the first period of privatization, domestic consumers in Britain have been paying a 'privatization premium' in their utility bills.

The tariff review process affords the regulatory bodies an opportunity to re-define the terms of the privatization settlement, and to allocate the financial benefits accruing from reduced costs and structural efficiencies more equitably amongst the industries and their sub-sets of consumers. The gas regulator took a significant step in this direction in his review of the tariff formula in 1991, although the resilience of the price/service package is likely to be fully tested by the fall-out from the MMC inquiry into the gas industry. The water and electricity regulators are both in the process of reviewing the price formulae in their industries. It remains to be seen whether they will be similarly successful in re-negotiating the financial settlement to the advantage of domestic consumers.

5

The management of debt and disconnection

Introduction

Changes in the level and structure of energy and water charges will have a disproportionate impact on low-income households simply because, as Chapter 2 showed, expenditure on utility services occupies a more prominent position in the budgets of these households than it does within the population generally. Increases in utility tariffs therefore, would be likely *a priori* to lead to greater levels of indebtedness and payment default, resulting ultimately in a growth in the number of disconnections. Conversely, the impact of reductions in tariffs would be manifested in a moderation in debt and disconnection.

To draw this direct causal link is to over-simplify, however, for movements in tariffs are only one part of the complex web of intersecting variables at play in utility debt and disconnection. Other factors at work include (i) the policy and practice of the utility companies regarding payment arrangements and options, debt retrieval and the like, (ii) the advent and use of technologies which enable the simultaneous maintenance of supply and recovery of debt and (iii) the degree to which social security benefits are up-rated in line with increases in utility charges. All of these factors need to be taken into account in examining the question of utility debt and disconnection.

The context of debt and disconnection

The correlation between fuel debt and low income has been well established. It has been estimated that in 1991, some 7 million households in Britain experienced fuel poverty, and there is both empirical (Boardman 1991b) and

Table 5.1   Households experiencing difficulties paying fuel bills

Pre-payment meters (June 1992)	2 918 124
Fuel direct (May 1992)	291 285
Disconnections (year ending June 1992)	50 440
Total	3 259 849

Sources: Gas Consumers Council (1992c); Office of Electricity Regulation (1991b); Benefits Agency (1992).

case-related evidence (NACAB 1991b) that the number of households living in fuel poverty has increased over the recent years.

If a very rough indicative measure of the number of households experiencing difficulty paying fuel bills can be constructed on the basis of the number of households with pre-payment meters, on fuel direct, or that have been disconnected, it can be seen (Table 5.1) that over 3 million households in Britain fell into this category in the first half of 1992. There is an element of 'double counting' in these figures as, for example, some households will use pre-payment meters as a method of paying both their electricity and gas bills.

By comparison with energy, there has been a dearth of empirical work in Britain on the interaction between water consumption and poverty, with the OFWAT-commissioned study on the social impact of water metering constituting one of the first (if limited) excursions into this field. There are, however, strong indications that water charges now occupy a much more significant, and problematic, place in the budgets of low-income households than has been the case hitherto (Social Security Advisory Committee 1990, 1992; NACAB 1992a; Huby and Dix 1992). Tangible measures of the increased manifestation of water debt (often described as 'water poverty') can be found in the way in which water companies are making greater use of the courts and their disconnection powers to retrieve outstanding debt (see below), and in the escalation in the number of direct payments for water being made through the social security system for income support recipients in debt. From the May quarter 1990 to the May quarter 1992, the number of direct payments for water increased from 32 499 to 126 979, a rise of over 290 per cent. This is shown graphically in Figure 5.1.

The rise in water-related debt might be seen to mirror the substantial increases in water charges over the past three years, but there have been other influences as well. Foremost among these have been the 1988 social security changes in the payment of water bills – previously the water rates of income support recipients were paid in full, now recipients have to pay directly out of their weekly benefit, and the abandonment by many local authorities and housing associations of the system of collecting water charges with the rent. The practice of tenants paying their water bills with their rent has the advantage of protecting them from disconnection, but it does result, in some instances in eviction or threatened eviction because of non-payment of water charges (NACAB 1992a).

Figure 5.1　Direct payments – water (May 1990–May 1992).

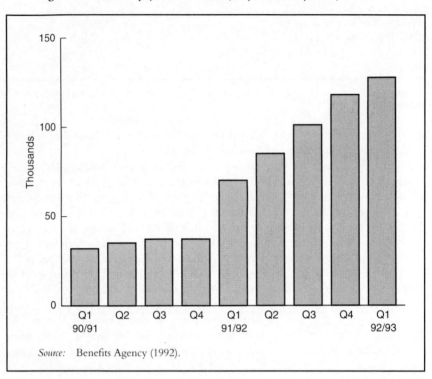

Source:　Benefits Agency (1992).

As with fuel there appears to be a strong correlation between water debt and socio-economic status. In the 1992 OFWAT survey *The Customer View-point*, 3 per cent of the customer sample (i.e. 123 respondents) had received a court summons for the non-payment of water bills in the past. Of these respondents, 66 per cent had a gross household income of less than £10000 (compared to 44 per cent of the entire sample) and 58 per cent identified themselves as being in social class DE (compared to 33 per cent of the full sample). The nexus between low income and water debt is underlined in the casework of citizens' advice bureaux throughout the country (NACAB 1992a; NACAB *Social Policy Bulletins*), in OFWAT's examination of the problem of debt and disconnection (Office of Water Services 1992g) and in the results of research into water debt commissioned by Welsh Water (Welsh Water, 1992).

The social security system has been slow to respond to the problems being experienced by low-income households as a result of rising water charges and the other changes alluded to above. The Social Security Advisory Committee (SSAC) had been arguing since 1990 that the Government make provision for water tariff increases in the annual up-rating of benefits. In the wake of the 1988 social security changes, water along with housing costs was excluded from the system of increasing benefits in line with inflation (the Rossi index). In October 1991, the Secretary of State for Social Security announced that water charges would in the future, be included in the Rossi index for up-rating benefits. This did not, however, address the water payment deficit experienced by beneficiaries over the previous three years, as the SSAC pointed out in its Annual Report (SSAC 1992: 18): 'there remains a shortfall in the income of those receiving income related benefits as no recompense was made for the period from 1988 to 1991, although water charges increased dramatically in that time'.

Nor does the notional element belatedly included in benefits to cover water charges directly correspond to the actual water bills of many low income households. Fitch (City of Bradford 1992) estimates that the water element paid to social security beneficiaries is currently £2.25 per week, whereas the average household water bill in England and Wales is £3.25 per week. In some parts of the country, consumers are paying bills well in excess of this average figure, with for example, consumers in the South West Water area paying on average £4.38 per week (Water Services Association 1992). In Autumn 1992, both the water industry and the OFWAT Customer Service Committees called on the Government to increase the water element in social security benefits (Welsh Water, 1992; *Water Bulletin*, 13/11/92; Office of Water Services 1992a*i*).

Disconnections for debt in the privatized energy and water industries

Prior to privatization, fears were held by community sector and consumer organizations that the advent of explicitly commercial regimes in the utility industries would lead to a more stringent approach to the handling of consumer debt. And that this, in conjunction with possible price increases, would be likely to result in the industries making greater use of their disconnection powers as a means of dealing with payment default. In actuality, the management of consumer debt by the privatized utilities thus far has been rather more variable, and in the case of the gas and electricity industries at least, more favourable, than this worst case scenario might suggest.

Over the initial period following the privatization of British Gas, and during the lead up to the sale of the water industry, a more assertive approach to payment default by domestic consumers was indeed in evidence. Domestic gas disconnections rose from 35626 in 1985 to 60778 in 1987, an increase of 70 per cent in the first two years of the industry's privatization. This increase was the result, in the view of British Gas, of worsening socio-economic conditions generally. But this argument was substantially refuted by the research of the Gas Consumers Council (1988) and, as reflected in the subsequent insertion of a new condition on debt and disconnection in the Licence of British Gas in early 1989, ultimately discounted by the regulator himself.

Disconnections (domestic and non-domestic) carried out by regional water authorities rose by 25 per cent between 1986–87 and 1988–89. This understated though, a longer-term trend in water disconnections which coincided with the industry's 'commercialization' in 1982, where disconnections rose from 1171 in 1981 to 9187 in 1987–88, almost an eightfold increase (Association of Metropolitan Authorities 1989b).

The electricity industry was the exception to this pattern of increased recourse to disconnection at or around the time of privatization, as the number of domestic disconnections had been in gradual and continuous decline since 1986 and remained that way over the period of privatization. The greater availability of token pre-payment meter technology in the ESI compared to the gas industry, may explain the downward trend in disconnections over this period (until recently, equivalent technology did not exist in the water industry – see below). Support for this thesis can be found in the way that the pre-payment meter became the critical element in the reversal of the disconnection trend in gas.

Responding to general community sector alarm and a request by the Gas Consumers Council to take action about the escalation in gas disconnections, the Director General of Gas Supply introduced a modification to British Gas' operating licence (known as Condition 12A) in April 1989. Condition

Figure 5.2   Gas and electricity domestic disconnections.

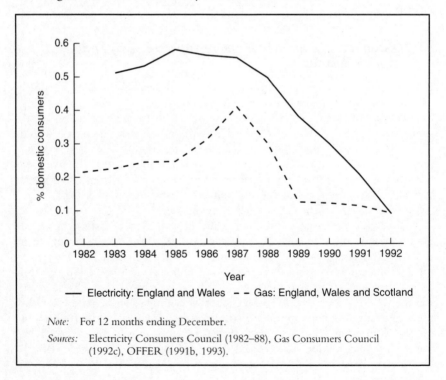

Note: For 12 months ending December.

Sources: Electricity Consumers Council (1982–88), Gas Consumers Council
(1992c), OFFER (1991b, 1993).

12A largely precluded the company from disconnecting a domestic customer experiencing difficulty paying their gas bill until a pre-payment meter had been offered as an alternative payment arrangement (Office of Gas Supply 1989b). The effect of this was to move the customer from paying for gas on credit, to paying for it in advance, with the meter calibrated to recover past debt. As a result of this change to the way that British Gas was allowed to pursue debt recovery, domestic disconnections dropped from a peak of 61 796 (or 4 disconnections for every 1 000 domestic customers) in the year ending 31 March 1988, to 19 266 in the year ending 31 March 1990 (just over 1 for every 1000 customers).

The dramatic success of the OFGAS-enforced licence modification encouraged the Government to add a similar provision, with almost exactly the same wording, to the draft licences of the regional electricity companies during the passage of the Electricity Bill. This subsequently became Condition 19 of the supply licence (Code of Practice on methods for dealing with tariff customers in default). Figure 5.2 shows the domestic disconnection trends in the two industries over the past decade. The part played by pre-payment meters in reducing the level of gas disconnections for debt is manifestly obvious in Figure 5.3, which compares the trends in pre-payment meter installation with domestic disconnections.

Figure 5.3   Pre-payment meters and gas disconnections.

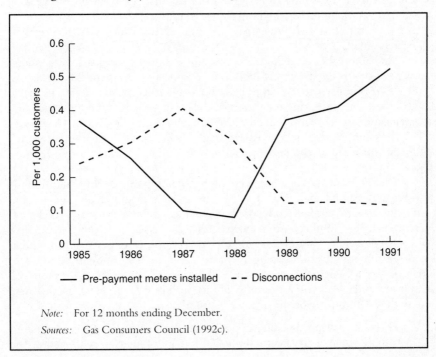

Note: For 12 months ending December.

Sources: Gas Consumers Council (1992c).

In the electricity industry, it would hardly be a coincidence that the number of disconnections in England and Wales fell by 43 per cent between July 1991 and June 1992, while at the same time, the number of domestic customers paying for their electricity via token meters rose by 41 per cent. Another illustration of the strong correlation between pre-payment meters and disconnection is found in the fact that in the June quarter 1992, the RECs with above average falls in the rate of disconnection were also those with above average rates of pre-payment meter installation during the quarter. Whereas in those RECs with a below average decline in disconnections, the level of pre-payment meter installation for the quarter was also below the average.

The Conditions 12A and 19 licence changes, and their impact in reducing disconnections, have been universally welcomed by consumer and community services agencies. Yet despite the broad intent of these codes of practice, which is to effectively eliminate withdrawal of supply because of inability to pay, a total of 33 725 households were disconnected by either electricity or gas companies in Britain in the year ending December 1992. In the case of gas, the decline in the rate of disconnection has hovered around the same level (1 per 1000 domestic customers) since March 1990. Theoretically, if Conditions 12A and 19 were being implemented to their optimum, the number of domestic disconnections should be very low indeed, involving only those consumers who have vacated properties without notifying the utility companies and those who for one reason or another refuse to pay their bills when they have a capacity to do so. This, of course, is based on the view – which has been supported by empirical research from Berthoud, 1983 onwards – that the proportion of 'won't pay' as opposed to 'can't pay' consumers is extremely small.

The factors that underlie the continuing residual of domestic disconnections have yet to be effectively identified, despite the efforts of the regulators (and OFGAS in particular) to find plausible explanations. An inability to make contact with the defaulting consumer has been identified by the industries and the regulators as the source of the problem. According to British Gas, 'over 95% of customers disconnected have made 'no contact' with the company' (OFGAS note *Gas Debt and Disconnection* to Public Utilities Access Forum, 29/4/92).

The 'no contact' issue has been a long-standing one in the utility industries, and Berthoud identified it as a major barrier to the resolution of debt problems in his seminal study of the operation of the voluntary codes of practice in 1983. While consumer advocates agree, as the companies argue, that without contact it is impossible to offer the customer either a pre-payment meter or to come to some arrangement over the payment of debt, there is less consensus over whether 'no contact' is the cause of the problem or merely a symptom, and over where the onus of responsibility for making contact lies, i.e. with the consumer or the utility (PUAF 1990a):

> There is a risk in dwelling upon no contact as a problem. It is arguable
> that the focus of concern should be on involuntary disconnection for

debt, and that no contact is an *explanation* for such disconnection. The explanation is one that is offered by suppliers, and the notion of no contact comprises a multitude of administrative and legal considerations. Perhaps observers should remain agnostic about the status of no contact as a problem, especially as suppliers are the main source of data about the issue, and information about it is collected and released in accordance with their requirements and interests.

The National Right to Fuel Campaign (1989) and the Gas Consumers Council (1991a), amongst others, have questioned whether the utility companies make sufficient efforts to contact consumers in default, and have sought clearer regulatory directions to the companies regarding the steps that need to be taken to establish customer contact.

The number of reconnections within a short period has been seen as a possible indicator of failure on the part of the companies to pursue contact as actively as they might, and certainly it raises questions about the validity of disconnection in the first place. Amongst the sample of gas disconnection cases regularly monitored by the Gas Consumers Council, the proportion of domestic consumers reconnected within 28 days has been consistently in the region of 37–40 per cent, which 'must represent a considerable waste of time and resources for British Gas and a cost to all consumers, in the long run' (Gas Consumers Council 1991b). In 1992, British Gas commissioned the Policy Studies Institute to carry out a qualitative research project on 'no contact' and the results of this research should assist in developing a more effective policy and practice response to this long-standing problem.

Despite the across-the-board downward trend in disconnections, individual company performance varies greatly as Figure 5.4 shows. The ability of companies like Norweb to implement a 'low disconnections policy' (in fact, in the year previously, a mere 129 customers were disconnected) is heavily predicated on the pre-payment meter solution. Norweb has adopted a vigorous policy on the installation of pre-payment meters for customers in default, which on occasions has apparently involved installing them without the agreement of, or even the presence of, the customer concerned.

Until recently, British Gas' capacity to reduce disconnections much below the March 1990 level had been constrained by an absence of appropriate coinless pre-payment meter technology. This, however, will change in the future with the mass production and installation of the new Quantum meter. Developed by Landis and Gyr, the Quantum pre-payment meter is a card-operated system with a number of the hi-tech features envisaged by Professor Littlechild in his metering consultation paper (*Gas World International*, April 1992; British Gas video *The Quantum System*). The meter is being tested throughout the country and British Gas plan to install around 20 000 Quantum meters per month from 1993 onwards.

Regulatory action and community sector advocacy notwithstanding, the pre-payment meter has manifestly been the key to the progress made in reducing

Figure 5.4 Electricity disconnections for year ending December 1992.

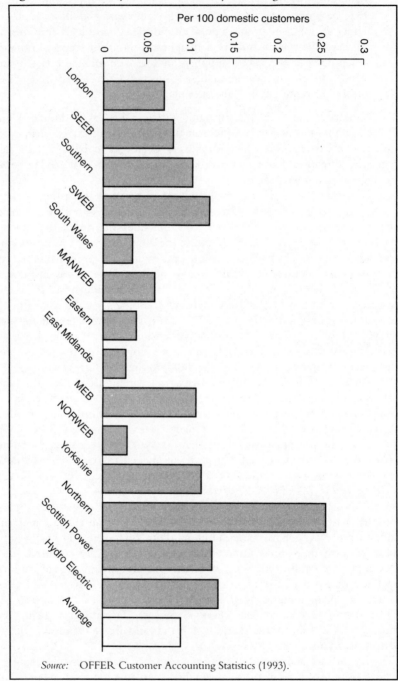

Source: OFFER Customer Accounting Statistics (1993).

the number of gas and electricity disconnections. Without the advent of coinless pre-payment meter technology, it is doubtful whether the dual objectives of reducing the level of domestic energy disconnections and enhancing the commercial capacity and freedom of the utility industries, could have been reconciled.

As well as giving customers in default the facility to remain on supply, pre-payment meters have clear advantages for the utility companies. They provide a continuous revenue stream in advance of the consumption of energy, which contrasts with the way that revenue is raised from the bulk of consumers, and they give the utilities a secured way of retrieving debt with minimal costs:

> [pre-payment meters] improve the cash flow of the supply business compared with quarterly payment methods, since payment is received . . . prior to consumption of the electricity . . . Consequently, the more customers that choose these payment methods [pre-payment meters and direct debit], the better the cash flow of the supply business, and the lower the necessary return of the supply business.
>
> (Office of Electricity Regulation (1992y: 37).

From the consumers' point of view, however, pre-payment meters are not without their costs. These are manifested in the additional charges borne by consumers paying for their electricity or gas through pre-payment meters, first, generally in the form of higher standing charges (and sometimes higher unit charges): pre-payment meter customers of Yorkshire Electricity and Northern Electricity, for example, on Economy 7 tariffs pay an additional 44 and 46 per cent, respectively, on their standing charge. Second, there is the financial and opportunity costs incurred by consumers having to travel to purchase supplies of tokens/cards to operate the meters.

At another level, a major and rather more insidious cost has been identified. The increasing use of pre-payment meters has been paralleled by rising concern about the possibility of self-disconnection amongst households unable to afford to buy the requisite tokens to operate pre-payment meters. By its very nature the level of self-disconnection within the community will remain largely hidden and undetected, although two qualitative studies – one in Leicester and the other in Birmingham and Bristol – have provided evidence that users of gas and electricity pre-payment meters tend to ration their use of energy (Law et al. 1990; Birmingham Settlement et al. 1992). Self-disconnection, in the sense of cutting back on essential energy use, can occur whether people have pre-payment meters or not, but in the more recent Birmingham and Bristol study, it was found that self-disconnection 'appears to be particularly prevalent among households with pre-payment meters – especially when the calibration is set high to recover a debt' (Birmingham Settlement et al.: 94).

The two studies present somewhat different accounts of the reaction of consumers to pre-payment meters. The Leicester study concluded that they assist with the more immediate problem of managing energy costs, as they enable 'consumers to be aware of the real costs of their fuel needs and to better budget for these. They are on the whole liked by those consumers who were using them' (Law et al. 1990: 33). The Birmingham and Bristol study (1992: 17) found that while pre-payment meters helped low-income households manage their fuel bills, this was often only because they 'forcibly alter[ed] the priority of repayment of debts' and that attitudes 'to pre-payment meters ranged widely from strong support to militant antagonism . . . [the] most common perspective on pre-payment meters was that they were a means to an end – typically debt repayment' (Birmingham Settlement et al. 1992: 92).

From a social policy perspective, pre-payment meters have more of the attributes of a 'quick fix' than a considered and effective approach to improving the access of low income households to essential utility services. Most fundamentally, they do little, in themselves, to address the underlying causes of fuel poverty. They have the propensity to simply 'privatize' the disconnection process, through the consumer rather the company acting as the mechanism for disconnection when fuel can no longer be afforded. Pre-payment meters also serve to reinforce the social division of utility service access through creating a second – and potentially stigmatized – class of gas and electricity customer.

Until recently pre-payment meter technology has not been available to the water industry. However, this is likely to change in the future as trials on 'budget metering' have been conducted by a number of water companies, the largest of which is the OFWAT-supervised trial of the Schlumberger budget meter by Severn Trent Water involving 3000 households. The Director General of Water Services has expressed a strong interest in the development of 'pay as you go' systems 'because budget meters may, in principle, have a valuable role to play in avoiding disconnection' (Office of Water Services *Annual Report* 1992: 40).

Beyond the current technological constraints which, for the present, limit the extended application of pre-payment metering systems in the water services industry, major reservations have been expressed about the use of this approach to debt management in the water industry, given the possible public health consequences of self-disconnection from water supply (Public Utilities Access Forum 1990b).

Until an equivalent to the gas and electricity industries' alternative to disconnection can be developed, more conventional measures have had to be applied in the privatized water industry. As a result of a House of Lords amendment to the Water Bill, Condition H (Code of Practice and Procedure on Disconnection) was added to the licences of the water companies. Under Condition H, the water companies could only disconnect domestic consumers after an application for a county court order on the repayment of the debt *and* if this order for repayment of the debt was subsequently breached. At the time, this appeared to represent a reasonable protective device for low-income consumers. It was also a considerable advance on the pre-privatization situation, where regional water authorities could disconnect consumers virtually without notice and minus any real form of external accountability.

Domestic water disconnections fell by just over 10 per cent in 1990–91 to 7560 (Office of Water Services 1991i). Total disconnections (domestic and non-domestic) by all 39 water companies fell from 15 255 in 1988–89 to 9092 in 1990–91 – a reduction of 40 per cent. Despite this substantial drop in the overall number of water disconnections, the Director General of the Office of Water Services warned that:

> the picture is a patchy one and the level of disconnections remain stubbornly high for some companies. There is reason to believe that the reduction in the level of disconnections is a temporary phenomena [sic], as companies adapt to the requirements of Condition H, and that disconnections can be expected to increase.
>
> Office of Water Services (1991b: 1)

This indeed, turned out to be the case. The Director General's caution, in the face of what looked to be a promising decline in disconnection trends in the industry, was stimulated by firstly, a knowledge that 'the companies were going softly, softly over the first couple of years of privatization' (interview with OFWAT policy officer, July 1992) and secondly, by evidence of the negative unintended consequences of the operation of Condition H (Perchard 1992). Through precipitately issuing summonses for county court determinations (often after only the most minor instances of payment default; NACAB 1991a; Office of Water Services 1991b), many of the water companies were able to breach the protective intent of Condition H.

In 1990–91, 900 000 summonses were issued by the water companies (representing approximately 1 in every 23 domestic and non-domestic premises in England and Wales), of which approximately half were brought to judgment. In a letter to the managing directors of the water companies (MD54), the Director General pointed out the seeming profligacy of this approach to the use of the courts. He also drew attention to the impost that this style of debt management placed on customers experiencing problems in paying their water bills:

> Because the court's costs and the company's legal costs in serving the summons can be recovered from the customer this means that each of those customers had to pay an additional £30 on top of their existing bill – a not inconsiderable burden for families struggling on a low income.
>
> Office of Water Services (1991b: 32–33)

In response to the haemorrhaging of Condition H, the regulator announced the setting up of a special working group to review its implementation and to recommend changes to its operation. The working group published its report in April 1992. While the working group rather surprisingly stopped short of recommending an immediate overhaul of Condition H, it indicated that this could occur in the future if the water companies failed to implement the published guidelines. A synopsis of the OFWAT *Guidelines on Debt and Disconnection* is produced in Figure 5.5, not only because it summarizes the flaws in

Figure 5.5   OFWAT *Guidelines on Debt and Disconnection.* (Source: Office of Water Services 1992g.)

OFWAT Guidelines on Debt and Disconnection

Reports on deliberations of a joint regulator/industry/CSC working group. Sets out guidelines for company practice, focusing on eight areas:

1. Contact with customers – companies should make contact with customers who are in arrears as soon as possible and 'seek to agree with them affordable payment arrangements to pay off the arrears' p.3.
2. Payment options – companies should consider extending the range of payment options available, including introducing frequent payment schemes.
3. Payment facilities – measures are required to assist customers who do not hold bank accounts (reports Policy Studies Institute finding that 20% of adults do not have bank or building society accounts); including assisting customers to meet the costs of 'individual transaction charges' (e.g. in Post Office, 70p counter fee charged).
4. Debt recovery timetable – considerable variation in company practice currently: 'The approach currently adopted by some companies can only be described as leisurely' p.9. 'Companies should avoid delay whilst giving customers adequate time to respond to the various stages in the debt recovery timetable' p.4. Timetable should consist of at least 5 stages and 'the disconnection visit should be preceded by at least one attempt to make direct personal contact with the customer' p.4.
5. Information – sets out details of the information that should be provided to customers at the reminder (or final notice) stage and at the pre-summons warning stage and includes an example letter.
6. Direct payment from income support – 'Companies should take positive steps to find out whether or not customers in arrears are in receipt of income support and, therefore, eligible for direct payments from benefit' p.5.
7. Non-standard payment arrangements – 'it is both reasonable and sensible that companies should take into account ability to pay when negotiating payment arrangements to clear arrears' p.12. Suggests seeking advice from local advice agencies and money advisers in relation to this.
8. Pre-disconnection visit – 'Few companies attempt to make contact, prior to the visit to disconnect, other than by letter or other written communication' p.13.

---

present industry practice but also because it is viewed by some members of the community sector as being a useful 'model' code of practice.

The need for urgent action to deal more effectively with the mounting problem of water-related debt was reinforced less than two months after the release of the *Guidelines* with the publication of the disconnection figures for 1991–92. Over the space of a year, domestic disconnections rose from 7673 to

Figure 5.6   Water disconnections. Regional Water Companies only, domestic consumers.

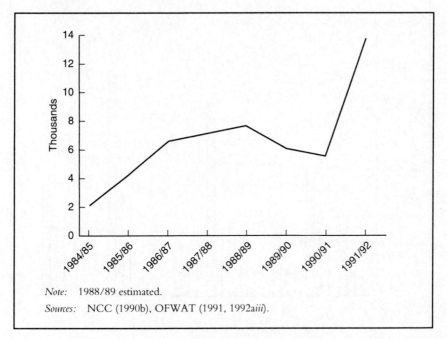

Note: 1988/89 estimated.
Sources: NCC (1990b), OFWAT (1991, 1992a*iii*).

21 286, an increase of 177 per cent. In proportional terms, water disconnections had reached a level akin to those for the gas industry (over 1 in every 1000 domestic water consumers). Over the same period, the number of summonses issued by the companies fell to just over 600 000, although the actual number of judgments remained roughly the same as the previous year (in excess of 400 000). Figure 5.6 shows the trends in water disconnections since 1984.

The variable disconnection practices of the water companies, alluded to by the Director General in MD54, is illustrated in Figure 5.7. The variations are even more extreme in the water only companies – with six companies having a rate of disconnection in excess of 2 per 1000 domestic customers in 1991–92. The South Staffordshire water company in the Midlands led the way with a disconnection rate of almost 8 in every 1000 households.

As a device for protecting water consumers from disconnection, Condition H has been a singular failure. As a mechanism for assisting low income consumers in debt negotiate arrangements based on capacity to pay, it has 'made the plight of customers worse' (OFWAT Director of Consumer Services, PUAF meeting, September 1992). John Winward sums up the misadventure of Condition H well when he says:

> For many years, consumer organisations argued that disconnection by water undertakings should only be allowed after recovery for debt had

Figure 5.7   Domestic water disconnections since privatization.

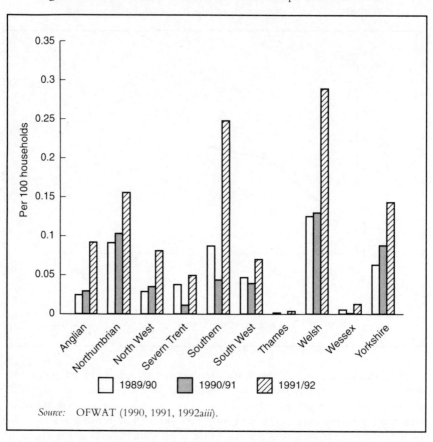

Source: OFWAT (1990, 1991, 1992a*iii*).

been sought through the county court. Since the passage of the Water Act 1989, this has effectively been the policy applied to the industry. It rapidly became apparent, however, that the policy was flawed. Rather than providing an independent body which could review the facts of each case and establish a repayment schedule, the courts have proved an extremely blunt instrument. The great majority of cases are never reviewed in detail; the consumer either clears the debt or fails to respond to the summons. At the same time, the courts have imposed additional costs on the consumer, and in some cases introduced significant delays.

Winward (1992: 2–3)

At the end of November 1992, 155 MPs signed an Early Day Motion initiated by the Sheffield MP, Helen Jackson. The motion called on the Government to, in effect, make water disconnections illegal through extending the Health and Safety Regulations to cover domestic premises.

Related issues in debt and disconnection

Action to retrieve serious debt is, in effect, the terminus in the relationship between the consumer and the utility company. It can either represent the end of the contractual relationship (at least temporarily) through disconnection, which in the context of essential services, leads to potentially serious consequences for the consumer concerned. It can also form the beginning of a re-negotiated relationship – one that is more attuned to the financial circumstances of the utility consumer. Therefore, the measures that make up the chain of interventions to resolve the problem of utility debt are as important to the framework of consumer protection as are specific prescriptions about disconnection itself. Indeed, they may be even more important for, from Berthoud's work in the early 1980s through to the operation of Condition H in the water industry, the message is clear. Action to circumscribe the disconnection powers of the utilities will be ineffective at best and positively harmful to the indebted consumer at worst, unless it is complemented by an array of measures aimed at confronting the underlying problem of managing fuel and water payments on a limited income.

The problem of fuel and water debt has been conventionally perceived by the utility industries to be one for the social security system to deal with, and along the demand dimension (i.e. whether households can obtain access to requisite amounts of water and energy and whether they have sufficient income to continue paying for these services) this view has some, but by no means incontestable, validity. On the supply side, however (i.e. how utility services are provided and how low-income consumers can be assisted to marshal their limited resources to maximum effect in purchasing and paying for utility services), the utilities have a direct and significant role to play. The provision that the utilities make for flexible and varied payment options, the method and frequency with which they bill customers, the levels of debt repayment set, the extent to which they engage the assistance of social security and social services agencies in support of the consumer in financial difficulty and the general attitude that they adopt to customers in debt, all exercise a considerable influence on the epidemiology of fuel and water debt.

Studies that have sought to document or assess the performance of the privatized utilities in this area suggest that the energy and water industries have some way to travel before the rubric of customer care attains much meaning for low-income consumers (NACAB 1991b, 1992; Birmingham Settlement et al. 1992; Office of Water Services 1992g; Berthoud and Kempson 1992). It should be said, however, that many of the defects identified mirror those exhibited over many years by the nationalized precursors of the present utility companies. In their *modus operandi* regarding low-income consumers, the publicly-owned energy and water industries were generally no better, and possibly in a number of respects, worse than their privatized counterparts.

In relation to payment and billing methods, analyses of current practice have shown that some utility companies have been reluctant to develop payment schemes which meld with the budgeting requirements of low-income households. The water industry in particular has displayed a marked reluctance to move away from the annual and biannual billing cycles towards more frequent payment systems. Untoward reliance is placed on estimated readings, which often results in low-income households having to confront unantici-pated large utility bills. Estimated readings are particularly rife amongst the RECs and the Director General of Electricity Supply has sought to revise the original performance standard (at least one 'firm reading' a year) in this area (Office of Electricity Regulation 1992x).

The actual terms of an agreement reached by the company and the customer for the recovery of debt will have a major bearing on whether the agreement succeeds or not. The logic of setting a debt repayment timetable in line with the customers' capacity to pay in order to optimize the prospect of debt recovery, however, seems to have escaped a number of companies. Case evidence from citizens' advice bureaux and the Birmingham and Bristol study on hidden disconnection indicates that the short-term commercial imperatives of the utility companies often overrides their longer-term commercial interests (i.e. the eventual recovery of the outstanding debt and maintaining the cus-tomer on supply), and seriously undermines the fragile budgeting systems of low-income households. Most companies aim to complete the debt-recovery process within 12 months, irrespective of the size of the debt or the customers' capacity to pay. Often the level of repayment is set well above the standard used by the Benefits Agency for direct payments (£2.15 per week for each utility debt). Access to fuel direct itself is a problem for some eligible con-sumers, i.e. those on income support with arrears greater than £42.45. This is notably the case for electricity consumers, as the RECs have balked at the additional administrative costs involved, preferring instead the pre-payment meter option (PUAF 1990a, 1991; Birmingham Settlement et al. 1992).

Disconnection action is an expression of a fundamental breakdown in the relationship between the utility and the consumer. If the debt-recovery systems used by the companies were being applied effectively and sensitively, it would be a rarely applied sanction, as the gas and water regulators have often pointed out. Although, in a context of rising utility tariffs, as in water, even the most dexterous of debt-recovery methodologies will run up against the reality that some households lack sufficient income to meet their utility and other debts. When disconnection does occur it should follow a process that is both trans-parent and accountable, and should not penalize the consumer beyond the termination of supply. Yet neither of these conditions presently apply in the utility industries.

Transparency and accountability in the process is precluded by the fact that the disconnection codes of practice are not published and hence are not subject to public scrutiny. Nor are they generally made available to consumer and welfare organizations who are often in the position of needing to advocate on behalf of customers who are facing imminent disconnection. The argument used by the companies – and by implication the regulators – that the publication of

Figure 5.8 Manweb's customer in default process. (*Source:* Manweb Licence Condition 19: *Methods for Dealing with Domestic Credit Customers in Default.*)

BILL SENT

16 DAYS LATER NO RESPONSE   REMINDER/FINAL NOTICE SENT [Unless
                                          customer who has paid last three most recent
                                          bills prior to a reminder 'sent a polite notice
                                          instead of the Reminder/Final Notice']

17 DAYS LATER NO RESPONSE★   NOTICE (CP1): ADVISES CUSTOMER OF CODE
                                          OF PRACTICE AND OFFERS THEM A CHOICE OF
                                          EITHER (a) A SPECIFIC PAYMENT
                                          ARRANGEMENT OR (b) A CARD METER

12 DAYS LATER STILL UNPAID★★   DISCONNECTION NOTICE SENT (CP2) BY
                                          FIRST CLASS POST 'notifying them of the date
                                          on which we intend to visit the premises to
                                          disconnect the supply and remove the meter.'
                                          The CP2 notice states that at this visit we
                                          will be prepared to install a card meter unless
                                          it is not safe or practical to do so'.

5 WORKING DAYS LATER   DISCONNECTION VISIT

TOTAL = 50–52 DAYS

[★ 'where the bill remains unpaid 33 days after billing'; ★★ by the 45th day after billing']

NO EFFECTIVE CONTACT   'If there is no adult at home with authority
                                          to give our disconnection operative access or
                                          if access is refused, he will leave a letter
                                          (CP3) at the premises which advises the
                                          customer that we now intend to apply for a
                                          Warrant of Entry under the Rights of Entry
                                          (Gas and Electricity Boards) Act 1954.' The
                                          cost of this visit will be added to the
                                          customer's account

                                          'The customer will always be notified, by
                                          first class post, of the date on which we
                                          intend to visit the premises with a Magistrates
                                          Warrant.' Additional expense of obtaining
                                          and actioning the Warrant added to
                                          customer's account

BUT NOTE: 'For customers who are continually late in settling their bills or late
in agreeing to payment arrangements, it would be impractical to follow
Procedure 1 every quarter. Therefore, we will only apply it once in any 12
month period' p.5. In this case, Procedure 2 is brought into play because it is
more 'streamlined': Disconnection Notice sent after 28 days from billing.

---

the disconnection codes (or 'methods') would enable certain customers and their advocates to exploit the system, is based on the false premise that the utility consumer world is inhabited by masses of 'won't pays', and it looks particularly frail when juxtaposed against the common law principle of due process. It also ignores the infinite human capacity for ingenuity. It would take, for example, little more than the studied observation of a neighbour's experience of disconnection to unpick the lock of the Manweb code set out in Figure 5.8.

Currently, the disconnected consumer effectively confronts a situation of 'double jeopardy', for in addition to losing supply, he or she is required to meet punitive disconnection costs. In water, for instance, disconnection charges range from £25.50 (Yorkshire) to £73 (Wessex) amongst the water and sewerage companies, and from £15 (York, Chester and Cambridge) to £80 (Hartlepool and North East) amongst the water only companies (Centre for the Study of Regulated Industries 1992: table B.7). These financial penalties are obviously designed to act as a deterrent against the wilful non-payment of utility bills. In their impact, however, they primarily serve to compound the financial difficulties of those groups of consumers whose problem is not one of wilfulness, but lack of income.

Despite the substantial defects in the debt-management procedures of the utilities, there are signs that some modest improvements are being effected in this area, although this varies across the industries and between the companies. The slow transformation of British Gas is probably the best exemplar of improving practice (Birmingham Settlement et al. 1992; Berthoud and Kempson, 1992; interviews with consumer and community sector organizations). Whether this has much to do with the forces for change within the companies themselves is a moot point. Certainly, the contribution of the regulatory bodies, underpinned by vigilant and effective advocacy of the community sector, has been important. The same applies to the development of systems of consumer protection generally across the three industries, as the next chapter reveals.

6

Consumer protection and representation

Consumer protection is meaningless if it is so complicated and inaccessible to ordinary people that they remain either unaware of their rights or unable to act on them.

Whitworth (PIRC 1989: 14)

Introduction

In the area of consumer rights, and to a lesser extent, service quality, the privatized utility industries began from what could be described as a relatively unambitious base. During their 40 years or so under public ownership, the water, electricity and gas industries had often been perceived as complacent, and even dismissive, in their approach to customer care (although interestingly, consumer surveys generally indicated a quite high level of satisfaction with service performance). But in the context of the 'new consumerism' of the late 1980s and 1990s (Taylor 1990a; Keat 1991), demands have been placed on the providers of public and essential services to display a stronger formal consciousness of consumer matters. The Conservative Government's Citizen's Charter (HMSO 1991b) is symbolic of the rhetorical shift from producer-led to customer-driven models of service delivery. The changes effected in the consumer orientation of the privatized utility industries, then, have to be viewed against this broader socio-political and cultural canvas.

Policy and organizational change, driven by consumerist objectives, often seem to be premised on an assumption that there is a homogeneity of interest amongst all consumers which transcends social class, income or relative need. However, programmes built on this assumption stand the danger of overlooking the different, and at times even conflicting, sets of interests that exist amongst particular groups of domestic consumers, in their desire to respond to a dominant and standardized customer prototype. Consumerist approaches also tend to focus more on procedural rights (e.g. the keeping of appointments and the answering of complaints) than on questions of access, affordability and equity. An examination of the 'social division' of service standards and quality prescriptions is an important dimension in the analysis of consumer protection and consumer representation in the privatized utilities. It will be introduced into the discussion below, and taken up at greater length in the final chapter.

Consumer protection

The convergence of regulatory responsibilities

Regulating for quality is every bit as important as regulating price in monopoly settings. In the absence of quality regulation, monopoly service providers have an opportunity to off-set the impact of price controls on profits, by making savings in the level and quality of service provided to the consumer. In the first period of utility privatization, with British Telecom and British Gas, the Government adopted a 'light touch' or 'hands off' approach to quality regulation, with the regulators being given quite muted consumer protection powers (Rovizzi and Thompson 1992). The regulatory provisions for consumer protection were strengthened in the water and electricity privatizations, and more recently, the Citizen's Charter legislation affecting the utilities, the Competition and Service (Utilities) Act 1992, has added further weight to the quality regulation powers of the four utility regulatory bodies. The decision by the Major Government to supplement the powers of the regulatory bodies would seem to indicate a belated recognition that the original powers given to a number of the regulators were insufficient for the task of quality regulation.

Partly because of the limitations in the regulatory framework, privatization was initially attended by very few service-related gains for domestic consumers. This was emphasized in a number of well-publicized surveys by organizations such as the Consumers' Association, which showed that most consumers believed that very little had changed in the service performance of the utilities in the years immediately after privatization. For example, the *Which?* survey taken in July 1989 (i.e. some three years after the birth of British Gas plc) found that 'only one in ten said the service had improved [since privatization] – the majority thought nothing had changed, or thought it was too early to say' (*Which?* 1989: 312).

The late 1980s and early 1990s witnessed an accretion of power by both the telecommunications and gas supply regulators in the area of consumer protection, as they sought to correct the deficits in their statutory powers *in situ*. Through a combination of negotiation, persuasion and threat, the telecommunications and gas regulatory bodies managed to stretch the bound-aries of their legislative mandate. Both regulators have had success in incor-porating quality of service criteria into the price control mechanism – directly in the case of OFGAS, indirectly in the case of OFTEL (Office of Gas Supply 1991e; Office of Telecommunications 1992a,b) – despite the fact that they have encountered resistance and opposition from the companies concerned:

> Because of British Gas' resistance to change and a lack of a purposeful, dynamic approach to customer service it has been a slow, difficult process to reach agreement with the company on many of these [i.e. customer protection] issues.
>
> Office of Gas Supply *Annual Report* (1991: Section 1)

The additional duties imposed on British Gas by OFGAS, including the intro-duction of *key service standards* along the lines of those in the electricity and water industries (see below), following its 1991 review of the gas tariff formula is a concrete illustration of the evolving strength of the regulatory machinery.

In the tariff review, the gas regulator sought to correct a fundamental deficit in the original Authorisation of British Gas, namely that 'there is no guarantee that lower prices will not be achieved at the expense of lower standards of service' (Office of Gas Supply 1991g: 3). Persistent calls by the regulator over the previous couple of years for the voluntary introduction of a clear and comprehensive system of service standards, had drawn an inadequate response from British Gas. Even though British Gas published a long-awaited customer standards statement in 1990, *Our Commitment to Banishing Gripes*, this was seen to lack both clarity and measurability:

> OFGAS did not consider that the published commitment covered the full area of services. Furthermore the services described in the document were qualified in relation to service delivery by the use of words like 'normally' and 'so far as possible'.
>
> Office of Gas Supply (1991f: 2)

The inability of British Gas to evaluate its service performance was fur-ther compounded by the absence of an effective information base on customer services:

> The review of the tariff formula revealed that British Gas did not operate an adequate system for monitoring and controlling the provision of spe-cific services. Thus British Gas has no assurance at present that best practices are consistently applied by all its service sector staff in its gas supply business, or that it is meeting service performance targets. If British Gas itself is unable to have that assurance it is in no position to provide it to its customers and OFGAS.
>
> Office of Gas Supply (1991f: 3)

In order to overcome the limitations of the rolling negotiation approach to standard-setting (and in order to move towards a position of regulatory parity with the water and electricity industries), the Director General of OFGAS introduced a new condition (Condition 13A) into the Authorisation of British Gas in October 1991, with effect from 1 April 1992. Condition 13A places a duty on the monopoly gas supplier to establish, publish and monitor a set of tariff customer performance standards relating to:

- Customer contact
- Obtaining a gas supply
- Continuity of supply
- Emergency services
- Appointments
- Customer accounting

The performance standards required under Condition 13A were subsequently published by British Gas in a series of brochures in 1992 (British Gas 1992a,b,c). These new standards of service cover both *overall* and *individual* performance targets. Overall standards encompass broader areas of practice – such as the recording of customer contacts, answering telephone calls within a specified period of time, capacity to deal with gas escapes and monitoring differences between actual and estimated gas usage by tariff customers – where the company is required to meet service targets between 90 and 100 per cent of the time (British Gas 1992e). Individual standards establish a more testing target (100 per cent in all cases) and relate to selected areas of the direct interface with consumers, for example, replying to correspondence, keeping appointments, connecting and interrupting supply, and requests for special meter readings. Failure to meet an individual standard can result in the payment of compensation, *on request* to the customer concerned, generally in the form of a credit to the customer's account (British Gas 1992e).

Provision has been made in seven of the 18 designated individual standards for fixed compensation payments to customers (£10–£20). In the tariff review, the Director General of Gas Supply decided against setting the level of compensation himself (as is done, effectively, by the water and electricity regulators) and left it up to British Gas to determine as 'OFGAS' examination of customer services in other countries during the review indicated that the imposition of external penalty payments would not suit the operation of the Total Quality Management concept. It is also self-evident that externally imposed penalties are by their nature somewhat inflexible and could be expensive to administer. They could also be open to abuse by either British Gas or its customers (Office of Gas Supply 1991e: 5).

The quality regulation powers secured by OFGAS in the tariff review were subsequently formalized, in the separate Citizen's Charter policy initiative of the Government under the Competition and Service (Utilities) Act 1992 (resulting in amendments to section 33 of the Gas Act). Ironically, this belated move by the Government to correct the deficit in the gas regulator's powers was not particularly welcomed by OFGAS, as:

it created something of a dilemma for us, we had to decide do we scrap what we've got and transfer it over to regulation under the Act or to continue with 13A . . . it muddied the waters and personally it was a bit of a nuisance.

Interview with OFGAS officer (July 1992)

As was seen in Chapter 1, the privatization of the water and electricity industries was accompanied by a stronger framework for quality regulation than that established for gas in 1986. The extensions to the consumer protection mandate of the water and electricity regulators in 1988–89 might be viewed as a manifestation of regulatory policy learning in what is still a comparatively new field of public intervention in Britain.

The three primary regulatory devices adopted for influencing service delivery by the water and electricity utilities are (i) enforceable codes of practice, (ii) overall standards of performance and (iii) guaranteed standards of performance schemes.

The codes of practice form part of the conditions of the operating licences of the companies, and are hence enforceable. Within the electricity industry, the RECs are obliged to produce and publish codes of practice in relation to:

- the payment of bills, e.g. information to consumers in respect of how bill is constructed, security deposits, alternative systems of payment, process for handling disputed bills (Licence Condition 18)
- methods for dealing with domestic tariff customers in default, including disconnections procedure, arrangements for paying outstanding debts, referrals to social security and social services (Licence Condition 19)
- services to the elderly and the disabled, i.e. that companies identify and respond to the particular needs of these consumers (Licence Condition 20)
- complaint handling procedures, i.e. company mechanisms for dealing with consumer grievances (Licence Condition 23)
- a code on the efficient use of electricity i.e advice to consumers on the efficient use of electricity, including the provision of a telephone advice service (Licence Condition 22)

The three codes of practice in the water industry are broadly similar, with Conditions G and H in the Instrument of Appointment of the Water and Sewerage Undertakers being equivalent to Conditions 18, 19 and 23 in the Public Electricity Suppliers' licence. The third code relates to the procedure for dealing with leakages in metered domestic premises. Curiously, no provision had been made in the licence for a code on services to the elderly and the disabled; a situation which the Director General drew attention to in his 1990 Annual Report:

British Telecom, British Gas and the electricity supply companies are each required under the terms of their respective licences to produce a code of practice on services for the disabled and elderly. Similar provision has not been made in respect of the water companies, even though the need for it is arguably every bit as important. OFWAT has completed a survey of the services provided by the water companies for the disadvantaged. The results are very disappointing. Only a handful of companies would seem to recognise the particular problems faced by such groups of customers.

Office of Water Services (1991: 52)

In September 1991, OFWAT produced a set of guidelines on services for disabled and elderly customers, which imitated some of the features of the British Gas code for these two groups of consumers – by, for example, setting up a register of disabled and elderly customers, providing a password system for company staff calling at the customer's home, assisting with aids and adaptations, and helping with bill reading (Office of Water Services 1991r). However as guidelines, they have none of the regulatory force of enforceable codes.

In the case of both the water and electricity companies the initial drafts of most of the codes of practice were rejected by the regulators, partly at the behest of the community sector:

> None of the submitted customer or disconnection codes were sufficiently well written, complete and accurate to meet the basic requirements of Conditions G and H. Suggested modifications were sent to the companies and as a result revised drafts were submitted.
>
> Office of Water Serices, *Annual Report* (1991: 51)

> The initial submissions made by the companies were disappointing and the Director General declined to approve them. OFFER made suggestions for improvements to each of the Codes.
>
> Office of Electricity Regulation, *Annual Report* (1991: 57–58)

The statutory consumer committees were formally involved, with varying degrees of success, in the screening of the draft codes of practice (this is discussed in the section on Consumer Representation below). After representations to the regulators, selected national consumer and community sector organizations and bodies such as the Public Utilities Access Forum, were given access to some of the draft codes. There was general agreement amongst these organizations that the draft codes were defective and required substantial re-working. Although the re-drafted codes of practice were finally approved by the water and electricity regulators some 15 months and 9 months, respectively after the date of privatization, disaffection was expressed about the limited nature of the consultative process. This was directed, in particular, at the electricity regulator:

> community representatives [other than the regional consumer committees] were only invited to comment on a limited number of draft codes. No response to our comments was received from OFFER, although a

response was promised by the summer of 1991, nor were our comments sought before the finalised Codes were approved and published.

Barbara Montoute, Foreword, *Fuel Rights Handbook 1992/93*

The efficacy of codes of practice as instruments for protecting consumers is ultimately dependent upon the rigour with which they are monitored and enforced. With the partial exception of the flawed Condition H code (water customers in default), the regulators have been dilatory in initiating action to monitor the codes of practice. The reason for this, on the part of at least one of the regulators, appears to be a reluctance to move too deeply into the operational domain of the privatized companies:

> It is a feature of the regulatory regime as a whole that regulation (including monitoring) is kept to a minimum consistent with the Director General's statutory duties. Accordingly, the framework for the monitoring of the Codes of Practice will reflect the Director General's wish that information requirements from the Companies should be kept to the minimum possible consistent with effectiveness.
>
> Office of Electricity Regulation (1991e: section 11)

The other two primary weapons in the regulators' consumer protection armoury are the setting of overall and individual standards of performance (the latter are usually described as *guaranteed standards schemes*). The standards of performance in water and electricity operate in a manner broadly similar to those devised more recently for British Gas, although in the former, the overall standards, up to this point in time, have been based on targets set by the companies themselves. In the electricity industry, eight overall standards of performance have been set by the regulator: reconnection of supply following faults, correction of voltage faults, new connections, reconnection after payment of bill (for disconnected customers), moving, changing and reading meters, and responding to written complaints. Different targets have been established for each of these eight standards and for each of the RECs, with the target rate of completion for most of the standards in the range of 85 to 100 per cent (Office of Electricity Regulation, 1992x: 17–21).

The guaranteed standards cover nine designated areas of service, including the provision and restoration of supply, notice of supply interruption, meter disputes, charges and payment queries and the keeping of appointments. In contrast to the scheme introduced by the gas regulator and the *original* scheme in the water industry, compensation – usually in the form of deductions from electricity bills – is *automatically* made in all but two areas for failure to meet the requisite standard.

In the second half of 1992, the electricity and water regulators made formal proposals for modifying aspects of the guaranteed standards schemes in their respective industries (see below).

Prior to the Competition and Service (Utilities) Act in 1992, the formal enforcement powers of the utility regulators varied substantially, with the

strongest powers held by OFFER and the weakest by OFGAS. As part of the
'levelling up' intent of the 1992 Act, all three regulators now have similar
powers of enforcement. This includes the ability to determine disputes between customers and the utility companies and to rule on these disputes with a
force equivalent to that of a county court decision. The regulators can also issue
enforcement orders on the companies for breaches of the codes of practice and
for failure to meet the specified standards of performance. In the event of
serious breaches of the licence conditions, the regulators can make references to
the Monopolies and Mergers Commission. In theory at least, major breaches of
the licence conditions could lead to the offending company having its operating licence revoked.

While there has been a convergence in the instruments for quality regulation and in the powers of the regulators, the potency of the consumer protection regime is still likely to be heavily dependent upon how each of the
Directors General interpret their mandate as stewards of the consumer interest.
In defending the interests of domestic consumers, the consumer protection zeal
of the regulator will be as significant as the statutory framework in which he/
she operates. This has been exemplified in the past by the Director General of
Gas Supply, who has managed to compensate for the deficits in his legislative
powers by adopting a vigorous and publicly-visible consumer advocacy approach to his relations with British Gas.

Outcomes

We have not been able to conduct a detailed examination of the new
standards and codes, nor to examine their effectiveness or compare them
with what existed before. We believe that they offer a prospect of improved standards of service, particularly if they are well published and
enforced, but it is too early to assess their effectiveness.
                    House of Commons Energy Committee (1992a: para 28)

The framework for protecting consumers from reductions in service quality
in the privatized utilities has evolved around the three key instruments of
codes of practice, overall and individual performance standards. This section
will examine preliminary evidence on the quality-related outcomes of the
privatized utilities from the perspective of domestic consumers, including an
assessment of the extent to which these instruments appear to be working. It
is still quite early days in the implementation of these measures and therefore
much of the discussion needs to be qualified. In the case of British Gas, most
of the relevant regulatory schemes have only been in place since April 1992
and hence information on their impact is obviously extremely limited at this
point.

Public opinion data on the service performance of the privatized utilities
is rather ambiguous but it tends to suggest that the bulk of ordinary consumers,
while being generally satisfied with the services delivered, do not believe that

Table 6.1 Satisfaction with public utility levels of service: 'How satisfied are you with the overall service you receive from . . . ?'

Utility	Mar 1990	Mar 1991	Jan 1992	Dec 1992
British Gas	77%	80%	85%	85%
Local electricity supplier	77%	78%	83%	79%
Local water supplier	58%	63%	69%	59%

Sources: National Consumer Council (1991a: 13); Office of Water Services (1992h: 2); MORI (1993: 7).

they have been the beneficiaries of improved service quality since privatization. British Gas, however, appears to be a partial exception to this.

There was evidence in the MORI surveys carried out between 1990 and early 1992 for the National Consumer Council and OFWAT, that the level of satisfaction with the service received from the utilities had increased over time (Table 6.1). This result was, however, confounded somewhat by the findings

Figure 6.1 Consumer satisfaction by class: electricity.

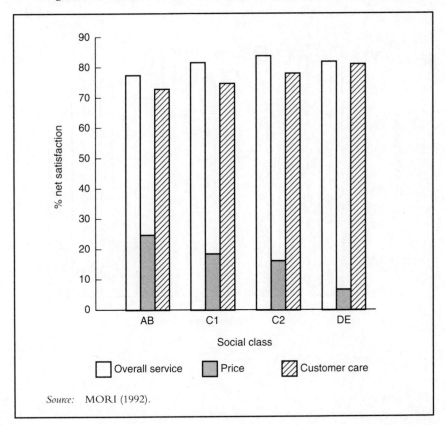

Source: MORI (1992).

of the more recent MORI survey for OFFER conducted in December 1992. In the later survey, the level of negative response to the question of satisfaction with overall service (and in which notably, respondents were asked to exclude their reaction to prices) had increased in the electricity and water industries compared to the earlier polls.

Public opinion surveys have consistently turned out a poor result for the 'privatization effect' when people have been asked to compare the performance of the utilities under private and public ownership. A poll conducted by ICM for *The Guardian* in July 1991 showed that the vast majority of respondents interviewed believed that the utilities had either *remained the same or got worse* since privatization – gas (73 per cent), electricity (88 per cent) and water (85 per cent). The December 1992 MORI survey commissioned by OFFER revealed even stronger evidence that the revolution in customer care, purported to attend privatization, has not materialized to date with 80, 87 and 89 per cent of respondents believing that the gas, electricity and

Figure 6.2   Consumer satisfaction by income: water.

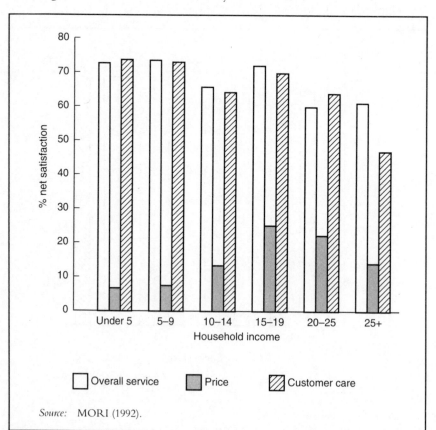

Source: MORI (1992).

water industries, respectively, have stayed the same or have got worse since they were privatized.

A closer examination of the MORI survey data also challenges the consumerist myth that the perspectives and interests of consumers are by and large similar. The survey data shows that responses to questions about the general and specific aspects of the performance of the utilities – most particularly in relation to prices – vary according to variables such as social class and income. This is illustrated in data on electricity and water from the MORI/OFWAT survey (Figures 6.1 and 6.2).

Another possible indicator of the performance of the utility industries is to be found in the volume of domestic customer complaints received by the regulators and their associated consumer committees over the past few years. The number of domestic consumer complaints rose across all three utility industries over the periods cited in Table 6.2. Not surprisingly perhaps, charging and billing disputes constituted the largest category of complaints in all cases. The Gas Consumers Council reported reductions in the volume of complaints about British Gas in 1992, which may indicate that the new service standards set in the tariff review are beginning to have some effect.

While the data on increased complaints to regulatory agencies seem clear enough (with the recent exception of British Gas), attempts to draw general conclusions about the performance of the privatized utilities from it are fraught with hazards. The increase in complaints may have, for instance, as much to do with the increasing profile and visibility of the regulatory bodies as it does with the behaviour of the utility companies. This may well explain part of the increase in complaints to the newer regulatory bodies like OFWAT and OFFER. Conversely, formal complaints to regulators, or indeed to the industries direct, will not necessarily capture the full extent of dissatisfaction with service quality amongst consumers. This is particularly likely to be the case amongst low income consumers. In the OFWAT customer survey, for example, 17 per cent of customers with incomes below £5 000 stated that they were aware of the existence of the water regulatory body (only 2 per cent of

Table 6.2 Consumer complaints to the regulatory bodies.

OFGAS:	Increased by 136 per cent in 1991 – largest single category of complaints: account disputes
GCC:	Increased by 4.6 per cent in 1991 – largest single category of complaints: gas bills
OFWAT:	Increased by 128 per cent between 1990–91 and 1991–92 – largest single category of complaints: charges or billing related
OFFER:	Increased by 19 per cent April 1991–March 1992 – largest single category of complaints: disputed accounts

Sources: Office of Gas Supply (1992); Gas Consumers Council (1992a); Office of Water Services (1992); Office of Electricity Regulation (1992x).

whom were able to name it), compared to 37 per cent of the full sample (15 per cent) (MORI 1992: tables 251 and 253). The study also found that the same group was far less likely to make contact with their local water supplier (8 per cent compared to 20 per cent of the full sample) (MORI 1992: table 37).

At a qualitative level, the evidence on standards of service in the privatized utilities is hardly conclusive, one way or another. This contrasts with the rather sharper outline of change in the areas of prices and debt and disconnection since privatization. The Select Committee on Energy was unable to conclude, after its investigation into the consequences of electricity privatization, whether the quality of service provided to the domestic consumer had improved or not. Positive accounts of the incipient transformation of the utility companies into customer care-driven organizations (United Research 1990; Lockwood 1991; Boys 1992a,b) need to be counterbalanced against the views of welfare rights and advice workers in the field and the experiences of low-income consumers themselves (Birmingham Settlement et al. 1992), which suggest that at the level of day-to-day practice at least, very little appears to have changed. Indeed some organizations maintain that in certain cases service delivery has deteriorated. The National Right to Fuel Campaign in its evidence to the Select Committee on Energy concluded that 'the standard of service provided by Public Electricity Suppliers has declined: there are more estimated bills . . . in some areas reduced staffing means long delays for telephone queries' (House of Commons Energy Committee 1992b: 82). The electricity company with the most ambitious labour-shedding programme – Manweb – admitted that customer services had suffered initially as a result of staffing cuts, but claimed that this has since been rectified (interview with customer relations staff, August 1992).

There are though, two common themes running through these seemingly contrasting evaluations: (i) that practice varies enormously between and even within the utility companies, and (ii) that considerable potential exists to improve the quality of utility service provision. For many people in the consumer and community sector, the key to promoting 'best practice' is held by the regulators and resides in the way in which they manage and exploit their consumer protection brief. In order for this to have optimum effect, changes will be necessary in the regulatory instruments they employ.

The regulatory instruments – codes of practice, overall and individual performance standards – in their original form are defective, both as a means of protecting the interests of domestic consumers generally and for protecting low-income consumers in particular. The codes of practice lack sufficient regulatory clout (as evidenced by the failure of Condition H in the water industry) and most consumers are unaware of their existence – in part because many companies have been parsimonious in their approach to the dissemination of copies of the codes. In an *ad hoc* survey on the availability of electricity codes of practice in company outlets in three cities, the National Right to Fuel Campaign found that 'none of those visited in London or Manchester had any copies of the Codes, and in Liverpool only 25 per cent had copies' (Barbara Montoute in Preface to *Fuel Rights Handbook 1992–93*).

The standards of performance, particularly in the water and electricity industries, provide relatively unchallenging targets for the companies to achieve. A leading example of which is the untaxing electricity meter reading standard, which the Director General of Electricity Supply has undertaken to rectify (Office of Electricity Regulation: 1992x). The original standards were also established with only minimal referencing to the views and service priorities of consumers and it is questionable whether the standards actually address those areas of service of greatest importance to consumers themselves. The requirement, added to the Competition and Service (Utilities) Act, after lobbying by organizations like the Consumers' Association and the National Consumer Council, that the regulators undertake consumer research prior to the setting of industry performance targets, should go some way towards rectifying this in the future.

The guaranteed standards of performance schemes seem to have had more force as public relations aids than as regulatory instruments designed to act as a real deterrent to service failure. The water industry is the most striking illustration of this, where the total compensation paid out by all water companies in 1990–91 and 1991–92 was less than £3500 and £4290 respectively. OFWAT estimate that 'no more than 1–2% of customers eligible for payments submit a claim' (Office of Water Services 1992y).

The poor take-up rate in the scheme might be the result of, amongst other things, a lack of information about the scheme; in the MORI survey for OFFER, less than one-quarter of electricity customers had heard of the guaranteed standards scheme (MORI 1993: 68). It could also have something to do with the derisory level of compensation available, which may deter customers from making the effort to claim (in those cases where compensation is not automatic). The companies can, of course, award higher payments, but this is entirely at their discretion. British Gas has shown more imagination and responsiveness in this regard than the electricity or water companies.

During the framing of the Competition and Service (Utilities) Bill, OFWAT sought to include a provision giving the regulators power to direct companies to award levels of compensation in line with the amount of damage or distress suffered by the customer experiencing service failure, but this was rejected by officials at the Department of Trade and Industry (interview with OFWAT policy staff, July 1992).

In reviews of the extant standards of performance in their industries in 1992, the water and electricity regulators proposed a number of changes to the guaranteed standards schemes, including adding the requirement that companies make more specific appointment times and a doubling of the compensation payment in many instances (Office of Electricity Regulation 1992x; Office of Water Services 1992i). The Director General of Water Services also recommended automatic compensation in a number of cases and introduced several additional provisions, including compensation for flooding from sewers. Importantly, he has removed two inequitable aspects of the original scheme –

the barrier to tenants and customers more than six weeks in arrears being compensated under the scheme.

On the whole, the provisions of existing guaranteed standards schemes are weighted substantially towards the interests of middle-class consumers. This is not to suggest that aspects of service delivery, like the keeping of appointments, replying to correspondence and notice of supply interruptions, are irrelevant to low-income households. However, there are other aspects of their relationship with the utilities that are likely to take precedence. This was underlined in the OFWAT customer survey, where, for example, low-income consumers showed less interest in specific appointment times than did more affluent consumers in the sample, but they expressed a higher degree of dissatisfaction with the choice of payment arrangements than other income groups. In the OFFER survey also, difficulties with estimated bills was a major cause of dissatisfaction for low-income households (MORI 1993: 43).

During the passage of the Competition and Service (Utilities) Bill in the House of Lords, a NACAB-initiated amendment to require the regulators to prescribe standards of performance specifically relevant to the needs of low-income consumers was rejected by the Government on the grounds that 'under this Bill the directors general can already set standards for any groups they choose, so that in effect the amendments would give the directors general no greater powers than they already receive under the Bill' (Lord Reay, House of Lords, 5/3/92, col. 1030).

Amongst the regulators, only the Director General of Gas Supply has shown any inclination thus far to exercise these latent powers. As part of the tariff review, the regulator introduced a standard requiring British Gas to be more proactive in its efforts to assist customers in debt: 'No later than 3 months after an unpaid bill has been despatched, clear action will be taken in accordance with Condition 12A to prevent debt build up.' British Gas (Key Standard No. 27) The other two regulators have resisted proposals made by the Public Utilities Access Forum to introduce company performance standards specific to low-income consumers.

Consumer representation

In the context of monopoly supply of essential services, it is important that domestic consumers be given structured opportunities to influence the policy and practice of the utility industries. In the absence of conventional consumer prerogatives, such as the power to exercise choice and the ability to adjudicate on service quality through changing supplier, formal mechanisms for representing and articulating the interests of consumers constitute a proxy for consumer sovereignty.

Effective consumer representation is also vital to the integrity of the regulatory system. Without regular consumer input, the regulators are likely to become detached from the everyday concerns of the users of utility services. Unless the perceptions of the utility industries are counterbalanced by the views of consumers, the information asymmetry problem endemic in regulation will become more acute. Consumer representation should act, in effect, to keep the regulators honest and accountable, an objective that is rendered all the more important in the prevailing situation where the regulators' responsibility for protecting the interests of consumers is secondary to other concerns.

Privatization provided an opportunity for the pre-existing structures of consumer representation in the nationalized industries to be substantially reformed. This was most particularly the case in the water industry, where the industry appointed and dominated local consumer committees, established under the Water Act 1983, were viewed virtually universally as defective mechanisms for consumer representation.

As Chapter 1 showed, there was considerable debate during the passage of the privatization legislation about the most appropriate consumer representation model, with the consumer movement (the Electricity Consumers Council aside) arguing strongly for the creation of national, industry-specific bodies independent of the regulator. This model was adopted for the gas industry, but displaced in the subsequent water and electricity privatizations by a regional, integrated-with-the-regulator's office approach. More recent attempts by the National Consumer Council and the Consumers Association

Table 6.3 Consumer representation in the utility industries.

Gas Consumers Council	National structure with regional branches; organizationally separate and independent of the regulator; budgetary and staffing control; functions: policy advice, advocacy, research, complaints' handling; aspects of 'consumer brief' wider than that of the regulator; national council members appointed by the President of the Board of Trade.
CSCs – OFWAT	Regional structure (CSC secretariat); *ad hoc* national forum of CSC chairs (subsequently National Customer Council); structurally linked to regulator; CSC chairs exercise limited budgetary and staffing control; functions: policy advice, advocacy, complaints' handling; members appointed by the Director General on the recommendation of the CSC chairs, chairs appointed by Director General in consultation with the President of the Board of Trade.
CCs – OFFER	Regional structure (OFFER regional offices service committees); legislative requirement for national forum of chairs (National Consumers' Consultative Committee); no budgetary or staffing control; functions: policy advice, advocacy, complaints' handling, delegated determination powers; members appointed by the Director General on the recommendation of the CC chairs.

during the passage of the Competition and Service (Utilities) Act, and the House of Commons Energy Committee (1992a: para 138) to have the Gas Consumers Council (GCC) model replicated in the water and electricity industries have not been successful.

While the dichotomy is usually drawn between the GCC model and the rest, it is possible to identify subtle differences in the structure and operation of the consumer committees in the water and electricity industries, which might suggest that there are three, rather than two, operational models of consumer representation in the privatized utilities. Recent changes in the way that the OFWAT Customer Service Committees (CSCs) operate, with for example the chairs taking on a more active, united and national role and an executive function (involving the supervision and appraisal of secretariat staff, and a degree of delegated control over the committees' budgets), distinguish them further from their ostensibly look alike counterparts in the electricity industry. The three models of consumer representation are set out in Table 6.3.

In addition to different structural arrangements, there appear to be significant differences in the *style* of the consumer representation bodies. This is exemplified in the contrast between the customer service committees (water) and the consumer committees (electricity). The OFWAT committees have the reputation of being much more open, domestic consumer-focused and independent than those in the electricity industry. The latter rarely publicize their meetings, limit the distribution of agendas and relevant papers and do not encourage non-member attendance and participation (the London Electricity Consumers' Committee is one apparent exception to this). The quality and content of the annual reports of the two sets of committees – with the OFWAT committees far superior in this respect – also reflect a very different philosophy of information dissemination and openness. The House of Commons Committee on Energy (1992a: para 138) drew attention to the poor quality of the formal reporting of the electricity committees and recommended that 'the Committee [i.e. the National Consumers' Consultative Committee] publish a report separate from the Director General's, containing the reports of individual committees and commenting on the Director General's work where appropriate'. The national council meetings of the Gas Consumers Council are not open to the general public.

Despite the virtual unanimity of support within the consumer movement for the structurally independent model, the superiority of this approach to consumer representation is not necessarily as self-evident as many of its proponents seem to suggest.

Manifestly, the siting of consumer committees within the structure of the regulator's office presents significant threats to the autonomy and independence of action of these committees. The experience of at least one of the committees in the water industry, where the regulator attempted to exercise a degree of censorial control over the sensitive issue of metering (interview, September 1992), is illustrative of the inherent tensions in the unitary model of regulation and consumer representation. It does not, however, follow that the existence of these tensions make the model unworkable, or should cause it to be dismissed out of hand.

While the regulatory body locus for consumer representation presents problems, it also brings with it particular advantages. Among other things, it structurally reinforces the regulator's responsibility for *social* as well as economic regulation and it should make for a freer two-way flow of information between the regulator and the consumer committee than would be the situation were the bodies organizationally separate. Most important of all, the presence of the Director General in the background, potentially places the consumer commit-tees in a far stronger position of influence with the regulated companies than would otherwise be the case. Certainly it would seem that the Customer Service Committees in the water industry believe this to be the case.

The performance of the Gas Consumers Council (GCC) and OFGAS (the archetypal model favoured by the consumer movement) partly confounds and partly supports the arguments above. The record of the Gas Consumers Council shows that generally it has been able to use its independence to good effect on behalf of domestic and industrial/commercial gas consumers, as evi-denced for example in its role as a catalyst for Condition 12A and in the OFT review of British Gas' industrial market. However, despite its structural auto-nomy, the GCC has had to exercise caution in deviating from the policy positions of the Director General of Gas Supply (let alone openly criticizing him), for at the end of the day, it has been substantially reliant upon him to provide the regulatory leverage to effect change in the gas industry.

It would seem that the Director General of Gas Supply has not required the presence of consumer committees within his own organization to alert him to his responsibilities for social regulation. But as Sir James McKinnon has become more involved in the affairs of domestic consumers, the respective roles of OFGAS and the GCC have become increasingly blurred and difficult to disentangle. This gives rise as a consequence to the danger of either duplica-tion in the functions of the two bodies (e.g. in handling consumer complaints), or to the possibility that a vacuum will be created in some areas, as both bodies incorrectly anticipate that the other will take action in particular instances. Something similar to this occurred following the introduction of Condition 12A, where OFGAS assumed that the GCC was pursuing the monitoring of British Gas' implementation of the new code of practice (and vice versa), with the effect that there was an unwarranted delay in the follow-up action on this important licence change.

Regardless of the debate over which set of structural arrangements con-stitute the best theoretical model, the efficacy of consumer structures will hinge ultimately upon the extent to which they (i) marshal the support and participa-tion of the major groupings within the domestic consumer population (i.e. their representativeness), (ii) provide a proactive, independent and informed analysis of the policy and practice issues at the centre of the consumer–utility interface and (iii) are able to back up their advocacy with powerful enough sanctions so that the industries take them seriously. Each of the existing

Table 6.4   Composition of the 10 OFWAT Customer Service Committees.

Component	Percentage of all members (n = 122)
Female members	34★
Non-Anglo-Saxon background	1
Consumer organization background	15
Community organization involvement	37
Current or ex-local government	27
Associated with water industry	11
Business/commerce background	37
Farming background	7
Academics	6
Declared interest in disability	3

Notes: ★ 2 out of 10 chairs are women; CSCs as at 31/3/92.

Source: CSCs annual reports (1992a*iv*).

consumer structures in the three industries, as they are presently constituted, would appear to be deficient in at least one of these respects.

The composition of the OFWAT customer services committees in early 1992 is shown in Table 6.4. The CSCs have been chosen, not because they are better or worse than the other bodies, but simply because in contrast to the others, information on the backgrounds of the members of each of the CSCs is published in their Annual Reports. It can be seen in Table 6.4 that the proportion of members with a background in business or commerce is high relative to those with experience in consumer advocacy organizations. The composition of the electricity consumer committees is unlikely to be any different in this respect, for a similar profile of strong business representation juxtaposed against a smaller base of members with consumer advocacy experience is indicated in the two electricity consumer committee annual reports where membership information is provided (there are, however, a larger number of members from the pre-existing nationalized consumer structures on the electricity committees). The absence of direct representation from low-income consumers and minority groups is characteristic of the water and electricity consumer committees, as well as the Gas Consumers Council. The water and electricity regulators have both expressed an interest in broadening the representative base of their respective consumer committees. The National Consumers Council and NACAB, amongst others, have argued that the brief of the regulatory body consumer committees and the Gas Consumers Council should be restricted to protecting the interests of domestic consumers only. This is based on a view that industrial/commercial consumers often have the means and the structures to influence the utility industries and the regulators independently of the formal consumer bodies. There is also a belief that the mandate encompassing all consumers creates an inherent conflict of interest for the committees, with the consequential fear that the interests of the least powerful and most disadvantaged will be overlooked.

As in any consumer representation process, the level of resourcing and support given to the committees impacts directly on the effectiveness of their work. To date, very little attention seems to have been given to the need to provide training to the members of the electricity and water consumer bodies, despite the fact that the majority of members appear to have had little background and experience in the area of consumer advocacy.

The difficulties faced by relatively inexperienced consumer representatives in the complex terrain of the regulated industries was amply illustrated in the electricity consumer committees' inauspicious encounter with the first drafts of the codes of practice. In 1990, the Director General gave the newly-established committees the task of examining the draft codes of practice produced by the RECs, which they subsequently endorsed. After an outcry from external consumer organizations about the quality of the codes, the Director General – against the earlier advice of his own consumer representatives – sent them back to the companies to be re-written. This incident affected the confidence of the committees and severely dented the credibility of the committees in the eyes of the consumer movement. The Energy Committee recommended that the Director General of Electricity Supply examine the level of training and information provided to the OFFER consumer committees (House of Commons Energy Committee 1992a: para 138).

The electricity and water committees are serviced by the regional staff of OFFER and OFWAT respectively, but unlike their peers in the gas industry, they have no capacity to commission research at a local level on consumer matters. The complaints' handling function of the committees provides an extremely useful casework database on consumer concerns, but without a research budget, they are limited in their ability to explore issues in greater depth, or to investigate areas of utility policy and practice outside of those identified by the regulator. Even more importantly, in the absence of resources for research, the committees have little capacity to check the verisimilitude of the information provided by the local utility companies. One of the criticisms levelled at the electricity consumer committees is that their analysis of the utility–consumer interface is too heavily dependent on the information provided by the RECs themselves (interviews with consumer sector workers, July–August 1992).

The British regulatory system has been criticized on the grounds that it is excessively secretive and closed, and certainly it suffers by comparison with the more open approach to regulatory decision-making that is generally found in America (as Chapter 2 showed). However, for all this, a greater degree of regulatory transparency – from the perspective of the ordinary consumer – now exists than was the case when the government acted as the regulator of the utilities. There is, unequivocally, more and better information available in the public domain about the operation of the utility industries than there was hitherto. In fact, the quantity and quality of data on the industries, being produced directly by or under the direction of the regulators, could be seen as one of the emerging strengths of the post-privatization regime. In respect to information, the Office of Water Services has led the field to date.

The availability of better information on the operation of the utility industries means that the scope for consumer bodies to comprehend, and hence to influence, the policy context in which the utilities operate has probably increased over recent years. Arguably, the consumer committees directly attached to the regulatory agencies (i.e. the OFWAT and OFFER committees) have an information edge over the Gas Consumers Council, as they are more likely to be privy to in-house, and possibly even commercially sensitive, information in addition to that released for public consumption.

Although the Directors General of Electricity Supply and Water Services convene regular meetings (usually quarterly) of the chairs of the committees, these national fora have yet to develop any real visibility or force. It is unlikely that this will happen until such time as they are given, or take, a more substantive and independent role in the overall regulatory framework.

The *potential* exists for more effective consumer representation under the regulated utilities than was the case when they were nationalized. This is almost entirely due to the buttressing function of the regulatory agencies in support of formal consumer interactions with the utilities. The Gas Consumers Council has realized some of this potential, yet whether this can be attributed to its independent status or to its superior resource base (compared to the other bodies) is debatable. The scope for this potential to be realized in the more recently established water and electricity committees is uncertain, although the signs look somewhat more propitious in the former – largely due to their more open style – than they do in the latter.

General conclusion on the consumer interest

On the evidence available to date (as discussed in this and the two preceding chapters) it would hardly be possible to conclude that the Government's bold prediction, at the time of privatization, that consumers would benefit in terms of lower prices and better services, has been realized. Equally, the evidence does not support the conclusion, sometimes drawn by political opponents of the Government, that privatization of the public utilities has been an unmitigated disaster.

The outcomes for consumers in general, along the four key dimensions of prices, debt and disconnection, consumer protection and consumer representation, appear to have been mixed. For the average consumer, privatization has been the proverbial 'curate's egg', with a gain in one area seemingly offset by a loss in another. There are clear indications, however, that low-income consumers have been affected more adversely than the generality of consumers. This has primarily been because of rises in water and electricity tariffs, in conjunction with a failure to recognize the particular needs of low-income households in the formulation of service standards. Even in the area where low-income consumers appear to have done best (i.e. energy disconnection practice) the gains may turn out to be illusory, if the changes effected lead to an increase in the incidence of self-disconnection.

In a number of instances where negative outcomes for domestic consumers have been apparent, it is difficult to separate out the 'privatization effect' from other contextual variables. This is exemplified in the changes to water tariffs, although even here there is strong evidence to support the view that consumers have been paying a 'privatization premium' in their water bills over the past five years.

The same problem of delineating the 'privatization effect' holds with even more force in those areas where positive outcomes have been achieved. The structural changes to the utilities may well have blown away some of the debris accumulated over decades of nationalization. Yet clearly, factors such as declining gas and coal purchase costs (not all the benefits of which have been passed through to domestic consumers) and technology (in the ambiguously beneficial area of pre-payment meters) have made an important, and from the Government's point of view timely, contribution. Also against the backdrop of rising consumer expectations, it was probably inevitable that the utility industries would be required to respond to the demand for improved services, irrespective of the variable of ownership change.

Unequivocally, the primary force for change has been the influence of the regulatory bodies. To this extent, the results of the utility privatization programme to date illustrate a striking paradox. The developing framework of stronger protection and procedural rights for utility consumers has been constructed using the instruments of the State (i.e. public intervention via the regulatory bodies), with the 'invisible hand' of market forces playing very much a secondary, and by no means always a supportive, role.

The contribution of the regulators has not, of course, been uniform. The Director General of Gas Supply and the Director General of Electricity Supply could be seen to proximate the two ends of a continuum of regulatory effort on behalf of domestic consumers – a continuum ranging from tenacity to torpidity. The water regulator appears to fall somewhere in between.

The prospect for future changes to the advantage of domestic consumers will also be substantially conditioned by the character and vigour of regulatory intervention. In the case of gas, this depends as much on the deliberations of the Monopolies and Mergers Commission as it does on the strong advocacy of the gas regulator. The Director General of Water Services' incremental incursions into the capital structure of the water companies and his positioning of consumer concerns towards the forefront in the Periodic Review could be interpreted as a positive sign for domestic consumers. However, his commitment to full economic pricing – in which metering is seen to occupy a central place – may act to negate any future gains for domestic consumers under revisions to the price formula. The ability of the electricity regulator to secure an improved settlement for domestic consumers could well be retarded by his implicit faith in the power of the market to advance the consumer interest. The broader implications of the outcomes of the first phase of utility privatization are considered in the final chapter.

7

Public utility privatization in perspective: policy and paradigm change

Introduction

There is a substantial gap between the promise and delivery of privatization in the field of energy and water services. One of the explanations for this can be found in the defective privatization settlement reached between successive governments, acting on behalf of the British public, and the privatized companies, over the period 1986 to 1991. But even more fundamentally, the current and in all probability, the continuing, gap between the rhetoric and reality of utility privatization suggests that there are endogenous and irresolvable contradictions in the model of privatization developed in Britain. In addition, the organizing principle around which utility privatization has been built – i.e. consumerism – is inconsistent with the provision of essential services like water and electricity supply.

At the same time, privatization of the public utilities has been attended by a number of positive outcomes for domestic consumers, particularly in the area of explicit and enforceable service standards. While these gains are related, first and foremost, to the influence of independent regulation, it would be churlish to deny any part in this to the utility companies themselves, as they strive to achieve a greater level of 'customer focus'. In substance though, these positive aspects of the privatization programme serve to emphasize the pivotal function that independent regulatory bodies can play in utility policy-making and organization. Importantly, this is likely to be the case irrespective of the ownership and structural character of the utility industries.

In this concluding chapter a number of the primary threads in the book will be drawn together through considering two sets of questions which get to the heart of the issue of why public utility privatization has failed to deliver thus far:

1. What are the limitations in the privatization settlement and the model of utility privatization and how might these be corrected?
2. Is the paradigm of consumerism appropriate to the domain of public utility services, or should it be replaced with an alternative paradigm based around the concept of social citizenship?

The limitations in the privatization settlement and model

In assessing the character of the privatization settlement and the efficacy of the model of utility privatization introduced in Britain, it is necessary to make a distinction between the outcomes of privatization at the point of sale on the one hand, and those that have arisen subsequently as a result of the implementation of the privatization regime, on the other. As Chapter 3 showed, the financial settlement negotiated by successive Conservative governments during the sale of the three utilities was defective in a number of significant respects. The sale of the utilities represented a net financial loss to the British public, both in terms of current valuation of assets and as a foregone future revenue stream. Overall, the management of the share flotation programme resulted in adverse distributional effects.

Despite the negative outcomes of the sale process for the British population at large, however, there is little from a public policy perspective that might now be done to correct this earlier failure, other than the politically unsustainable action of renationalizing the utility companies without compensating shareholders. However, the 'social welfare losses involved in the transfer of money from the state (i.e. UK citizens) to those who obtained shares' (Waterson 1988: 129) does provide a salutary lesson to the British Government and to governments elsewhere about how not to proceed with privatization sales in the future.

In contrast, the post-sale impact of privatization warrants further analysis. This is because the outcomes, in some instances, are more equivocal than is the case with the privatization sales and also because there is scope for introducing policy changes aimed at correcting existing defects. In this section, four major features of the privatization settlement/model introduced in Britain will be briefly discussed, namely:

  (i) the financing rules of the utility companies
 (ii) the regulatory framework
(iii) competition assumptions
(iv) market-led utility policy making

These features reveal problems both in the original privatization settlement and in the way that the current model of public utility privatization has evolved over time.

The financing rules of the utility companies

Under a privatized model of public utility practice, the price – and hence the affordability – of utility services is ultimately conditioned by the financial structure within which the utility companies operate. Consequently, policy action aimed at influencing or moderating utility tariffs (other than through direct public subsidies) cannot be pursued in isolation from the question of what constitutes an appropriate set of financing rules for private utility providers. These financing rules include such matters as allowable rates of return on capital, efficiency targets, capacity to 'pass-through' purchasing and other costs, and the 'ring-fencing' of expenditure on core areas of service provision from non-core activities.

In Chapters 3 and 4 it was shown that the terms of the original settlement between the Government and the privatized companies substantially favoured the companies, particularly in respect to the setting of inflated rates of return on capital, unchallenging efficiency targets, and generous provision for cost-pass-through (with the exception of the RECs over the first three years of privatization in the case of cost-pass-through). This has resulted, as a consequence, in artificially high tariffs for consumers and substantial profits for the companies.

The 'privatization premium' that the population in Britain has been paying over the past several years could be viewed as a supplement to the income transfers made to company shareholders at the time of privatization, although this time in the guise of consumers rather than as taxpayers.

The key to the formulation of 'fair' utility tariffs for domestic and other consumers, where benefits are evenly distributed between consumers and shareholders, lies in a trilogy of measures involving:

- the determination of rates of return on capital which recognize the low risk and relatively secure customer base of the utility industries;
- the setting of targets which directly reflect the assumptions on efficiency gains to be achieved through conversion to plc status;
- and the structuring of cost-pass-through provisions in a way that provides an incentive for economic and efficient purchasing.

The Government singularly failed to apply these measures at the time of privatization for each of the three utilities.

In their various ways, the three utility regulators have expressed muted criticism of the privatization settlement (Office of Gas Supply 1991d; Office of Water Services 1992o,z; Office of Electricity Regulation 1992y). In recent times, the gas and, to a lesser extent, the water and electricity regulators have taken action, via adjustments to the price formula, aimed at striking a better deal for tariff customers.

The Director General of Water Services has been somewhat more explicit in his criticisms of the original set of financing rules than have his regulatory colleagues, presumably because under the original price formula in the water industry he has been presented with the difficult task of selling continuing tariff increases well above the rate of inflation. It may also have something to do with the more open communication style that he has adopted. The water regulator has foreshadowed major changes following the 1994 Periodic Review of the price formula, although it remains to be seen whether these can be delivered. It would be most surprising if the electricity regulator did not seek likewise to stiffen the efficiency targets for the regional electricity companies in his review of the distribution price control. To this extent, the corrective action of the regulators could well represent a triumph for independent public regulation over political expediency and the accumulation zeal of private enterprise.

It is by no means certain that regulatory action will continue to move irresistibly in a direction favouring domestic consumers over the longer term, however. The regulated companies, shareholders and the City are likely to become increasingly restive about what they perceive as 'over-regulation'. Some commentators are already claiming that the modest advances made by the regulators breach the 'regulatory bargain' struck between the government and shareholders at the time of privatization: 'regulators . . . are railing against the original regulatory bargain by progressively edging the rules against the utilities' (Veljanovski 1991: 22). The request by British Gas to the President of the Board of Trade for a wide-ranging MMC inquiry into the gas industry as a defence against the regulatory assault on their market dominance, and the active resistance of the water companies to the Director General of Water Services proposals for a reduction in the notional rate of return on capital, possibly herald the beginnings of a corporate counter-attack against public regulation.

The headlong rush to diversify their activities by many utility companies and the move to shift as much of their business as possible from regulated to non-regulated areas, are also indicative of the desire to 'break the shackles' of regulation. While the regulators have statutory powers to prevent the cross-subsidization and cross-financing of core and non-core activities (strengthened in the case of the water industry under the provisions of the Competition and Service (Utilities) Act 1992), diversification serves to make the regulatory task considerably more complex and imposes high information and enforcement costs. There is also the danger that in expanding their entrepreneurial horizons, nationally and globally, the utility companies may lose sight of their primary *raison d'être* as providers of essential services to the people of Britain.

Ultimately, however, the ability of the regulatory bodies to negotiate new sets of financing rules to the advantage of domestic consumers may well be constrained, regardless of their own predilections, by two of the salient features of the British regulatory system – the statutory injunction on the regulators to protect the profitability of the utility companies, and the declared political preference for 'light-touch', non-intrusive regulation. Consequently, if domestic consumers are to become the beneficiaries of the efficiency dividend implicit in the privatization settlement, the legislative and regulatory framework will require change in the future.

The regulatory framework

The merits in overlaying the operation and management of public utility services with a system of independent public regulation is probably the most positive lesson to have emerged thus far from the privatization programme. Although the regulators have been hamstrung by a defective structure, they have been able to progress the case of the general consumer interest. This is not to suggest though that each of the utility regulators has been equally vigorous or effective in championing the cause of domestic consumers, let alone protecting the interests of low-income households. Indeed, the variability in the performance of the regulators – which relates, in large part, to how they interpret and balance their statutory duties – is an endemic weakness in the British model of regulation.

The model of public utility regulation in Britain has evolved considerably over the life of the privatization programme. From its beginnings in the Office of Telecommunications and the Office of Gas Supply as a limited device for price regulation and an even more limited device for social regulation, it has been re-shaped, over time, into a rather more comprehensive vehicle for economic regulation and consumer protection. The fact that this has occurred owes at least as much to the energy and dynamism of the leading regulators (particularly, the past Director General of Telecommunications and the Director General of Gas Supply) as it does to the graduated refinement of the statutory framework in later privatizations. As suggested earlier, the need to introduce legislation to supplement the powers of the regulators, well after the last of the three privatizations had been concluded, could be seen as a covert admission by the Government that the regulatory structure introduced as part of the privatization settlement was inadequate to the task.

Under the Competition and Service (Utilities) Act 1992, the powers of the four utility regulators (i.e. including OFTEL) have been standardized and this is likely to lead to a more uniform approach to consumer protection across the utility sectors in the future. A 'best practice' model constructed from the existing strengths of the regulatory bodies would incorporate the advocacy, community outreach and networking attributes of the Office of Gas Supply with aspects of the decisional transparency and information dissemination of the Office of Water Services and, to a more limited extent, the Office of Electricity Regulation. OFWAT's practice of publishing the general correspondence of the Director General to water company executive officers and of disseminating comprehensive comparative pricing data, along with OFFER's excellent customer accounting statistics are features which should be replicated by all of the regulatory bodies.

Despite a sense of progression in the development of the regulatory framework, and notwithstanding the endeavour of the individual regulators and their staff, the British model of regulation continues to display a number of serious flaws which serve, in aggregate, to denude its strength as an instrument of consumer protection. These include (i) the treatment of the consumer interest as a secondary and contingent dimension of regulation, (ii) the absence of a specific requirement to protect low-income consumers, (iii) the limited power of the regulators in respect to strategic development and management of utility industry resources, (iv) variable transparency of decision-making and (v) the opaque lines of regulator accountability. It will be recalled from Chapter 1 that each of these areas was identified, in one form or another, as substantive gaps in the regulatory system by community and consumer sector organizations at the time of privatization. The fact that they remain unresolved indicates that the degree of regulatory progression is nowhere near as great as it may seem at a superficial glance.

It could well be argued, by the Director General of Gas Supply for instance (see for example, OFGAS Annual Report 1991a), that the absence of formal powers in each of these areas is essentially academic, as he has been able to achieve progress in most of them despite the apparent deficiencies in the regulatory framework. The virtue of the British model lies in its ability to adapt to the particularities and circumstances of each of the utility sectors at any given point of time. But the weakness in this argument is that the scope and strength of the regulatory regime is substantially dependent upon the character, ethos and capacity of the Director General. In the hands of a Sir James McKinnon this may present no real difficulties, but in the hands of a lesser regulator, it may well expose domestic consumers to considerable risk.

Each of the five problems in the existing regulatory structure, mentioned above, has been considered at some length in Chapter 2, and hence it is unnecessary to reproduce those arguments here. However, two issues require additional comment – the absence of a specific duty to protect low-income consumers and the constraints on regulatory involvement in strategic policy-making – the first in the light of the material in the previous three chapters, and the second as a result of the crisis in the coal industry.

During the passage of the Competition and Service (Utilities) Bill the Government rejected amendments to place a specific duty on the regulators to protect low-income and vulnerable consumers of utility services:

> The purpose of this group of amendments. is to enable each of the Regulators to require that standards of performance to be met by the suppliers in individual cases are relevant to the needs of the most vulnerable consumers, and particularly to those who may experience difficulty in paying for supply. Such standards could include, for example, procedures to be followed prior to disconnection, information to be supplied to customers in debt, offering a choice of payment methods to low

income consumers, and access to token supply points for coinless pre-payment meters.

NACAB (1992b: 1)

These amendments were consistent with the 'standard setting' (Gilbert and Gilbert 1989: 174) model of British regulation, as opposed to a more active 'redistributional' approach to regulation, where for instance, the regulator would be much more active in influencing company practices on pricing and energy efficiency as these effect low-income households.

However, in refusing to admit the amendments on the grounds that the regulatory bodies had sufficient powers under the legislation to address the needs of this group of utility consumers if they so desired, the Government missed (consciously or unconsciously) the essential point of the amendment. While the Bill gave the regulators discretionary power to set performance standards in reference to any sector of the consumer population, the purpose of the amendment was to *ensure* that each of the utility regulators would actually make use of their latent powers on behalf of those groups at greatest disadvantage in their interactions with utility service providers.

The rejection of the unexceptional NACAB amendment expressed a continuation of the dominant British theme of maximizing regulatory discretion. It also displayed the perennial sensitivity of utility policy-makers in this country to charges of 'undue preference' and 'undue discrimination'. Yet this apparent reluctance to discriminate did not prevent the Government, on earlier occasions, from explicitly directing regulatory attention towards the particular needs of elderly, disabled and rural consumers.

Even though there may be a case for providing a relatively wide field of regulatory discretion in particular arenas of utility industry practice, the ability to act on, or to stand aloof from, issues to do with the maintenance of lifeline services to disadvantaged groups of utility consumers is not one of them. This is particularly so in a context, where through a combination of factors – not the least of which is the rise in tariffs – the level of utility debt has increased sharply in recent years.

In the absence of a statutory duty to institute measures to protect this sector of the consumer population, an untoward reliance is placed on the 'social responsiveness' of the individual regulators. This is rendered all the more problematic by the constraints on community sector involvement in the relatively closed process of regulatory decision-making process. Apart from the Director General of Gas Supply, the performance of the regulators, thus far in this area, has hardly been of a character to inspire unreserved confidence in their ability to act as guardians of the interests of low-income consumers. However, even OFGAS has been rather complacent in some areas, such as monitoring the impact of the pre-payment meter 'solution' to debt and disconnection on the consumption behaviour of low-income households. The Director General of Electricity Supply has displayed little observable interest in the welfare of low-income consumers *per se*. Although the water regulator has continually alluded to the deleterious impact of environmentally-driven water tariff increases on the budgets of low-income customers, he has at the same time actively promoted an approach to water charging (i.e. metering) which is likely to act to the greatest disbenefit of low-income households.

The failure to mandate an explicit role for the regulators *vis-à-vis* low-income consumers also, arguably, sends exactly the wrong message to the utility companies. It implies that like the regulators they do not need to give particular attention to consumers who are poor. The companies should be responsive, of course, to the needs of all their customers, but because of the particular characteristics of some consumers this responsiveness will often need to be more proactive and sensitive. Nowhere will this be more so than in regard to those on low incomes. Yet the commercial unattractiveness of the low-income sector of the market – and particularly that sub-set of low-income consumers which Fitch (1992) describes as 'difficult customers' – will in many instances inhibit the development of such an approach, unless it is supported by regulatory sanction.

Competition assumptions

It is one of the unpleasant facts of life that certain capacities (and also certain advantages and traditions of particular organizations) cannot be duplicated, as it is a fact that certain goods are scarce. It does not make sense to disregard this fact and to attempt to create conditions 'as if' competition were effective.

Hayek (1960: 265)

competition . . . is the Government's ark of the covenant . . .
Lord Stoddart of Swindon, House of Lords, Second Reading Debate on the Gas Bill, 10/4/86, col. 318

The utility privatization programme is premised centrally on a form of 'competitive Utopianism', i.e. an intuitive belief in the emergence and efficacy of competition in the utility industries. The advent of competitive forces into the erstwhile monopoly domains of gas, electricity and water supply, it is held, will open up new horizons for industry efficiency and consumer sovereignty, and ultimately eliminate the need for external regulation altogether.

The extent to which competition will actually become a pervasive feature of the utility industries in the future, particularly in the area of domestic supply, is impossible to determine at this point. However, there is a degree of scepticism amongst commentators, including members of the past Select Committee on Energy, about the prospect of competition flourishing in the domestic sector in the future.

Even if competition does develop, it does not necessarily follow that it will produce unalloyed benefits for domestic consumers in general, and for low-income consumers in particular. A sense of agnosticism about the merits of competition, from the perspective of the poor, could be derived from the *a priori* observation that the competitive marketplace has conventionally done little to promote access and equity objectives; indeed its 'natural laws' work in a way that is antithetical to social justice objectives. However, in addition to this, the case for 'competitive agnosticism' can be supported by more specific concerns arising from the particular characteristics of the utility industries.

The consumer is presently at a considerable information disadvantage in their relationship with utility providers and imperfect information, or the problem of being able to select amongst competing suppliers on the basis of an informed assessment of price and service quality, is manifestly a barrier to the attainment of consumer sovereignty:

> Without perfect information, however, agents are unable to exercise their choice rationally; nor can they tell whether competitive cost reductions are associated with an unacceptable reduction in quality. An important conclusion follows – that the efficiency advantages of competition are contingent on perfect information.
>
> Barr (1987: 82)

Consequently, the present high level of information asymmetry that exists between utility suppliers and their consumers would need to be addressed, in order for competition to function to the benefit of domestic consumers. Perfect information may be expecting too much, but certainly consumers would need to be markedly more informed about the utility marketplace, as well as their own pattern of consumption and expenditure than currently appears to be the case (see DoE 1991a; Office of Water Services 1992b). This will mean, as a consequence, that consumers will incur higher 'transaction costs', i.e. the costs 'associated with discovery, information gathering, bargaining and enforcement' (Miller 1990: 722) of their prerogatives in the market. In contrast to the supermarket or shopping mall, where the array of consumption choices are laid out before prospective purchasers, utility consumers will probably need to go to some trouble to become more fully informed. For some consumers, these transaction costs will outweigh the benefits gained in terms of price or service quality. For others, either because of disability, language, or the sheer complexity of the task, the opportunity to shop around for utility services is likely to be foreclosed.

Future advances in technology, under the Littlechild scenario (Office of Electricity Regulation 1992b), may well obviate these information search problems for many domestic consumers. However, technology will come at a price, and there is a clear danger that low-income consumers may be excluded from the possibility of exercising choice (via advanced metering technology) because of an inability to afford access to the technology. This, along with the prospect of utility suppliers targeting the more commercially attractive and income elastic sectors of the domestic market, would act to entrench the present social division of utility services in Britain. The removal of the obligation to supply, which would seem to be a necessary precondition for the introduction of open competition in the domestic sector, also could mean that customers with a track record of debt and payment default may experience problems gaining access to supply at all.

The received wisdom in competition theory is that the introduction of multiple and competing suppliers almost invariably leads to decreases in prices. But for some consumers of utility services, the advent of competition is likely to have the reverse result. This will be particularly the case for consumers in some rural areas, and may well also apply – in relation to electricity supply – to consumers in the south of England, as most electricity is currently sourced from the north of the country. The removal of uniform tariffs and the elimination of geographical cross-subsidization would appear to be an inevitable corollary of the removal of monopoly franchises in the gas and electricity industries. Under a competitive regime, utility tariffs for customers who have hitherto been the beneficiaries of a degree of cross-subsidization will almost certainly increase, unless public expenditure is deployed to maintain a level of uniform pricing. On the obverse side, the removal of cross-subsidies will potentially result in a welfare gain (in the form of lower prices) for consumers who live in areas where the distribution and supply costs are relatively low. From an equity perspective, the winners and losers from these tariff adjustments premised on economic pricing principles will be defined indiscriminately and without reference to 'ability to pay' or social impact.

In addition to variable pricing outcomes, which may run counter to equity objectives and the strategic interests of the country, there could well be a number of negative byproducts of competition. These might include a decline in overall service quality, the abandonment of special services for the elderly and the disabled and a reduction in research and development output. The Gas Consumers Council and Neighbourhood Energy Action (1992d) argued along these lines in their defence of the retention of British Gas' monopoly in the gas tariff market.

Another byproduct is the devolution of strategic management of utility industries resources to competitive forces, which could result in duplication, resource wastage, over- and under-supply in particular areas and a neglect of the critical externality dimensions of utility service provision:

> Clearly regulation itself is not a costless endeavour. On the other hand, should our focus on the virtues of competition blind us regarding the ubiquitous nature of externalities and advantages of coordination?
>
> Gegax (1989: 214)

The operation of market forces in the electricity industry thus far, which has resulted *inter alia* in a projected mismatch between electricity generation capacity and demand in Britain by the middle of the decade and arguably, the misuse of a finite natural resource, i.e. gas in electricity generation, for short-term commercial gain (Fells and Lucas 1991), could hardly be seen as a ringing endorsement of the self-regulating capacity of the market.

A number of these problems could possibly be overcome, or at least abated, if competition was extended under the aegis of strong framework of public policy and regulatory accountability. Consequently, in marked contrast to the expressed intention of the Government, which is to gradually displace the regulatory system through the creation of a competitive market in domestic utility services, the framework of regulation will need to be retained and, in some areas, extended if consumers are to be effectively protected.

There are lessons to be learnt in this respect from the American experience, and in a highly critical account of the history of telecommunications regulation in the United States, Melody (1989: 685) dismisses the idea of replacing regulation with competition:

> Competition is not a substitute for policy and regulation. It is a potential tool of policy that, under some circumstances, can facilitate the achievement of the objectives both of economic efficiency and universal telephone service; under other circumstances it can promote efficiency at the expense of social policy; under still other circumstances it can promote neither . . . Despite a definite shift toward an increased role for market forces, the primary influence upon future developments will not be the 'invisible hand' of the competitive market, but rather the more visible hands crafting policy and regulatory decisions.

At a minimum, additions to the regulators' powers in the area of protection for low-income consumers will be necessary, as they are likely to be the group most exposed under competitive conditions. This will need to be complemented with an extension to the existing mechanisms for consumer representation, through, for example, strengthening the resource base and national structures of the electricity and water consumer bodies, for as McHarg (1992: 396) concludes:

> regulation of monopoly and regulation for competition are complex tasks which have already required increased, rather than less, regulation . . . In the improbable event of full competition developing, however, there will still be a role for consumer 'voice' alongside 'exit', in order to influence the range of services on offer as well as the ability to choose between them and to protect those disadvantaged in the marketplace: utility services are too important for us to be able to contemplate market failure.

Market-led utility policy-making

Electricity privatisation requires a clear choice between the claimed advantages of centralised co-ordination and management and the less certain outcomes of the free play of competitive market forces.

Helm et al. (1988b: 41)

> We are not certain of what new mechanisms will best serve us to produce useful, practical and acceptable guidelines for managing the energy sector . . . what we are certain of is that we cannot go blindly into the future armed only with the comforting simplicities of market economics, uncertain of what might happen and what we should do about it if it does.
>
> Fells and Lucas (1992: 389)

The formulation of energy and water resources policy has not been a major focus of this book, but as Chapters 2 and 4 in particular suggest, it constitutes a critical contextual influence on the service delivery system for domestic consumers. The implications of utility policy decisions are manifested directly in the domestic arena in the form of prices, quality and security of supply, and indirectly in the management of externalities and in their macro-economic consequences in such areas as employment and industrial development. In essence, the welfare of current and future generations of consumers – and citizens – is integrally connected with the direction of utility policy.

The privatization of the public utilities has been founded on a strong presumption in favour of devolving the instruments for policy-making from the State to the private market, although this has been rather more the case in the energy field than in the water industry, where the Department of the Environment and the National Rivers Authority continue to perform significant functions in relation to water resource management. The ideological roots of this project of decentralization lie in an abhorrence for centralized planning and an intuitive belief in the superiority of the market over other forms of economic organization. The derogation of energy policy has been expressed at a concrete level in the abolition of the Department of Energy and the House of Commons Select Committee on Energy, and in the Government's unwillingness to cede anything more than a peripheral function to the regulatory bodies in the domain of energy industry strategic planning.

The limitations of an essentially *laissez-faire* model of energy policy-making, as well as the interconnectedness between major energy-related decisions and other areas of public policy, were substantially exposed in October 1992 in the Government's unpopular decision to close 31 of the 50 remaining coal mines in Britain. The intersecting factors leading to this decision were extremely complex and included:

- The increasing lack of interest of the major generating companies and the RECs (all but one of whom are currently investing in electricity generation) in purchasing locally produced coal as a result of the availability of cheaper imported coal and because of extensive investment in gas-fired electricity generating plant.
- The Government's interest in maximizing the return on the sale of its 40 per cent stake in National Power and PowerGen sometime after April 1993 – a new contract between the generating companies and British Coal, involving a reduced intake of coal at cheaper prices, would further this end by enhancing the profitability of the generators.

- The plans to privatize British Coal have created an imperative to close unprofitable pits in order to turn British Coal into a saleable commodity.

Putting to one side the question of the relative influence of each of these factors, the clear message to emerge from the announcement on the future of British Coal was that energy policy set adrift in the turbulent waters of the marketplace will inevitably collide, at some point, with broader issues of economic and social policy, and the national interest.

The damaging impact that the privatization of the electricity industry would have on British Coal had been anticipated by a number of energy commentators well ahead of the events of October 1992 (Vickers and Yarrow 1988; Robinson 1989; Fells and Lucas 1991; House of Commons Energy Committee 1992a). But electricity privatization has had other negative policy-related consequences as well, as Fells and Lucas (1991) outline in their forthright analysis of *UK Energy Policy Post-Privatisation*:

> The short-term commercial perspective of the privatised electricity supply industry conflicts with the public interest in several ways: insufficient attention to environmental externalities, insufficient or inappropriate R & D, inappropriate choice of fuel especially by ignoring long term security from domestic coal or nuclear power.
>
> Fells and Lucas (1991: vi)

> The limitations of the market apply especially to climate change; market forces do not transmit the signals to make the proper allocations. Given that nuclear energy and renewable energies are the only means of expanding supply outside the fossil fuel corset; given that they can only practically be introduced into the electricity supply system: it makes no sense to burn high grade fossil fuels like natural gas for power generation.
>
> Fells and Lucas (1991: 77)

In their report, Fells and Lucas emphasize that energy policy is simply too important to leave in the hands of the private sector (and indeed, too strategically significant to delegate to the industry regulators), and they call for the development of a 'comprehensive energy strategy' (Fells and Lucas 1991: ix) involving direct government intervention.

A more recent review of the state of British energy policy in the wake of the coal débâcle (Jones 1992: 38) similarly advocates the development of a clear public policy framework on strategic energy issues, complemented by energy regulatory bodies directly accountable to Parliament with responsibility for overseeing 'tactical issues of market conduct'. To delineate between strategic and tactical issues in this way, however, ignores the critical interaction between policy-making and policy implementation, and overlooks the important function that economic and social regulation performs in the practical formulation of utility industry policy.

In the aftermath of the decision to close down much of the domestic coal industry, the electricity regulator was publicly castigated for not intervening to prevent the exponential growth in gas-fired generating capacity (the so-called 'dash for gas') and for failing to take a strategic view of current and future energy needs in Britain. Yet Professor Littlechild had a point when he argued in his defence that it is the role of Government rather than the regulator to determine the *broad* parameters of energy policy:

> For the regulator to have that responsibility would be to confer enormous power on that person to shape the market and dictate the investment decisions on which future generations of customers will depend. If there is to be more general direction about the form and pace at which the generation market evolves surely it would be better to take that forward in a more democratic framework.
>
> Office of Electricity Regulation (1992z)

In letting the market dictate the character and resource content of electricity generation, the regulator was merely following the thread-bare outlines of the Government's existing energy policy.

To direct the blame for strategic policy omissions, like the coal débâcle, at the formal regulatory bodies is really to expect too much of the industry-specific regulatory apparatus. Responsibility for the vital social, economic and environmental policy issues, related to the operation of public utilities, is most appropriately the preserve of democratically-elected governments, not quasi-independent, regulatory bureaucrats. The loss of strategic control of primary areas of national and local infrastructure is the first – and perhaps in the long term, the most significant – casualty of public utility privatization. Privatization has, in effect, cut these profoundly important matters of public policy adrift from the democratic process.

The two inquiries into the present state of the British energy market, announced in response to the clamorous public reaction to the coal mine closures, *may* result ultimately in the development of an energy policy with something more substantial to it than the shadow of the market. But if it is to engage with key areas of economic, environmental and social policy, substantial modifications to the original blueprint of electricity privatization will be required. At the same time, the Government might constructively use this policy space to re-think the fundamental paradigm upon which privatization is based.

Reformulating the paradigm

. . . the project of the 1990s is surely to think and to popularize the task of reform and reconstruction of free market economies in the name of social justice but also in the interest of the authentic, rather than merely ideological, attainment of efficiency in the production and distribution of goods in a modern international economy.

Taylor (1990a: 3–4)

Privatization of the public utilities has involved more than the transfer of ownership and the physical restructuring of the water and energy industries in Britain. It has also sought to redefine the relationship between the individual and the State and the way in which individual needs for essential utility services are met. At its heart, the privatization programme is founded on the paradigm of consumerism.

Consumerism is built on the central dynamic of commodification, involving the designation of most forms of service and exchange as commodities which can be priced and sold. Virtually all human needs are translated into individual wants and market-based interactions become the primary mechanism for satisfying these wants. Consumerism gives expression to this core social and material relationship of the 'individual in the marketplace' and articulates a set of procedural rights designed to protect the individual in their engagement with the market. The corpus of these rights are choice, information, the power of 'exit' and the ability to seek redress in the event of service failure (e.g. through complaints procedures and compensation measures). This paradigm of consumerism is enshrined in the privatization legislation and the Citizen's Charter-related supplements to the original legislation.

In the context of public utility services characterized however, as Chapter 2 showed, by a composite of features which distinguish them from other commodities (e.g. essentialness, substitution problems, inelasticity of demand, natural monopoly and positive and negative externalities), is the paradigm of consumerism appropriate? It will be argued here that it is not, both because the consumerist model breaks down when applied to utility services and because consumerism fails to address the central issue of 'entry' or access. It will be suggested that a superior alternative paradigm lies in the conception of citizenship, or more specifically, social citizenship.

The limits of consumerism

The efficacy of consumerism as an organizing principle in the public utility arena ultimately rests on the extent to which choice and 'exit rights' can be realized in practice. The other procedural rights are in effect secondary and contingent rights, whose power is only fully realized once the choice and exit conditions are met. For example, the right to information has little meaning (from a consumerist, 'shopping around' perspective) if there is no capacity to choose between different service options and providers. Equally, the ability to complain is likely to have rather less potency in a situation where the service provider, against whom the complaint is being directed, is aware that the complainant does not have the option of taking their business elsewhere, or of substituting one product with another. A right to compensation in the event of service failure can assist as a proxy in this regard, but unless it is extremely punitive, it will have none of the power of actually losing custom through customer 'exit'.

The field of choice available to domestic consumers of electricity, gas and water services in contemporary Britain is little different now than it was over decades of public ownership. The inability to choose between different water or energy service providers, in tandem with the lack of substitutes for many utility services, effectively forecloses the opportunity for ordinary consumers to exercise their 'power of exit'.

In effect, the present structure of the utility industries gives domestic consumers about as much chance of expressing the key attributes of consumerism as did those seventeenth century travellers seeking to hire a horse from the Cambridge carrier – the eponymous Mr Hobson – where the choice on offer was the one nearest the door, or nothing!

It is anticipated, of course, that these severe impediments to the consumerist ideal will be removed by 1998, in the case of electricity, and probably earlier in the case of gas. Only the future will tell if this environment of choice will be created in the domestic energy sector, although there is some doubt as to whether many of these hopes will be realized. But leaving aside the issue, to paraphrase Prospero, as to whether this is such stuff as dreams are made on, it is important to ask whether the extension of choice will be all that useful to many domestic consumers of utility services. As suggested above, the manufacturing of choice in utility services will be attended by costs as well as potential benefits. The opportunity costs involved in becoming informed and discerning consumers may well be high, and the transaction costs in switching between suppliers could outweigh, for some consumers, the savings made in reduced tariffs or improvements in service quality. The advent of competition could also discriminate against those groups of domestic consumers who might be described as 'information poor', as well as households who are materially poor (they are in practice, of course, often the same).

In addition to these practical issues, which cast doubt on the universal benefits of, and indeed prospects for, choice, in public utility services, the elevation of choice as a valued end in itself needs to be questioned. The image of the village market, where sellers openly ply their wares and where customers pick and choose amongst a wide array of consumption possibilities, has been an important symbolic metaphor of the market economy in liberal political thought from Adam Smith onwards. However, water and energy services are not like commodities traded in the village market or the late twentieth century variant, the hypermarket. The capacity to select one's utility services on the basis of an immediate visual evaluation of the price/quality combination obviously does not exist. But more importantly, consumers are likely to want a utility service that is reliable, safe, and value for money, rather than have the ability to exercise fine graduations of choice equivalent to making a decision between a plain white garment or a striped white one. It is the end product rather than the means of getting there that will be of most importance to consumers of energy and water services. Dowding (1992: 314) places the relevance of choice in perspective when he says:

> Increased choice, as opposed to better products or efficient markets, is not necessarily something to be valued at all. Firstly, the whole notion of

'increased choice' is problematic and, secondly, it is not obvious that we should always value it anyway. Rather what we value is getting what we want. Markets are often good at that, and they do it by offering us a choice of products; but it is the goods we value, not the choice itself. In any particular area of public policy the usefulness of the market must be examined in relation to the ease of shifting from one alternative to another, the costs of making decisions and the ability of individuals to have clearly defined preference schedules. Whether or not it brings greater choice is not something to be valued at all. The value of choice in the market is merely instrumental in that it enables preferences to be revealed or discovered.

Even if the conditions of actual, as opposed to rhetorical, choice and 'exit rights' were to be satisfied in the future, it would still leave untouched the fundamental flaw in the consumerist paradigm, namely its failure to address the question of access/entry rights.

Access to reasonable water and energy services is universally regarded as a fundamental quality-of-life requirement in today's society. Yet clearly, the capacity to gain, and retain, access to requisite levels of utility services is not equally shared by all individuals and households in contemporary Britain. The 'social division' of utility services characteristic of Britain (as well as in other countries) is related substantially to the prevailing structure of income inequality, and the consequent disparities which exist in the ability to pay for energy and water. In addition, most notably in relation to energy consumption, higher demand costs are imposed on many low-income households as a result of their living conditions, i.e. poorly insulated housing, expensive forms of heating, inefficient appliances and the like (Boardman 1991a,b).

In the face of these structural barriers to entry and access, however, the consumerist paradigm is mute. Procedural rights are important, but in themselves they are insufficient. A panoply of procedural rights is largely ineffective in assisting consumers negotiate their way through the utility service system if, at the core, lies the problem of fuel or water poverty, as the regulatory bodies in Britain are beginning to find out. Consumerism is essentially an expression of the negative, one-dimensional view of citizenship favoured by adherents of New Right political theory. It constitutes a repertoire of individualistic protections for those able to make their way in the economic system. It undercuts the very notion of *public* utilities in the sense of collective provision for the collective good. For a more positive framework of social, as well as consumer, protection we need to look elsewhere.

Social citizenship

... it [social citizenship] implies some limit to commodification and commercialisation, in the sense that the basic welfare goods to which individuals have rights are not ultimately to be subject to the market mechanism, since the market cannot guarantee the provision of these goods, as of right, on a fair basis to all citizens.

Plant (1992: 16)

It is hardly likely to be coincidental that after well over a decade of New Right ascendancy in Britain, academic commentators and politicians alike have begun to search for different answers to contemporary social and economic problems. A fertile source of material in this post-Thatcherism debate about the nature of the British polity has been found in the theory of citizenship, involving *inter alia* a return to T.H. Marshall's seminal account of citizenship written in 1949 (Marshall 1992). The resurrection of citizenship as an intellectual counterpoint to neo-liberal ideas is evident, at the political level in the formulation of citizens charters by each of the three political parties and at an academic level in the proliferation of published works on the subject.

As well as possibly heralding the beginnings of a shift in the tide of political ideas, the return to citizenship also underscores, interestingly, the hegemony of capitalism in late twentieth-century society. For the template of citizenship – consisting of the triad of political, civil and social rights – is superimposed on the extant structure of the market economy (albeit often redefined as the 'social market'), and indeed it was for these reasons that Marshall's ideas were generally dismissed by neo-Marxist theorists in the 1960s and 1970s. The immediate relevance of this, for our purposes here, is that the framework of citizenship is likely to be more congruent with the privatized structure of the public utilities, than would more radical, and possibly more desirable, political formulations.

The present generation of writers on citizenship have sought to apply and adapt Marshall's fairly simple thesis about citizenship to the contemporary era, with Lister (1990, 1993), Plant (1991, 1992), Bottomore (1992) and Ignatieff (1991) in particular, doing effective updating work. Yet the basic construction of citizenship, with notably its elevation of social rights to an equivalent status with civil and political rights, remains pretty much the same as that originally articulated by Marshall:

> By the social element I mean the whole range from the right to a modicum of economic welfare and security to the right to share to the full in the social heritage and to live the life of a civilised being according to the standards prevailing in the society.
>
> Marshall (1992: 8)

Marshall did not specifically allude to energy and water services in his account of the evolution of citizenship rights (nor, for that matter, do most contemporary commentators), but the character and importance of these services in present-day Britain would place them firmly within the last part of his definition, i.e. 'to live the life of a civilised being according to the standards prevailing in the society'.

Locating public utility services within a paradigm of social citizenship, as opposed to the paradigm of consumerism, changes the theoretical and practical relationship of the consumer to the privatized water and energy industries. It connotes a recognition of substantive as well as procedural rights (Plant 1991: 58) and mandates public policy and utility company action aimed at ensuring that access rights are guaranteed and protected. Because social citizenship, in contrast to consumerism, recognizes *collective* as well as individual rights and responsibilities, it firmly locates strategic decision-making on the utility industries firmly within the domain of democratic accountability and public policy.

The social security system, energy efficiency programmes and the regulatory bodies would be the key instruments for the enactment of a social citizenship model of utility service provision, at the level of public policy. Over recent years, relatively little effort has been made to target assistance to households experiencing difficulties paying energy and water bills (with the exception of the desultory cold weather payments scheme), and this has been exacerbated by the post-1988 changes to the social security system (Crowe 1991). A form of fuel and water allowances for social security beneficiaries with disproportionately high bills, or discounts made at source by the utility companies – which would subsequently be reimbursed out of public revenue – would seem to be a minimum requirement.

The causal link between housing quality, in terms of energy efficiency, and fuel poverty is well established (e.g. Boardman, 1991a,b; DoE 1991b). Therefore, without concentrated action to deal with the demand side of the energy equation in many low-income households, through a comprehensive domestic energy efficiency strategy, fuel allowances would, in a sense, be simply throwing good money after bad. An energy efficiency-led approach to fuel poverty would also, as Boardman (1990, 1991a) has persuasively argued, intersect with the public policy objective of reducing energy-related environmental externalities.

It is little more than wishful thinking, of course, to airily propose substantial increases in public expenditure in the recent political and economic climate of Britain. A climate, where at first, social policy was to be rendered irrelevant by the 'economic miracle' and then when this failed to materialize, the cries of the most disadvantaged have become distant echoes to the thunderous demands of an ailing economy. The demise, over the past 20 years in Britain, of the idea of social justice as a legitimate end of public policy serves to underscore the need for paradigmatic change. What is needed in relation to public programmes aimed at giving low-income households full participation rights in energy and water services, is a replication of the political will which sanctioned the surcharging of all electricity consumers, in order to underwrite the costs of the nuclear power industry, to the tune of something in excess of £4 billion between 1990 and 1993.

A social-citizenship approach to utility services would demand a far more active role for the regulators than has been, with one partial exception, the case to date. This would require, amongst other things, not only the setting of specific service standards to provide a minimum floor of protection to low-income consumers, but the delineation of performance targets aimed at promoting competitive 'best practice' in relation to social and environmental responsiveness. These would include targets designed to raise the level of energy efficiency in low-income households, to prevent the build up of consumer debt and to eliminate the archaic and barbaric practice of disconnection for debt. Like quality standards generally, these measures should be tied to the price formula.

One of the most enduring and disingenuous myths perpetrated by the public utility industries – which well and truly pre-dates privatization – is that they are a set of basically physical services, with no mandate, nor responsibility, for social welfare. However, as Fitch (1992: 5) cogently asks 'What is it that these providers of essential services supply if not welfare? Enjoyment of the services of the water, fuel and telecommunications utilities is the foundation of well-being – of welfare – in modern societies'.

In a very real sense, public utilities are the bedrock of social welfare in contemporary societies and in contrast to the consumerist paradigm, where this is hidden beneath a morass of commercial and technical imperatives, the social citizenship model of the public utilities would explicate and formalize the central contribution that the industries make to economic and social well-being.

This does not necessarily mean though, that the utility companies would be required to engage in *extensive* cross-subsidization or 'tariff-tilting' in order to facilitate access to services for designated sections of the population, although the current obsession with expunging all vestiges of cross-subsidy from utility practice altogether, makes little sense on practical, commercial or social justice grounds. Measures aimed at giving financial assistance to low-income consumers are best handled, arguably, through the taxation/social security system, for the reason that this is likely to be a more distributionally progressive and transparent approach. External measures also would not have the negative impact on efficiency that has been seen to be the case when internal price manipulation has been used (Dilnot and Helm 1987). On the 'down-side', transparent and externally-funded measures are directly exposed to the vagaries of government budgetary processes and to shifting political priorities.

Irrespective of the mechanism employed for subsidizing access, tariffs would be strictly controlled under the social citizenship paradigm. Constraints would be placed on the companies' ability to generate excessive profits, much of which is derived from the capacity to extract 'monopoly rents'. At the moment only shareholders benefit from efficiency and purchasing savings in excess of those anticipated under the price formula. Provision could be made for the 'claw-back' of a proportion of the additional profits made by the utility companies (in the form of lower tariffs), without negating the in-built incentives for efficiency. In this way, consumers as well as shareholders would gain a dividend from improved industry performance.

There is much that the companies could do at a service-delivery level to help low-income households maintain access to utility services, for example, in payment and debt rescheduling on the supply side, and in energy efficiency initiatives on the demand side. This will inevitably involve an element of cross-financing, including the possibility of slightly higher charges for consumers in general, but if the MORI survey commissioned by the water regulator (MORI 1992: table 207) is anything to go by, this is a price that the majority of consumers are willing to pay in order to assist low-income households. Above all under the citizenship paradigm, 'social responsiveness' (Frederick et al. 1988: 468) would form a primary criterion, along with commercial success, for adjudging industry performance, as it 'will only be possible to create a more socially responsible economy with more socially responsible companies, which recognise social obligations as well as financial and economic ones' (Leadbeater 1991: 24).

In combination, the public policy and regulatory actions implicit in the adoption of a social citizenship approach would effectively entail a re-negotiation of the terms of the privatization settlement between the Government, the industries and the people of Britain.

Conclusion

The defects in the British model of utility privatization are such that more than marginal policy tinkering will be required to correct them. The paradigm around which the privatization programme has been framed is inconsistent with the basic function and importance of public utility services in the lives of individuals and families, and in the economy generally. If the rhetoric of privatization, notably in respect to the provision of new consumer rights and opportunities for *all* households in the country, is to be matched with concrete outcomes, then major changes will be required. In this sense, the privatization project remains substantially incomplete.

Within the circumscribed frame of reference set for them, the regulatory bodies have made, generally speaking, a positive contribution to the broad welfare of ordinary consumers. The procedural rights that domestic consumers have gained in recent years are certainly superior to those which existed during the decades of nationalization in Britain. But these have not been delivered by the operation of the market, as the thesis of consumerism asserts, but through public intervention in the market via regulation. However, the regulators have been relatively ineffectual in dealing with the important issues of social equity and strategic policy in the provision and management of public utility services.

The privatization programme has illustrated that, rather than leading to the withering away of the state, the mechanisms of public policy need to remain centrally engaged within the milieu of public utility activity, if consumers are to be protected and if the strategic resources of the utility industries are to be optimized to the benefit of society as a whole.

Arguments that the levers of regulation should be released in order to let the markets in energy and water operate without constraints, or that regulation should be progressively displaced in line with the emergence of competition, are based on a set of fallacious premises about the commodity nature, and unexceptional character, of water and energy services. Public utility services are different from other commodities and a failure to recognize this is likely to result in deep and long-lasting economic and social damage.

The British privatization programme has been rife with contradictions. This was in evidence right at the beginning in the objectives of the programme and it has continued to be a pervasive feature of the programme ever since. To suggest that a social citizenship paradigm of public utility services could be built onto the quintessentially individualistic model of privatization might be seen to be a contradiction in terms, as well as being wildly unrealistic. Yet, in theory at least, such an approach is possible. It would be a remarkable contradiction indeed, if a project designed, in part, to entrench the severely unequal distribution of property rights in this country could be transformed into an instrument for the promotion of social justice and collective welfare in Britain in the 1990s.

Bibliography

Abercrombie, N., Hill, S. and Turner, B.S. (eds) (1990) *Dominant Ideologies*, London, Unwin Hyman.

Andrews, G. (1991) (ed.) *Citizenship*, London, Lawrence and Wishart.

Archibald, G. (1988) Household water metering, the national trials, *Public Finance and Accountancy*, 11 March.

Ashworth, W. (1991) *The State in Business: 1945 to the mid-1980s*, Basingstoke, Macmillan.

Association of Metropolitan Authorities (1989a) *Briefing Papers for House of Commons Committee on Water Bill*, London, AMA.

Association of Metropolitan Authorities (1989b) *Parliamentary Briefings for House of Lords on Water Bill*, London.

Association for the Conservation of Energy (n.d.) *Evidence from the Association for the Conservation of Energy to the Select Committee on Energy on the Regulation of a Private Sector British Gas Corporation*, London, ACE.

Barr, N. (1987) *The Economics of the Welfare State*, London, Weidenfeld and Nicolson.

Beauchamp, C. (1990) National Audit Office, its role in privatisation, *Public Money and Management*, 10 (2), 55–8.

Beaver, M. (1988) Water charges post-1990, is metering the answer?, *Public Finance and Accountancy*, 28 October.

Beckerman, W. (1986) How large a public sector?, *Oxford Review of Economic Policy*, 2, 2.

Beesley, M. and Littlechild, S. (1986) Privatisation, principles, problems and priorities, in Kay, J. et al., op. cit., pp. 35–7.

Beesley, M.E. (1991) Current themes in regulation, in Veljanovski, C., op. cit., pp. 152–5.

Benefits Agency (1992) *Direct Payment Statistics*, Leeds.

Berry, D. (1992) Electricity utility least cost planning, *Journal of Economic Issues*, 26 (3), 769–89.

Berthoud, R. (1983) Disconnection, preventing debt and disconnection, in Bradshaw, J. and Harris, T., op. cit., pp. 69–84 and 125–42.

Berthoud, R. (1989) *Credit, Debt and Poverty*, Social Security Advisory Committee, Research Paper 1, London, HMSO.

Berthoud, R. and Kempson, E. (1992) *Credit and Debt: The PSI Report*, London, Policy Studies Institute.

Bibby, D. (1992) Efficiency in private and public sectors, *Economic Review*, 10 (1), 9–11.

Birmingham Settlement, Community Energy Research & Bristol Energy Centre (1992) *The Hidden Disconnected* (Draft), Birmingham.

Bishop, M. and Kay, J. (1988) *Does Privatization Work? Lessons from the UK*, Centre for Business Strategy, London, London Business School.

Boardman, B. (1990) *Fuel Poverty and the Greenhouse Effect*, Glasgow, FoE/NEA/NRTFC/Heatwise.

Boardman, B. (1991a) *Fuel Poverty, From Cold Homes to Affordable Warmth*, London, Belhaven Press.

Boardman, B. (1991b) *Ten Years Cold, Lessons from a Decade of Fuel Poverty*, Newcastle, Neighbourhood Energy Action.

Boardman, B. and Houghton, T. (1991) *Poverty and Power, The Efficient Use of Electricity in Low-Income Households*, Bristol, Bristol Energy Centre.

Booker, A. (1992) 'Issues Involved in Regulation of Privatised Water Utilities.' Speech delivered to the Institute for International Research, Malaysia, 'Financing Water Utilities Symposium', *OFWAT Information Pack*, Birmingham.

Boorman, T. (1992) 'New Dimensions in Regulation.' Speech to Economist Conference, 19 June, Birmingham, Office of Electricity Regulation.

Borrie, G. (1991) 'Regulation in the United Kingdom.' Speech to the Institute of Economic Affairs' Regulation in the United Kingdom Conference, London.

Bottomore, T. (1992) Citizenship and social class, forty years on, in Marshall, T.H. and Bottomore, T., op. cit., pp. 55–93.

Boys, P. (1992a) Speech for Power to Change Conference, Queen Elizabeth Conference Centre, 3 June.

Boys, P. (1992b) 'Competition and Regulation in the Electricity Industry.' Speech for Ente Vasco de la Energia, Bilbao, 12 June.

Bradshaw, J. and Harris, T. (eds) (1983) *Energy and Social Policy*, London, Routledge and Kegan Paul.

Bradshaw, J. and Hutton, S. (1983) Tariff tilting, in Bradshaw, J. and Harris, T., op. cit., pp. 143–54.

Bradshaw, J. (1986) *The Impact of the Social Security Act on Electricity Consumers*, Occasional Paper No. 15, London, Electricity Consumers' Council.

Brain, A. (1990) Paying for water. Simplicity comes top of the bill, *Public Finance and Accountancy*, 7 December, 16–17.

Brechling, V. and Smith, S. (1992) *The Pattern of Energy Efficiency Measures Amongst Domestic Households in the UK*, London, Institute for Fiscal Studies.

British Gas (1989) *Principles for the Collection of Domestic Gas Debt*, London.

British Gas (1990) *Payment of Gas Bills. A Guide Concerning the Payment of Gas Bills, Including Guidance to Domestic Customers if they have Difficulty in Paying*, London.

British Gas (1992a) *Standards of Service*, London.

British Gas (1992b) *Complaints Handling Procedure and Compensation Scheme*, London.

British Gas (1992c) *Commitment to Customers*, London.

British Gas (1992d) *BG Press Information. British Gas Delivers its Price Promise*, London, 14 May.

British Gas (1992e) *Financial and Operating Statistics for the Year Ended 31 December 1991*, London.

British Gas (1993a) *Directors' Report and Accounts for the Year Ended 31 December 1992*, London.

British Gas (1993b) *Financial and Operating Statistics for the Year Ended 31 December 1992*, London.

Brown, I. (1986) *Lessons from America No. 5, The Regulation of Gas and Electric Utilities in the USA*, London, Association for the Conservation of Energy.

Brown, I. (1990) *Least-Cost Planning in the Gas Industry*, London, Office of Gas Supply.

Buckland, R. (1987) The costs and returns of the privatization of nationalized industries, *Public Administration*, 65, Autumn.

Bunn, D. and Vlahos, K. (1988) Evaluation of the Nuclear Constraint in a Privatised Electricity Supply Industry, *Fiscal Studies*, 10, 1.

Bunn, D. and Vlahos, K. (1989) Evaluation of the long-term effects on UK electricity prices following privatisation, *Fiscal Studies*, 10 (4), 104–16.

Button, K. and Swann, D. (1989) *The Age of Regulatory Reform*, Oxford, Clarendon Press.

Byatt, I.C.R. (1990a) The Office of Water Services, structure and policy, *Utilities Law Review*, Summer 1990, 85–90.

Byatt, I.C.R. (1990b) *The Regulation of the Water Industry, The Office of Water Services, Structure and Policy* (Hume Occasional Paper No. 16), Edinburgh, The David Hume Institute.

Byatt, I.C.R. (1991) 'Regulation of Water and Sewerage.' Speech to the Institute of Economic Affairs' Regulation in the United Kingdom Conference, London.

Carney, M. (1991) Is OFWAT turning its back on incentives?, *Water Bulletin*, 479, 10–12.

Carney, M. (1992) *Water Services before and after Privatisation – The Facts*, London, Water Services Association.

Central Statistical Office (1991a) *Family Spending, A Report on the 1990 Family Expenditure Survey*, London, HMSO.

Central Statistical Office (1991b) *Retail Prices 1914–1990*, London, HMSO.

Central Statistical Office (1991c) The 1989 Share Register Survey, *Economic Trends*, 447, 116–21.

Central Statistical Office (1992a) *Financial Statistics*, September, London, HMSO.

Central Statistical Office (1992b) *Financial Statistics*, October, London, HMSO.

Centre for the Study of Regulated Industries (1991) *The UK Water Industry. Charges for Water Services 1991–92*, London, Public Finance Foundation.

Centre for the Study of Regulated Industries (1992a) *The UK Water Industry. Charges for Water Services 1992–93*, London, Public Finance Foundation.

Centre for the Study of Regulated Industries (1992b) *The UK Water Industry. Water Services and Costs 1990–91*, London, Public Finance Foundation.

Chalkey, M. (1989) Water – A question of demand? Water at the right price, *Economic Review*, September 1989, January 1990.

Chapman, C. (1990) *Selling the Family Silver. Has Privatisation Worked?*, London, Hutchinson.

Chesshire, J. (1992) Why nuclear power failed the market test in the UK, *Energy Policy*, August, 744–53.

Chesshire, J. and Surrey, J. (1988) UK electricity privatization, *Energy Policy*, April.

Childs, M. and Huby, M. (1992) The Social and Environmental Implications of Domestic Water Metering, York, unpublished.

CIPFA (1989) *The Water Industry*, London.

City of Bradford (1992) *Report on Conference on Water Metering*, Bradford, 5 October.

Clarke, P. (1987) Essay on privatisation, in Neuberger, J. (ed.) *Privatisation. Fair Shares for All or Selling the Family Silver*, London, Macmillan.

Colton, R.D. (1990) Client consumption patterns within an income-based energy assistance program, *Journal of Economic Issues*, 24(4), 1079–93.

Commission of the European Communities (1990) *Eurobarometer: The Perception of Poverty in Europe in 1989*, Brussels.

Conservative Central Office (1979) *The Conservative Manifesto 1979*, Westminster.

Conservative Central Office (1983) *The Conservative Manifesto 1983*, Westminster.

Conservative Central Office (1987) *The Conservative Manifesto 1987*, Westminster.

Consumers' Association (1989a) Power for people, *Which?*, March, 146–7.

Consumers' Association (1989b) *The Water Bill*, London.

Consumers' Association (1989c) Water works?, *Which?*, May, 230–1.

Consumers' Association (1991a) *Consumers' Association's Response to OFGAS' Consultation Document 'New Gas Tariff Formula – Proposed Modifications of the Conditions of British Gas' Authorisation'*, London.

Consumers' Association (1991b) Consumer Briefing, Competition and Service (Utilities) Bill, Committee Stage, December, London.

Consumers' Association (1992a) Consumer Briefing, Competition and Service (Utilities) Bill, Report Stage, House of Lords, January, London.

Consumers' Association (1992b) Consumer Briefing, Competition and Service (Utilities) Bill, 2nd Reading Debate, House of Lords, February, London.

Consumers' Association (1992c) Putting Gas to the Test, *Which?*, June, 318–21.

Consumers' Association (1992d) Data from CA. The quality of service in the utility industries. Part 2. Gas and electricity, *Consumer Policy Review*, 2 (1), 48–52.

Consumers' Association (1992e) *Response to OFFER Consultation Paper on Metering*, June, London.

Consumers' Association (1992f) *Response to OFFER Consultation Paper on Energy Efficiency*, July, London.

Cook, J. (1989) *Dirty Water*, London, Unwin Hyman.

Cook, P. and Kirkpatrick, C. (eds) (1988) *Privatisation in Less Developed Countries*, Brighton, Wheatsheaf Books.

Coote, A. (ed.) (1992) *The Welfare of Citizens, Developing New Social Rights*, London, IPPR/Rivers Oram Press.

Cornes, R. and Sandler, T. (1986) *The Theory of Externalities, Public Goods and Club Goods*, Cambridge, Cambridge University Press.

Cox, A. (1987) The politics of privatisation in Robins, L., op. cit., pp. 150–79.

Crew, M.A. and Kleindorfer, P.R. (1979) *Public Utility Economics*, London, Macmillan.

Crowe, J. (1991) *Colder by Decree, Income Support – For Poorer, For Colder, in Sickness and in Bad Housing*, Birmingham, National Right to Fuel Campaign.

Cullis, J.G. and Jones, P.R. (1989) *Microeconomics and the Public Economy: A Defence of Leviathan*, Oxford, Basil Blackwell.

Curwen, P. (1986) *Public Enterprise. A Modern Approach*, Brighton, Wheatsheaf.

Davies, L. (n.d.) *The Electricity Supply Trade Union Council Campaign on the Electricity Bill*, London, ESTUC.

Demsetz, H. (1988) *Ownership, Control, and the Firm. The Organization of Economic Activity*, Volume I, Oxford, Basil Blackwell.

Demsetz, H. (1989) *Efficiency, Competition, and Policy. The Organization of Economic Activity*, Volume II, Oxford, Basil Blackwell.

Department of Energy (1990) *Public Electricity Supply Licence for East Midlands Electricity plc*, London.

Department of Energy (1991) *Digest of United Kingdom Energy Statistics 1991*, London, HMSO.

Department of Energy (1992) *Energy Trends*, London.

Department of the Environment (1990) This Common Inheritance, Britain's Environmental Strategy, Cm 1200, London, HMSO.

Department of the Environment (1991a) *Attitudes to Energy Conservation in the Home*, London, HMSO.

Department of the Environment (1991b) *English House Condition Survey, 1988, Supplementary (Energy). Report*, London, HMSO.

Department of the Environment (1992) *Environment News Release, New Energy Savings Trust Announced*, London, 13 May.

Department of the Environment/Welsh Office (1989) *Instrument of Appointment of the Water and Sewerage Undertakers*, London, HMSO.

Department of the Environment/Welsh Office (1991a) *Water Supply, Sewerage Disposal and the Water Environment, A Guide to the Regulatory System*, London.

Department of the Environment/Welsh Office (1991b) *Competition in the Water Industry, A Consultation Paper*, London.

Department of the Environment/Welsh Office (1992) *Using Water Wisely. A Consultation Paper*, London.

Department of Trade and Industry (1992a) *DTI Press Notice, Michael Heseltine orders comprehensive MMC investigation of the Gas Market*, London 31 July.

Department of Trade and Industry (1992b) *Monopoly Reference to the Monopolies and Mergers Commission*, London.

Department of Trade and Industry (1992c) *Digest of United Kingdom Energy Statistics 1992*, London, HMSO.

De Oliveira, A. and MacKerron, G. (1992) Is the World Bank approach to structural reform supported by experience of electricity privatization in the UK?, *Energy Policy*, 20 (2), 153–62.

Devlin, J. and Miall, R. (1990) Paying for water, getting the balance right, *Public Finance and Accountancy*, 7 December, 12–14.

Dilnot, A. and Helm, D. (1987) Energy policy, merit goods and social security, *Fiscal Studies*, 8, 3.

Dnes, A.W. (1989) How to privatise natural monopolies, *Policy*, Summer, 13–16.

Donahue, J.D. (1989) *The Privatization Decision, Public Ends, Private Means*, New York, Basic Books.

Dorgan, J. (1989) Privatisation. A review of some issues, *Administration*, 37, 1.

Dowding, K. (1992) Choice, its increase and its value, *British Journal of Political Science*, 22 (3), 301–14.

Drucker, P.F. (1969) *The Age of Discontinuity*, London, Heinemann.

Dunleavy, P. (1986) Explaining the privatization boom, public choice versus radical approaches, *Public Administration*, 64, Spring.

Dunleavy, P. (1991) *Democracy, Bureaucracy and Public Choice*, Hemel Hempstead, Harvester Wheatsheaf.

Dunleavy, P. and O'Leary, B. (1987) *Theories of the State. The Politics of Liberal Democracy*, Basingstoke, Macmillan.

Dunsire, A., Hartley, K., Parker, D. and Dimitriou, B. (1988) Organizational status and performance. A conceptual framework for testing public choice theories, *Public Administration*, 66, Winter.

Dunsire, A., Hartley, K. and Parker, D. (1991) Organizational status and performance. Summary of findings, *Public Administration*, 69, Spring, 21–40.

East Midlands Region Electricity Consumers Committee (1991) *Annual Report 1 April 1990–31 March 91*, Nottingham.

Eaton, J.W. (1989) Bureaucratic, capitalist and populist privatization strategies, *International Review of Administrative Sciences*, 55, 467–92.

Electricity Association (1991a) *UK Electricity Tariff Rates*, London.

Electricity Association (1991b) *UK Electricity 91*, London.

Electricity Consumers Council. *Statistics on Disconnection of Domestic Consumers*, London.

Electricity Consumers Council (1980–1988/89), *Annual Reports* London.

Electricity Council (1990) *Handbook of Electricity Supply Statistics 1989*, London.

Emery, C.T. and Smythe, B. (1986) *Judicial Review*, London, Sweet and Maxwell.

Estrin, S. and Whitehead, C. (eds) (1988) *Privatisation and the Nationalised Industries*, London, Suntory-Toyota International Centre for Economics and Related Disciplines.

Fells, I. and Lucas, N. (1991) *UK Energy Policy Post-Privatisation*, Scottish Nuclear Ltd.

Fells, I. and Lucas, N. (1992) UK energy policy post-privatization, *Energy Policy*, 20 (5), 386–89.

Fimister, G. (1989a) Tapping the resources, *Community Care*, 18 May.

Fimister, G. (1989b) Pleased to meter you, *Insight*, 7 June.

Fimister, G. (1989c) 'Life on the edge', *Insight*, 11 October.

Fine, B. (1989) Privatization of the ESI. Broadening the debate, *Energy Policy*, June.

Fitch, M. (1992) Public Utilities, Regulation and the Welfare of 'Difficult Customers', unpublished.

Forbes, J.D. (1987) *The Consumer Interest. Dimensions and Policy/Implications*, London, Croom Helm.

Fraser, R. (ed.) (1988) *Privatization. The UK Experience and International Trends*, Harlow, Longman.

Frayman, H. (1991) *Breadline Britain 1990s*, London, Domino Films/LWT.

Frederick, W.C., Davis, K. and Post, J.E. (1988) *Business and Society: Corporate Strategy, Public Policy, Ethics, 6th edn*, New York, McGraw-Hill.

Friends of the Earth (1990) *Pollute Electric? Twelve Regional Electricity Companies, Privatisation and the Environment*, London.

Gadbury, D. (1991) Will we use water more wisely?, *Water Bulletin*, 488, 10.

Gamble, A. (1988) *The Free Economy and The Strong State. The Politics of Thatcherism*, Basingstoke, Macmillan.

Gamble, A. (1989) Privatization, Thatcherism, and the British State, *Journal of Law and Society*, 16 (1), 1–19.

Garrett, P. (1989) The four year journey to privatisation, *Water Bulletin*, 374, 10–13.

Gas Consumers Council (1988) *An Analysis of Gas Disconnections*, London.

Gas Consumers Council (1990) *Annual Report 1989*, London.

Gas Consumers Council (1991a) *Annual Report 1990*, London.

Gas Consumers Council (1991b) *Gas Consumers Council Report to OFGAS, Monitoring British Gas' Debt and Disconnection Procedure*, November/December 1991, London.

Gas Consumers Council (1992a) *Annual Report 1991*, London.

Gas Consumers Council (1992b) Statement by Ian Powe, Director, Gas Consumers Council, London, 14 May.

Gas Consumers Council (1992c) *British Gas Debt and Disconnection Statistics*, London.

Gegax, D. (1989) Natural monopoly measures and regulatory policy, in Nowotny, K. et al., op. cit., pp. 185–216.

George, M. (1990) Squeezing every last drop, *Community Care*, 15 November.

George, M. (1992) Waterlogged, *Social Work Today*, 6 August.

Gibson, M. and Price, C. (1988) *Privatising the electricity industry*, in Estrin, S. and Whitehead, C., op. cit., pp. 33–43.

Gilbert, N. and Gilbert, B. (1989) *The Enabling State: Modern Welfare Capitalism in America*, New York, Oxford University Press.

Gilmour, I. (1992) *Dancing with Dogma, Britain under Thatcherism*, London, Simon and Schuster.

Glennerster, H. and Midgley, H. (eds) (1991) *The Radical Right and the Welfare State: An International Assessment*, Hemel Hempstead, Harvester Wheatsheaf.

Glynn, D. (1988) Economic regulation of the privatized water industry, in Johnson, C., op. cit., pp. 77–92.

Glynn, D. (1990) Paying for water. The company's right to choose, *Public Finance and Accountancy*, 7 December, 14–16.

Green, R. (1991) Reshaping the CEGB. Electricity privatization in the UK, *Utilities Policy*, 1 (3), 245–54.

Grout, P. (1987) The wider share ownership programme, *Fiscal Studies*, 8 (3), 59–73.

Halsey, A.H. (ed.) (1988) *British Social Trends since 1900*, Basingstoke, Macmillan.

Hammond, E.M., Helm, D.R. and Thompson, D.J. (1986) Competition in electricity supply. Has the energy act failed?, *Fiscal Studies*, 7 (1), 11–33.

Harden, I. (1992) *The Contracting State*, Buckingham, Open University Press.

Hardten, R.D. and Sheffield, N. (1988) Water supply tariffs in the United States, *Public Finance and Accountancy*, 10 June.

Hare, P.G. (ed.) (1988) *Surveys in Public Sector Economics*, Oxford, Basil Blackwell.

Harrison, R.Z. (1992) *Paying for Fuel*, Edinburgh, Right to Warmth/Fuel Policy Forum.

Hawes, D. (1992) Parliamentary Select Committees, some case studies in contingent influence, *Policy and Politics*, 20 (3), 227–236.

Hayek, F.A. (1960) *The Constitution of Liberty*, London, Routledge and Kegan Paul.

Heal, D.W. (1990) From monopoly to competition. Marketing natural gas in the UK, *Utilities Policy*, 1 (1), 54–64.

Heald, D. (1984) Privatization and Public Money, in Steel, D. and Heald, D., op. cit., pp. 21–43.

Heald, D. and Steel, D. (1986) Privatising public enterprises. An analysis of the Government's case in Kay J. et al., op. cit., pp. 58–77.

Helm, D. (1986) The economic borders of the state, *Oxford Review of Economic Policy*, 2 (2), i–xxiv.

Helm, D. (1987) Nuclear power and the privatisation of electricity generation, *Fiscal Studies*, 8 (4), 69–73.

Helm, D. (1988a) Regulating the electricity supply industry, *Fiscal Studies*, 9, 86–105.

Helm, D. (1988b) The privatisation of electricity, in Helm, D. et al., op. cit., pp. 1–24.

Helm, D. (ed.) (1989) *The Economic Borders of the State*, Oxford, Oxford University Press.

Helm, D., Kay, J. and Thompson, D. (1988a) Energy policy and the role of the State in the market for energy, *Fiscal Studies*, 9 (1), 41–61.

Helm, D., MacKerron, G., Miklewright, J., Robinson, B. and Skea, J. (1988b) *Privatising Electricity, Impact on the UK Energy Market*, London, Institute for Fiscal Studies.

Helm, D. and Yarrow, G. (1988) The Assessment. The Regulation of Utilities, *Oxford Review of Economic Policy*, 4, 2.

Helm, D. and Pearce, D. (1990) Assessment, economic policy towards the environment, *Oxford Review of Economic Policy*, 6 (1), 1–16.

Helm, D. and Powell, A. (1992) Pool prices, contracts and regulation in the British electricity supply industry, *Fiscal Studies*, 13 (1), 89–105.

Hill, M., Aaronovitch, S. and Baldock, D. (1989) Non-decision making in pollution control in Britain, nitrate pollution, the EEC Drinking Water Directive and agriculture, *Policy & Politics*, 17 (3), 227–40.

Hill, S. (1990) Britain: The dominant ideology thesis after a decade, in Abercrombie, N. et al., op.cit., pp. 1–37.

HMSO (1986a) Gas Act 1986, London.

HMSO (1986b) *Privatisation of the Water Authorities in England and Wales*, London, Cm 9734.

HMSO (1988a) *Privatising Electricity. The Government's proposals for the privatisation of the electricity supply industry in England and Wales*, London, Cm 322.

HMSO (1988b) Water Bill, London.

HMSO (1989a) Electricity Act 1989, London.

HMSO (1989b) Water Act 1989, London.

HMSO (1991a) Water Industry Act 1991, London.

HMSO (1991b) The Citizen's Charter, London, Cm 1599.

HMSO (1991c) Competition and Service (Utilities) Bill, London.

HMSO (1992d) Competition and Service (Utilities) Act 1992, London.

HM Treasury (1992) Public Expenditure Analyses to 1994–95, Cm 1920, London, HMSO.

Hoffland, A. and Nicol, N. (1992) *Fuel Rights Handbook*, 8th edn, London, Child Poverty Action Group.

Hogwood, B.W. (1992) *Trends in British Public Policy, Do Governments Make Any Difference?*, Buckingham, Open University Press.

Honderich, T. (1991) *Conservatism*, London, Penguin.

Hood, C. (1986) *Administrative Analysis. An Introduction to Rules, Enforcement and Organizations*, Brighton, Wheatsheaf.

House of Commons Committee of Public Accounts (1992) *Sale of the Water Authorities in England and Wales*, HC 140 (1992–3), London, HMSO.

House of Commons Energy Committee (1992a) *Consequences of Electricity Privatisation*, Volume 1, Report, HC 113-I (1991–2), London, HMSO.

House of Commons Energy Committee (1992b) *Consequences of Electricity Privatisation*, Volume 2, Memoranda of Evidence, HC 113-II (1991–2), London, HMSO.

House of Commons Energy Committee (1992c) *Consequences of Electricity Privatisation*, Volume 3, Minutes of Evidence, HC 113-III (1991–2), London, HMSO.

House of Commons Library Research Division (1991a) *Background Paper. The Regulation of Privatized Utility Companies*, London, 1 July.

House of Commons Library Research Division (1991b) *Research Note*, Competition and Service (Utilities) Bill, London, 14 November.

House of Commons Parliamentary Debates (1989) *Official Report of Standing Committee D*, Water Bill, London, HMSO.

House of Commons Parliamentary Debates (1991) *Official Report of Standing Committee E,* Competition and Service (Utilities) Bill, London, HMSO.

Huby, M. and Dix, G. (1992) *Evaluating the Social Fund,* Department of Social Security Research Report No. 9, London, HMSO.

Hutchinson, G. (1991) Efficiency gains through privatisation of UK industries, in Ott, A.F. and Hartley, K., op. cit., pp. 87–107. ·

Hutton, S. and Hardman, G. (1992) *Expenditure on Fuels 1987,* London, Gas Consumers Council.

Ignatieff, M. (1991) Citizenship and moral narcissism, in Andrews, G., op. cit., pp. 26–36.

International Energy Agency (IEA) (1991) *Utility Pricing and Access. Competition for Monopolies,* Paris, OECD.

Jackson, P. and Terry, F. (eds) (1989) *Public Domain. The Public Sector Yearbook 1989,* London, Public Finance Foundation.

James Capel Research (1992) *Regional Electricity Package Split Look at the Core Business,* London 12 May.

Johnson, C., (ed.) (1988a) *Lloyds Bank Annual Review, Privatization and Ownership,* London, Pinter.

Johnson, C. (1988b) The economics of Britain's electricity privatization, in Johnson, C., op. cit., pp. 60–76.

Johnson, C. (ed.) (1989) *The Market on Trial, Lloyds Bank Annual Review,* Volume 2, London, Pinter.

Johnson, C. (1992) Public spending – a break with the past?, *The Economic Review,* 10 (1), 13–16.

Johnson, P., McKay, S. and Smith, S. (1990) *The Distributional Consequences of Environmental Taxes,* IFS Commentary No. 23, London, Institute for Fiscal Studies.

Jones, D. (1992) *Energy Policy Now,* London, Institute for Public Policy Research.

Jowell, R. et al. (eds) (1990) *British Social Attitudes. The 7th Report,* Aldershot, Gower.

Jowell, R. et al. (eds) (1991) *British Social Attitudes. The 8th Report,* Aldershot, Dartmouth.

Kamerman, S.B. and Kahn, A.J. (eds) (1989) *Privatization and the Welfare State,* Princeton, Princeton University Press.

Kay, J., Mayer, C. and Thompson, D. (eds) (1986) *Privatisation and Regulation. The UK Experience,* Oxford, Clarendon.

Keat, R. (1991) Introduction. Starship Britain or universal enterprise? in Keat, R. and Abercrombie, N., op. cit., pp. 1–17.

Keat, R. and Abercrombie, N. (eds) (1991) *Enterprise Culture,* London, Routledge.

Kikeri, S., Nellis, J. and Shirley, M. (1992) *Privatization. The Lessons of Experience,* Washington, The World Bank.

King, D.S. (1987) *The New Right, Politics, Markets and Citizenship,* Basingstoke, Macmillan.

King, M. (1992) *Cold Shouldered. A Report from Winter Action on Cold Homes,* Bedford, Winter Action on Cold Homes.

Kinnersley, D. (1988) *Troubled Water, Rivers, Politics and Pollution,* London, Hilary Shipman.

Kleinwort Benson Ltd (1990) *The Regional Electricity Companies Share Offers Main Prospectus,* London.

Kling, R.W. (1988) Building an institutional theory of regulation, *Journal of Economic Issues,* 22, 1.

Labour Party (1990a) *Looking to the Future,* London.

Labour Party (1990b) *An Earthly Chance,* London.

Law, B., Sealy, J., Elliott, C. and Cornhill, P. (1990) *Contains No Cash. The Experience and Opinions of 50 Users of Gas Key Meters*, Leicester, Leicester Family Service Unit.

Law, B. and Downes, D. (1991) *Disability and Coinless Prepayment Meters*, Leicester, Leicester Family Service Unit.

Leadbeater, C. (1991) Whose line is it anyway?, *Marxism Today*, July, 20–4.

Le Grand, J. (1991) *Equity and Social Choice. An Essay in Economics and Applied Philosophy*, London, HarperCollins Academic.

Le Grand, J. and Robinson, R. (eds) (1984) *Privatisation and the Welfare State*, London, Allen and Unwin.

Letwin, O. (1988) *Privatising the World*, London, Cassell.

Levacic, R. (1987) *Economic Policy-Making*, Brighton, Wheatsheaf.

Lewis, R. (1991) Reforming Industrial Relations, Law, Politics and Power, *Oxford Review of Economic Policy*, 7 (1), 60–75.

Lister, R. (1990) Women, economic dependency and citizenship, *Journal of Social Policy*, 19 (4), 445–67.

Lister, R. (1993) Tracing the contours of women's citizenship, *Policy and Politics*, 21 (1), 3–16.

Littlechild, S. (1988) Economic regulation of privatised water authorities and some further reflections, *Oxford Review of Economic Policy*, 4, 2.

Littlechild, S. (1991a) 'Regulation of the British Electricity Industry.' Speech to *Investing in Power Seminar*, Birmingham, Office of Electricity Regulation.

Littlechild, S. (1991b) 'Competition, Efficiency and Emission Reduction. A Regulator's View.' *Royal Institute of International Affairs Energy Conference*, London, 3 December.

Lockwood, P.W. (1991) Repositioning Delivery Quality in the Water Industry, MBA thesis, School of Accountancy, Law and Management Studies, Huddersfield Polytechnic.

Lundqvist, L.J. (1988) Privatization. Towards a concept for comparative policy analysis, *Journal of Social Policy*, 8 (1).

Lyons, J. (1989) Privatizing electricity supply cannot be justified, *Energy Policy*, April.

MacAvoy, P.W., Stanbury, W.T., Yarrow, G. and Zeckhauser, R.J. (1989) *Privatization and State-Owned Enterprises*, Boston, Kluwer Academic Publishers.

Mack, J. and Lansley, S. (1985) *Poor Britain*, London, Allen and Unwin.

MacKerron, G. (1990) Contractual relationships and electricity privatisation, *Public Finance and Accountancy*, 5 January, 15–16.

Macrory, R. (1989) *The Water Act 1989, Text and Commentary*, London, Sweet and Maxwell.

McAllister, I. and Studlar, D.T. (1989) Popular versus elite views of privatization, The case of Britain, *Journal of Public Policy*, 9 (2), 157–78.

McGowan, F. (1988) Public ownership and the performance of the UK ESI, *Energy Policy*, June.

McGregor, G. (1992) *Gas and Energy Efficiency The 'E' Factor*, London, Office of Gas Supply.

McHarg, A. (1992) The Competition and Service (Utilities) Act 1992, Utility Regulation and the Charter, *Public Law*, Autumn, 385–96.

McIntosh, A. (1990) *What to do about Water, Industrial Policy Paper No. 4*, London, Institute for Public Policy Research.

McKinnon, J. (1991) 'Regulation of the Gas Sector.' Speech to the *Institute of Economic Affairs' Regulation in the United Kingdom Conference*, London.

Mann, P.C. (1989) Urban water supply. The divergence between theory and practice, in Nowotny, K. et al., op. cit., pp. 163–84.

Manweb (1991) *Codes of Practice, Complaint Handling Procedures; Paying Electricity Bills; Services for People with Disabilities or Older People; Electricity Efficiency*, Chester.

Manweb (n.d.) *Licence Condition 19, Methods for Dealing with Domestic Customers in Default*, Chester.

Marsh, D. (1991) Privatization under Mrs Thatcher. A review of the literature, *Public Administration*, 69 (4), 459–80.

Marsh, D. and Rhodes, R.A.W. (eds) (1992) *Implementing Thatcherite Policies. Audit of an Era*, Buckingham, Open University Press.

Marshall, T.H. (1992) Citizenship and social class, in Marshall, T.H. and Bottomore, T., op. cit., pp. 3–51.

Marshall, T.H. and Bottomore, T. (1992) *Citizenship and Social Class*, London, Pluto.

Martin, R.C. and Wilder, R.P. (1992) Residential demand for water and the pricing of municipal water services, *Public Finance Quarterly*, 20 (1), 93–102.

Melody, W.H. (1989) Efficiency and social policy in telecommunication: lessons from the US experience, *Journal of Economic Issues*, 23 (3), 657–88.

Metcalf, D. (1991) British unions, dissolution or resurgence, *Oxford Review of Economic Policy*, 7 (1), 18–32.

Meyer, R.A. (1975) Publicly owned versus privately owned utilities. A policy choice, *Review of Economics and Statistics*, 57, 4.

Micklewright, J. (1988) Towards a household model of UK domestic energy demand, in Helm, D. et al., op. cit., pp. 49–62.

Midlands Electricity plc (1991a) *Codes of Practice. Handling Complaints; Payment of Bills; Services for Older or Disabled People; Using Electricity Efficiently*, Halesowen.

Miller, E.S. (1990) Economic efficiency, the economics discipline, and the 'affected-with-a-public-interest' concept, *Journal of Economic Issues*, 24 (3), 719–32.

Millward, R. (1986) The comparative performance of public and private ownership in Kay J. et al., op. cit., pp. 119–44.

MMBW (Melbourne and Metropolitan Board of Works) (1991) *Pricing to Conserve Water, Issues and Options for the 1990s*, Melbourne.

Moore, J. (1986) Why privatise? *and* The success of privatisation in Kay J. et al., op. cit., pp. 78–93 and 94–7.

MORI (1992) *The Consumer Viewpoint. A Quantitative Survey – Computer Tables*, Volumes I and II, London.

MORI (1993) *Electricity Services: The Customer Perspective*, Report prepared for the Office of Electricity Regulation, London.

Musgrave, R.A. and Musgrave, P.B. (1984) *Public Finance in Theory and Practice*, 4th edn., New York, McGraw-Hill.

NACAB (National Association of Citizens Advice Bureaux) (1989) *Parliamentary Briefings on the Water Bill*, London.

NACAB (National Association of Citizens Advice Bureaux) (1991a) *Paying for Water*, London.

NACAB (National Association of Citizens Advice Bureaux) (1991b) *Problems with Electricity – April 1990–March 1991*, NACAB submission to the Office of Electricity Regulation, London (August).

NACAB (National Association of Citizens Advice Bureaux) (1992a) *High and Dry*, CAB evidence on water charges, debt and disconnection, London (June).

NACAB (National Association of Citizens Advice Bureaux) (1992b) *CAB Briefings on the Competition and Service (Utilities). Bill to House of Lords*, London.

NACAB (National Association of Citizens Advice Bureaux) *Social Policy Bulletin (1990–1992)*, London.

National Audit Office (1987) *Report by the Comptroller and Auditor General, Department of Energy, Sale of Government Shareholding in British Gas plc*, London, HMSO.

National Audit Office (1989) *National Energy Efficiency*, London, HMSO.

National Audit Office (1992a) *Report by the Comptroller and Auditor General, Department of the Environment, Sale of the Water Authorities in England and Wales*, London, HMSO.

National Audit Office (1992b) *Report by the Comptroller and Auditor General. The Sale of the Twelve Regional Electricity Companies*, London, HMSO.

National Consumer Council (n.d.) *Second Reading Briefing on Gas Privatisation*, London.

National Consumer Council (1986) *Comments on the Gas Bill and Draft Licence to Standing Committee on the Gas Bill (9/1/86)*, London.

National Consumer Council (1988a) *Electricity Privatisation, Policy Paper No. 1*, London.

National Consumer Council (1988b) *Privatisation of the Electricity Industry, Policy Paper No. 2*, London.

National Consumer Council (1989a) *In the Absence of Competition. A Consumer View of Public Utilities Regulation*, London, HMSO.

National Consumer Council (1989b) *National Consumer Council Response to Water Bill 1989 – Proposed Regulations to Establish a Guaranteed Standards Scheme*, London.

National Consumer Council (1989c) *Parliamentary Briefings for House of Commons on Water Bill*, London.

National Consumer Council (1989d) *Parliamentary Briefings for House of Lords on Water Bill*, London.

National Consumer Council (1989e) *Parliamentary Briefings for House of Lords on Electricity Bill*, London.

National Consumer Council (1990a) *Consumer Concerns 1990. A Consumer View of Public Services*, London.

National Consumer Council (1990b) *Credit and Debt. The Consumer Interest*, London, HMSO.

National Consumer Council (1991a) *Consumer Concerns 1991. A Consumer View of Public and Local Authority Services*, London.

National Consumer Council (1991b) *'Paying for Water'. National Consumer Council Response to the OFWAT Consultation*, London.

National Metering Trials Co-ordinating Group (1990) *National Metering Trials*, Second Interim Report, July.

National Metering Trials Group (1992) *Water Metering Trials Newsletter*, September.

National Right to Fuel Campaign (1991) *Energy Efficiency, OFGAS and British Gas*, Comments from the National Right to Fuel Campaign, June, Birmingham.

National Right to Fuel Campaign (1992) Comments from the National Right to Fuel Campaign on the OFFER Energy Efficiency Consultation Document, Birmingham, June.

National Utility Services Ltd (1992) *News Information, International Water Price Survey July 1991–July 1992*, Croydon.

Neighbourhood Energy Action (1991) *Fighting the Cold. 10 Years of Energy Efficiency Achievement*, Newcastle.

Neighbourhood Energy Action (1992a) *Proposed EC Directive on Carbon/Energy Tax, Consultation*, Newcastle.

Neighbourhood Energy Action (1992b) *Standards of Performance and Customer Appointments*, Newcastle.

Neighbourhood Energy Action (1992c) *British Gas Standards of Service and Compensation Scheme*, Newcastle.

Neighbourhood Energy Action (1992d) *Response to Monopolies and Mergers Commission Inquiry on British Gas plc*, Newcastle.

Nelson, R.A. (1990) The effects of competition on publicly-owned firms; evidence from the municipal electric industry in the US, *International Journal of Industrial Organization*, 8, 37–51.

Neuberger, J. (ed.) (1987) *Privatisation. Fair Shares for All or Selling the Family Silver*, London, Macmillan.

NOP Omnibus Services (1992) *A Report Produced for Office of Population Censuses and Surveys on Behalf of the Treasury and ProShare on Share Ownership 1992*, London.

Northern Electric (1991) *Codes of Practice, Procedures for Handling Complaints from Customers; Payment of Electricity Bills by Domestic Customers; Provision of Services for Elderly or Disabled Persons; Efficient Use of Electricity*, Newcastle upon Tyne.

North West Electricity Consumers Committee (1991) *Annual Report 1990–1991*, Manchester.

Norton, G.A. (1984) *Resource Economics*, London, Edward Arnold.

Nowotny, K., Smith, D.B. and Trebing, H.M. (eds) (1989) *Public Utility Regulation. The Economic and Social Control of Industry*, Boston, Kluwer.

OECD (Organisation for Economic Co-operation and Development) (1987) *Pricing of Water Services*, Paris, OECD.

Office of Electricity Regulation (1990) *Annual Report 1989*, London, HMSO.

Office of Electricity Regulation (1990a) *Statement by the Director General of Electricity Supply. The Regulatory System and the Duties of the DGES*, Birmingham, October.

Office of Electricity Regulation (1990b) Determination by Director General of a matter referred under Section 23 of the Electricity Act 1989, Meter Tampering, Birmingham, 13 December.

Office of Electricity Regulation (1991) *Annual Report 1990*, London, HMSO.

Office of Electricity Regulation (1991a) Speech by the Director General, New Metering Presentation, Birmingham, 22 January.

Office of Electricity Regulation (1991b) *Customer Accounting Statistics, Quarters ending March 1991, June 1991, September 1991, December 1991, March 1992, June 1992*, Birmingham.

Office of Electricity Regulation (1991c) Monitoring the Codes of Practice. A Discussion Paper, Birmingham, 18 April.

Office of Electricity Regulation (1991d) Press Release. *Standards of Performance – New Service Guarantees for Electricity Customers*, May.

Office of Electricity Regulation (1991e) *Monitoring the Codes of Practice. A Discussion Paper for the Public Utilities Access Forum*, Birmingham, 16 July.

Office of Electricity Regulation (1991f) Determination No. S23/C/002/(B), Birmingham, August.

Office of Electricity Regulation (1991g) Determination No. S23/C/003/(B), Birmingham, 8 August.

Office of Electricity Regulation (1991h) *Customer Accounting Statistics, Quarter ending June 1991*, 21 August, Birmingham.

Office of Electricity Regulation (n.d.) *Connection Charges Discussion Paper*, Birmingham.

Office of Electricity Regulation (1991i) Press Release. *DGES Approves Renewables Contracts*, Birmingham, 6 November.

Office of Electricity Regulation (1991j) Press Release. *OFFER Helps Save Money for Electricity Customers*, Birmingham, 12 November.

Office of Electricity Regulation (1991k) Press Release. *Competition in Electricity Market Benefits Environment*, Birmingham, 3 December.

Office of Electricity Regulation (1991l) *Report on Distribution and Transmission System Performance 1990–91*, Birmingham, 12 December.

Office of Electricity Regulation (1991m) *Report on Pool Price Inquiry*, Birmingham, December.

Office of Electricity Regulation (1991n) Press Release. *Levy Rate to Remain at 11 Per Cent*, Birmingham, 16 December.

Office of Electricity Regulation (1991o) Press Release. *Offer Launches Energy Efficiency Consultation*, Birmingham, 18 December.

Office of Electricity Regulation (1991p) *Energy Efficiency Consultation Paper*, Birmingham.

Office of Electricity Regulation (1992a) Press Release. *Modern Metering is the Way Forward*, Birmingham, 21 January.

Office of Electricity Regulation (1992) *Annual Report 1991*, London, HMSO.

Office of Electricity Regulation (1992b) *Metering Consultation Paper*, Birmingham.

Office of Electricity Regulation (1992c) Press Release. *Offer Calls for More Information on Security Deposits to be given to Business Customers*, Birmingham, 25 January.

Office of Electricity Regulation (1992d) Press Release. *Electricity Price Controls, Results of Director General's Investigations*, Birmingham, 6 February.

Office of Electricity Regulation (n.d.) *Electricity Price Controls Statement*, Birmingham.

Office of Electricity Regulation (n.d.) *Maximum Resale Price of Electricity. A Guide for Domestic Tenants and their Landlords*, Birmingham.

Office of Electricity Regulation (1992e) Press Release. *Director General of Electricity Supply's Decision on Direct Sales Limits*, Birmingham, 7 and 12 February.

Office of Electricity Regulation (1992f) Press Release. *Offer Switches on Combined Heat and Power Database*, Birmingham, 17 February.

Office of Electricity Regulation (1992g) Determination No. S23/R/011/(B), Birmingham, 25 February.

Office of Electricity Regulation (1992h) Determination No. S23/R/016/(B), Birmingham, 25 February.

Office of Electricity Regulation (1992i) Press Release. *Director General of Electricity Supply Publishes 1991 Annual Report*, Birmingham, 9 March.

Office of Electricity Regulation (1992j) Press Release. *Electricity Resale. Advice for Landlords and Tenants*, Birmingham, 1 April.

Office of Electricity Regulation (1992k) Press Release. *Director General Gives Guidance on Price Discrimination*, Birmingham, 16 April.

Office of Electricity Regulation (1992l) Press Release. *Multi-Occupation Rule Relaxed*, Birmingham, 23 April.

Office of Electricity Regulation (1992m) Press Release. *Director General Gives Guidance on Connection Charges*, Birmingham, 30 April.

Office of Electricity Regulation (1992n) Determination No. S23/C/015/B, Birmingham, 6 May.

Office of Electricity Regulation (1992o) Press Release. *Privatisation Leads to Improved Customer Services*, Birmingham, 3 June.

Office of Electricity Regulation (1992p) Press Release. *Licence Modification Proposed for National Power, Powergen and Nuclear Electric*, Birmingham, 5 June.

Office of Electricity Regulation (1992q) Press Release. *Director General of Electricity Supply Responds to Energy Select Committee*, Birmingham, 9 June.

Office of Electricity Regulation (1992r) *Energy Committee Consequences of Electricity Privatisation. Response from the Director General of Electricity Supply, Birmingham,* 9 June.

Office of Electricity Regulation (1992s) *Report on Gas Turbine Plant,* Birmingham, June.

Office of Electricity Regulation (1992t) Press Release. *Director General of Electricity Supply Comments on REC Results,* Birmingham, June.

Office of Electricity Regulation (1992u) Determination No. S23/R/017/(B), Birmingham, 19 June.

Office of Electricity Regulation (n.d.) *Electricity Consumers' Committees. A Brief Guide,* Birmingham.

Office of Electricity Regulation (n.d.) *Report on Distribution and Transmission System Performance 1990–91,* Birmingham.

Office of Electricity Regulation (1992v) *A Statement by the Director General of Electricity Supply, Future Control on National Grid Company Prices,* Birmingham, 7 July.

Office of Electricity Regulation (1992w) Press Release. *Higher Standards Proposed for Customers,* Birmingham, 23 July.

Office of Electricity Regulation (1992x) *Report on Customer Service 1991–92,* Birmingham, July.

Office of Electricity Regulation (1992y) *The Supply Price Control Review Consultation Paper,* Birmingham, October.

Office of Electricity Regulation (1992z) Press Release. *Director General Clears Up Some Misconceptions,* Birmingham, 11 November.

Office of Electricity Regulation (1993) *Customer Accounting Statistics, Quarter Ending December 1992,* Birmingham.

Office of Gas Supply (1988) *Annual Report 1987,* London, HMSO.

Office of Gas Supply (1989) *Annual Report 1988,* London, HMSO.

Office of Gas Supply (1989a) *Notice Under Section 23 (2) of the Gas Act 1986,* London, 11 January.

Office of Gas Supply (1989b) *Modification of the conditions of British Gas plc's Authorisation by Agreement,* London, 18 April.

Office of Gas Supply (1989c) OFGAS News Release. *Time to End the Misery of Gas Disconnections,* London, 20 April.

Office of Gas Supply (1989d) OFGAS Information. *Safeguards for Gas Consumers Against Disconnection for Debt,* London.

Office of Gas Supply (1990) *Annual Report 1989,* London, HMSO.

Office of Gas Supply (1990a) OFGAS to review gas tariff formula, *OFGAS News,* June.

Office of Gas Supply (1991) *Annual Report 1990,* London, HMSO.

Office of Gas Supply (1991a) Consumer Affairs Extract from *Annual Report 1990,* London, HMSO.

Office of Gas Supply (1991b) Gas users get new 'Green Code', *OFGAS News Release,* London, 30 January.

Office of Gas Supply (1991c) *New Gas Tariff Formula. Tariff Structures,* London.

Office of Gas Supply (1991d) *New Gas Tariff Formula. Economic Aspects,* London.

Office of Gas Supply (1991e) *New Gas Tariff Formula. Standards of Service,* London.

Office of Gas Supply (1991f) *Gas Regulation. The Environment and Energy Efficiency,* London.

Office of Gas Supply (1991g) *New Gas Tariff Formula. Proposed Modifications of the Conditions of British Gas' Authorisation,* London.

Office of Gas Supply (1991h) OFGAS News Release. *Watchdog Secures Value for Money for 17m. Gas Users,* London, 29 April.

Office of Gas Supply (1991i) OFGAS News Release. *Watchdog Says British Gas Could Renege on Agreement*, London, 14 October.

Office of Gas Supply (1992) *Annual Report 1991*, London, HMSO.

Office of Gas Supply (1992a) OFGAS News Release. *'Busiest-Ever Year' Claims Gas Watchdog*, London, 11 February.

Office of Gas Supply (1992b) OFGAS News Release. *Watchdog Hits Home With Service 'Ace'*, London, 26 March.

Office of Gas Supply (1992c) OFGAS News Release. *Gas Price Cuts Needed Now – Industry's Watchdog*, London, 6 May.

Office of Gas Supply (1992d) OFGAS News Release. *Gas Price Cuts Not To Be Sniffed At*, London, 14 May.

Office of Gas Supply (1992e) OFGAS News Release. *Price Cuts for Tenants Using Gas Announced*, London, 1 July.

Office of Gas Supply (1992f) OFGAS News Release. *Gas Transmission Problem Referred to Monopolies Commission*, London, 31 July.

Office of Gas Supply (1992g) *Reference by the Director General of Gas Supply to the Monopolies and Mergers Commission under section 24 of the Gas Act 1986*, London, 31 July.

Office of Gas Supply (1992h) OFGAS News Release. *Further Reference to the Monopolies Commission*, London, 7 August.

Office of Population Census and Surveys (1989) *General Household Survey 1987*, London, HMSO.

Office of Population Census and Surveys (1990) *General Household Survey 1988*, London, HMSO.

Office of Population Census and Surveys (1991) *General Household Survey 1989*, London, HMSO.

Office of Telecommunications (1992a) *The Regulation of BT's Prices*, London.

Office of Telecommunications (1992b) *Future Controls on British Telecom's Prices*, London.

Office of Water Services (1990). *Annual Report 1989*, London, HMSO.

Office of Water Services (1990a) Press Notice. *Water Watchdog Appoints Local Champions of Customer Interests*, 27 February.

Office of Water Services (1990b) OFWAT News Release. *1989/90 Water Supply Disconnection Figures Published*, Birmingham, 15 August.

Office of Water Services (1990c) *Paying for Water. A Time for Decisions*, Birmingham.

Office of Water Services (1990d) *Paying for Water. A Time for Decisions – Annexes 1–10*, Birmingham.

Office of Water Services (1990e) *Charging Policy Consultation Document. Synopsis*, Birmingham.

Office of Water Services (1990f) *Paying for Water – Annexe 3, Current Water and Sewerage Charges*, Birmingham.

Office of Water Services (1991) *Annual Report 1990*, London, HMSO.

Office of Water Services (1991a) *Water and Sewerage Bills 1991–92*, Birmingham.

Office of Water Services (1991b) *Debt and Disconnection, Letter from the Director-General to Managing Directors of Water Companies and Water and Sewerage Companies (MD54)*, Birmingham.

Office of Water Services (1991c) OFWAT News Release. *Director General of Water Services Agrees to Rationalisation of Three Water Companies in South East – Customers to Benefit*, Birmingham, 30 April.

Office of Water Services (1991d) OFWAT News Release. *Water Industry Must Consider its Customers says Watchdog*, Birmingham, 9 May.

Office of Water Services (1991e) *Profits and Dividends (MD 55)*, Birmingham, 23 May.

Office of Water Services (1991f) *Paying for Water. OPCS Omnibus Survey*, Birmingham, June.

Office of Water Services (1991g) OFWAT News Release. *OFWAT to Take Action on Water Company Diversification*, Birmingham, 5 June.

Office of Water Services (1991h) OFWAT News Release. *Data on Financial Performance of Water Industry in 1990/91 Published by OFWAT*, Birmingham, 1 July.

Office of Water Services (1991i) OFWAT News Release. *Water Supply Disconnection Figures Published for 1990–91*, Birmingham, 17 July.

Office of Water Services (1991j) OFWAT News Release. *OFWAT to Reset Water Company Price Limits from 1995*, Birmingham, 31 July.

Office of Water Services (1991k) OFWAT News Release. *OFWAT Consults on Rates of Return for Water Industry*, Birmingham, 31 July.

Office of Water Services (1991l) *Cost of Capital. A Consultation Paper*, Birmingham, July.

Office of Water Services (1991m) *Report of the views of OFWAT's Yorkshire Customer Service Committee on the consultation paper 'Paying for Water – a Time for Decisions'*, Leeds, September.

Office of Water Services (1991n) OFWAT News Release. Water Metering Hardship Survey Commissioned, Birmingham, 2 September.

Office of Water Services (1991o) OFWAT News Release. *OFWAT Implements Licence Amendments to Protect Water and Sewerage 'Core' Business*, Birmingham, 3 September.

Office of Water Services (1991p) OFWAT News Release. *Regional Water Watchdogs Have Their Say on How You Pay*, Birmingham, 9 September.

Office of Water Services (1991q) OFWAT News Release. *Water Watchdogs to Ask Water Customers What Services They Want*, Birmingham, 19 September.

Office of Water Services (1991r) *Guidelines on Services for Disabled and Elderly Customers*, Birmingham, September.

Office of Water Services (1991s) OFWAT News Release. *Water Companies Cut Price Increases – Capital Programmes on Track*, Birmingham, 1 October.

Office of Water Services (1991t) OFWAT News Release. *OFWAT Publishes Report on Water Industry Standards of Service Delivery for 1990–91*, Birmingham, 5 December.

Office of Water Services (1991u) *Paying for Water. The Way Ahead – The Director General's Conclusions*, Birmingham, December.

Office of Water Services (1991v) OFWAT News Release. *Director General Commends Selective Approach to Water Metering*, Birmingham, 12 December.

Office of Water Services (1991w) *Plans for Periodic Review (MD 67)*, Birmingham, 23 December.

Office of Water Services (1991x) *Determination by the Director General of Water Services of an Application for Interim Adjustment of Price Limits by South West Water Services Limited*, Birmingham, 23 December.

Office of Water Services (1992a) *Water and Sewerage Bills 1991–92*, Birmingham.

Office of Water Services (1992b) *Meter Installation Report. A Survey of Customers in the Water Metering Trial Areas*, Birmingham, January.

Office of Water Services (1992c) *The Approach to the Periodic Review (MD 72)*, Birmingham, 3 March.

Office of Water Services (1992d) *Meter Installation Survey (MD 71)*, Birmingham, 2 March.

Office of Water Services (1992e) OFWAT News Release. *Customer Involvement Essential in Review of Water Industry Charges says Byatt*, Birmingham, 4 March.

Office of Water Services (1992f) *Debt and Disconnection. Guidelines and Monitoring Information, Letter from the Director-General to Managing Directors of Water Companies and Water and Sewerage Companies (MD76)*, Birmingham.

Office of Water Services (1992g) *Guidelines on Debt and Disconnection*, Birmingham, April.

Office of Water Services (1992h) *The Customer Viewpoint. A Quantitative Survey (MORI)*, Birmingham, May.

Office of Water Services (1992i) *Compensation for Customers. A consultation paper*, Birmingham, May.

Office of Water Services (1992j) *Guidelines on Optional Metering*, Birmingham, May.

Office of Water Services (1992k) OFWAT News Release. *Water Companies' Disconnections Increase, OFWAT Expresses Concern*, Birmingham, 5 June.

Office of Water Services (1992l) OFWAT CSC Chairmen's Group News Release. *Customer Watchdogs Call for Stronger Powers for Director General*, Birmingham, 6 July.

Office of Water Services (1992m) *Market Plans and Customer Involvement in the Periodic Review (MD 80)*, Birmingham, 9 July.

Office of Water Services (1992n) OFWAT News Release. *Director General Sets Out his Policy on Provision of First Time Rural Sewerage*, Birmingham, 10 August.

Office of Water Services (1992o) *The Cost of Quality. A Strategic Assessment of the Prospects for Future Water Bills*, Birmingham, August.

Office of Water Services (1992p) *Periodic Review. Autumn Consultations and Progress on Guidelines for the Strategic Business Plans (AMP2) (MD 81)*, Birmingham, 10 August.

Office of Water Services (1992q) *Review of Codes of Practice and Approval of Complaints Procedures (MD 82)*, Birmingham, 17 August.

Office of Water Services (1992r) *Proposed Amendment of Condition F -Cross-Subsidisation and Transfer Pricing, Letter from the Deputy Director-General to Managing Directors of Water Companies and Water and Sewerage Companies*, Birmingham, 21 August.

Office of Water Services (1992s) *Competition and Service (Utilities) Act 1992, Determination of Disputes, Letter from the Deputy Director-General to Managing Directors of Water Companies and Water and Sewerage Companies (MD 83); and Draft Note on the Determination of Disputes under Section 30A of the Water Industry Act*, Birmingham, 24 August.

Office of Water Services (1992t) *The Social Impact of Metering. First Report*, Birmingham.

Office of Water Services (1992u) *The Social Impact of Metering. Second Report*, Birmingham.

Office of Water Services (1992v) *The Social Impact of Metering*. Summary, Birmingham.

Office of Water Services (1992w) OFWAT News Release. *Water Metering Hardship Survey Published*, Birmingham, 11 September.

Office of Water Services (1992x) *Review of the Guaranteed Standards Scheme, Letter to Managing Directors of the Water Companies and Water and Sewerage Companies (MD84)*, Birmingham, 21 September.

Office of Water Services (1992y) *Application to the Secretary of State for the Environment and the Secretary of State for Wales for the modification and extension of the Water Supply and Sewerage Services (Customer Service Standards). Regulations 1989 (as Amended)*, Birmingham, September.

Office of Water Services (1992z) *1991–92 Report on Capital Investment and Financial Performance of the Water Companies in England and Wales*, Birmingham, October.

Office of Water Services (1992a*i*) OFWAT News Release. *Local Watchdogs Urge Government Action to Alleviate Impact of Rising Water Prices*, Birmingham, 30 October.

Office of Water Services (1992a*ii*) *Assessing Capital Values at the Periodic Review. A Consultation Paper on the Framework for Reflecting Reasonable Returns on Capital in Price Limits*, Birmingham, November.

Office of Water Services (1992a*iii*) *Annual Report 1991*, London, HMSO.

Office of Water Services (1992a*iv*) Customer Service Committees, *Annual Reports*.

Ogden, S.G. (1991) The trade union campaign against water privatisation, *Industrial Relations Journal*, 22 (1), 20–35.

O'Leary, M.C. and Smith, D.B. (1989) The contribution of economic theory to the regulatory process: Strengths, weaknesses, and future directions, in Nowotny, K. et al., op. cit., pp. 223–38.

Orchard, L. and Dare, R. (eds) (1989) *Markets, Morals and Public Policy*, Sydney, Federation Press.

Ott, A.F. and Hartley, K. (eds) (1991) *Privatization and Economic Efficiency*, Aldershot, Edward Elgar.

Owen, G. (1990) *Energy Efficiency, Low-Income Households, and the Fuel Utilities, Challenges and Opportunities, Policy Discussion Paper No. 4*, Newcastle upon Tyne, Neighbourhood Energy Action.

Oxford Economic Research Associates (OXERA) (1992) *Energy Utilities*, February.

Parker, D. and Hartley, K. (1991) Status change and performance, economic policy and evidence, in Ott, A.F. and Hartley, K., op. cit., pp. 108–25.

Parry, R. (ed.) (1990) *Privatisation. Research Highlights in Social Work 18*, London, Jessica Kingsley.

Paterson, J. (1987) The privatisation issue, water utilities, in Abelson, P. (ed.), *Privatisation. An Australian Perspective*, Sydney, Australian Professional Publications.

Pearce, D., Markandya, A. and Barbier, E.B. (1989) *Blueprint for a Green Economy (Report for the UK Department of the Environment)*, London, Earthscan.

Pearson, M. and Smith, S. (1990) *Taxation and Environmental Policy. Some Initial Evidence*, IFS Commentary No. 19, London, Institute for Fiscal Studies.

Pearson, M. and Smith, S. (1991) *The European Carbon Tax. An Assessment of the European Commission's Proposals*, London, Institute for Fiscal Studies.

Perchard, T. (1992) Water debt and disconnections, *Consumer Policy Review*, 2 (1), 18–20.

Pint, E.M. (1990) Nationalization and privatization. A rational-choice perspective on efficiency, *Journal of Public Policy*, 10 (3), 276–98.

PIRC (1989) *Water Privatisation and Pension Fund Investors*, PIRC Briefing Paper No. 2, London.

Pirie, M. (1988) *Privatization*, Aldershot, Wildwood House.

Pitelis, C. (1991) Market failure and the existence of the state, a restatement and critique, *International Review of Applied Economics*, 5 (3), 325–40.

Plant, R. (1991) Social Rights and the Reconstruction of Welfare, in Andrews, G., op. cit., pp. 50–64.

Plant, R. (1992) Citizenship, rights and welfare, in Coote, A., op. cit., pp. 17–29.

Pollitt, C. (1988) Bringing consumers into performance measurement; concepts, consequences and constraints, *Policy and Politics*, 16 (2), 77–87.

Potter, J. (1988) Consumerism and the public sector. How does the coat fit? *Public Administration*, 66, Summer.

Powe, I. (1992) Competition in gas supply, paradox or policy?, *Consumer Policy Review*, 2 (1), 4–13.

Price Waterhouse (1992) *Regulated Industries. The UK Framework* (Regulatory Brief 2), London, Centre for the Study of Regulated Industries.

Pryke, R. (1986) The comparative performance of public and private enterprise in Kay, J. et al., op. cit., pp. 101–18.

Pryke, R. (1987) Privatising electricity generation, *Fiscal Studies*, 8, 3.

PSPRU (Public Services Privatisation Research Unit) (1992) *Privatisation, Disaster for Quality*, London.

PUAF (Public Utilities Access Forum) (1990a) *Payment Direct for Water, Electricity and Gas. A Discussion Paper*, London.

PUAF (Public Utilities Access Forum) (1990b) *Water Pre-Payment Metering. The Social Policy Implications*, PUAF Discussion Paper, London.

PUAF (Public Utilities Access Forum) (1990c) *Water, Electricity and Gas Disconnection of Supply for Non-Payment. The No Contact Problem – a Discussion Note*, London.

PUAF (Public Utilities Access Forum) (1991–92) *Information Bulletins*, London.

PUAF (Public Utilities Access Forum) (1991) *Payment Direct. Report of Round-Table Discussion*, London.

Quiggin, J. (1988) Private and common property rights in the economics of the Environment, *Journal of Economic Issues*, 22, 4.

Ramanadham, V.V. (ed.) (1989) *Privatisation in Developing Countries*, London, Routledge.

Redwood, J. (1988) *Popular Capitalism*, London, Routledge.

Rees, J. (1981) Urban water and sewerage services, in Troy, P.N., op. cit., pp. 85–103.

Rees, J. (1989) Regulating private water, *Public Finance and Accountancy*, 14 April.

Rees, J. (1992) Winners and losers, paying for water, *Consumer Policy Review*, 2 (1), 14–17.

Rhodes, R.A.W. (1988) *Beyond Westminster and Whitehall. The Sub-Central Governments of Britain*, London, Unwin Hyman.

Richardson, J.J., Maloney, W.A. and Rudig, W. (1992) The dynamics of policy change, lobbying and water privatization, *Public Administration*, 70 (2), 157–75.

Roberts, J., Elliot, D. and Houghton, T. (1991) *Privatising Electricity. The Politics of Power*, London, Belhaven Press.

Roberts, S. (1992) Beyond the hunch?, *Energy Utilities*, February, 12–13.

Robins, L. (ed.) (1987) *Politics and Policy-Making in Britain*, London, Longman.

Robinson, C. (1989) Electricity privatization. What future now for British Coal?, *Energy Policy*, 17, 1.

Roche, M. (1992) *Rethinking Citizenship. Welfare, Ideology and Change in Modern Society*, Cambridge, Polity Press.

Roper, B. and Snowdon, B. (eds) (1987) *Markets, Intervention and Planning*, London, Longman.

Roth, G. (1987) *The Private Provision of Public Services in Developing Countries*, Oxford, Oxford University Press.

Rovizzi, L. and Thompson, D. (1992) The regulation of product quality in the public utilities and the Citizen's Charter, *Fiscal Studies*, 13 (3), 74–95.

Saunders, P. and Harris, C. (1990) Privatization and the consumer, *Sociology*, 24 (1), 57–75.

Savage, S.P. and Robins, L. (eds) (1990) *Public Policy under Thatcher*, Basingstoke, Macmillan.

Schroders (1989) *Prospectus. The Water Share Offers*, London.

Scottish Power (1992) *Codes of Practice. On Handling Complaints; On The Payment of Electricity Bills; On Providing Services for Elderly or Disabled People; On Efficient Use of Electricity in The Home*, Hamilton.

Secretary of State for Energy (1988) *Privatising Electricity. The Government's Proposals for the Privatisation of the Electricity Supply Industry in England and Wales*, Cm 322, London, HMSO.

Secretary of State for the Environment et al. (1977) *The Water Industry in England and Wales. The Next Steps*, Cm 6876, London, HMSO.

Secretary of State for the Environment et al. (1986) *Privatisation of the Water Authorities in England and Wales*, Cm 9734, London, HMSO.

Seeboard (1991a) *Codes of Practice. On the Procedure for Handling Complaints from Customers; On the Payment of Electricity Bills by Domestic Customers; On the Provision of Services for Elderly or Disabled Persons; On the Efficient Use of Electricity (Domestic)*, Hove.

Seldon, A. (1990) *Capitalism*, Oxford, Basil Blackwell.

SHAC/WRUG (1989) *Fuel Rights Handbook*, 7th edn, London.

Sharkey, W.W. (1982) *The Theory of Natural Monopoly*, Cambridge, Cambridge University Press.

Sharpe, T. (1992) Undue price discrimination and undue preference, a legal perspective, *Consumer Policy Review*, 2 (1), 33–35.

Sherman, R. (1989) *The Regulation of Monopoly*, Cambridge, Cambridge University Press.

Simpson, R. (1992) Will we buy it?, *Consumer Voice*, July, London, National Consumer Council.

Smith, A. and Bell, J. (1992) The consumer v. the public utility, *Consumer Policy Review*, 2 (1), 42–7.

Social Security Advisory Committee (1990) *Direct Deductions and Water Charges*, Paper to the Secretary of State for Social Security.

Social Security Advisory Committee (1992) *Social Security Advisory Committee, Eighth Report*, London, HMSO.

South Western Electricity (1991) *Codes of Practice, Paying Your Electricity Bill; If You Have a Complaint; Services for Older and Disabled People; Using Electricity Efficiently in Your Home*, Bristol.

Starr, P. (1989) The meaning of privatization, in Kamerman, S.B. and Kahn, A.J., op. cit., pp. 15–48.

Steel, D. and Heald, D. (eds) (1984) *Privatizing Public Enterprises: Options and Dilemmas*, London, Royal Institute of Public Administration.

Stelzer, I.M. (1991) Regulatory methods. A case for 'Hands across the Alantic', in Veljanovski, C., op. cit., pp. 59–75.

Stevens, B. (1992) Prospects for privatisation in OECD Countries, *National Westminster Bank Quarterly Review*, August, 2–22.

Stigler, G. (1971) The theory of economic regulation, *Bell Journal of Economics*, 2, 3–21.

Stiglitz, J.E. (1988) *Economics of the Public Sector*, New York, W.W. Norton.

Swaney, J.A. (1988) Trading water, market extension, social improvement, or what?, *Journal of Economic Issues*, 22, 1.

Swann, D. (1988) *The Retreat of the State. Deregulation and Privatisation in the UK and US*, Hemel Hempstead, Harvester/Wheatsheaf.

Swann, D. (1989) The regulatory scene. An overview, in Button, K. and Swann, D., op. cit., pp. 1–23.

Taylor, D. (1991–92) A big idea for the nineties? The rise of the Citizen's Charter, *Critical Social Policy*, 33, Winter, 87–94.

Taylor, I. (1990a) The concept of 'social cost' in free market theory and the social effects of free market policies, in Taylor, I., op. cit., pp. 1–26.

Taylor, I. (ed.) (1990b) *The Social Effects of Free Market Policies*, Hemel Hempstead, Harvester Wheatsheaf.

Taylor-Gooby, P. (1989) The role of the state, in Jowell, R., Witherspoon, S. and Brook, L. (eds) *British Social Attitudes 6th Report, Special International Report*, Aldershot, Gower.

Taylor-Gooby, P. (1991) Attachment to the Welfare State, in Jowell, R. et al., op. cit., pp. 23–42.

Terry, F. and Jackson, P. (eds) (1992) *Public Domain 1992*, London, Chapman and Hall.

Thackray, J. (1988) Towards rationality in water charging, *Public Finance and Accountancy*, 11 March.

Thomas, D. (1986) The union response to denationalisation in Kay, J. et al., op. cit., pp. 299–321.

Thompson, D., Bishop, M. and Rovizzi, L. (1991) Regulatory reform and public enterprise performance, productivity and prices, *Consumer Policy Review*, 1 (4), 204–210.

Thompson, S., Wright, M. and Robbie, K. (1990) Management buy-outs from the public sector. Ownership form and incentive issues, *Fiscal Studies*, 11 (3), 71–88.

Tillsley, C. (1988) Water, Cause for Concern – The Privatisation of the Water Industry, Implications for Consumers and Public Accountability, MA Dissertation, Department of Social Policy and Social Work, University of York.

Towers, B. (1989) Running the gauntlet. British trade unions under Thatcher, 1979–1988, *Industrial and Labour Relations Review*, 42, 2.

Troy, P.N. (1981) *Equity in the City*, Sydney, Allen and Unwin.

United Research (1990) *Privatisation. Implications for Cultural Change*, London.

Vane, H. (1992) The Thatcher years. Macroeconomic policy and performance of the UK economy, 1979–1988, *National Westminster Bank Quarterly Review*, May, 26–43.

Vass, P. (1992) Regulated public service industries, in Terry, F. and Jackson, P., op. cit., pp. 209–37.

Veljanovski, C. (1987) *Selling the State. Privatisation in Britain*, London, Weidenfeld and Nicolson.

Veljanovski, C. (1989a) Privatization. Experience with regulation, *Energy Policy*, August, 351–5.

Veljanovski, C. (ed.) (1989b) *Privatisation and Competition. A Market Prospectus*, London, Institute of Economic Affairs.

Veljanovski, C. (ed.) (1991) *Regulators and the Market. An Assessment of the Growth of Regulation in the UK*, London, Institute of Economic Affairs.

Vickers, J. (1991) Government regulatory policy, *Oxford Review of Economic Policy*, 7 (3), 13–30.

Vickers, J. and Yarrow, G. (1988) *Privatization. An Economic Analysis*, Cambridge (MA), MIT Press.

Vickers, J. and Yarrow, G. (1989) Privatization in Britain, in MacAvoy, P.W. et al., op. cit., pp. 209–45.

Vickers, J. and Yarrow, G. (1991) The British electricity experiment, *Economic Policy*, April, 188–227.

Vining, A.R. and Weimer, D.L. (1990) Government supply and government production failure: A framework based on contestability, *Journal of Public Policy*, 10 (1), 1–22.

Vogelsang, I. (1988a) Regulation of public utilities and nationalized industries, in Hare, P.G., op. cit., pp. 45–67.

Vogelsang, I. (1988b) Deregulation and privatization in Germany, *Journal of Public Policy*, 8, 2.

Walker, D. (1990) Enter the regulators, *Parliamentary Affairs*, 43 (2), 149–58.

Water Services Association (1991) *Waterfacts 1991*, London.

Water Services Association (1992) *Water Bulletin 1989–1992*, London.

Waterson, M. (1988) *Regulation of the Firm and Natural Monopoly*, Oxford, Basil Blackwell.

Webb, M.G. (1985) Energy policy and the privatisation of the UK energy industries, *Energy Policy*, February, 27–36.

Welsh Water PLC (1992) *Welsh Water Press Release, Water Industry Calls for Benefit Changes*, Brecon, 19 October.

West Midlands Low Pay Unit (1989) *Water Privatisation. The Effects of Water Metering*, Birmingham.

Weyman-Jones, T. (1986) *The Economics of Energy Policy*, Aldershot, Gower.

Weyman-Jones, T. (1989) US and UK energy policy, in Button, K. and Swann, D., op. cit., 279–99.

Weyman-Jones, T. (1990) RPI – X price cap regulation. The price controls used in UK electricity, *Utilities Policy*, 1 (1), 65–77.

Whitfield, D. (1992) *The Welfare State. Privatisation, Deregulation, Commercialisation of Public Services, Alternative Strategies for the 1990s*, London, Pluto Press.

Winward, J. (1989) The privatization programme and the consumer interest, *Energy Policy*, October, 511–17.

Winward, J. (1991) Consumers, competition and services, *Consumer Policy Review*, 1 (4), 194–95.

Winward, J. (1992) Public utilities, *Consumer Policy*, 2 (1), 2–3.

Yarrow, G. (1986) Privatisation in theory and practice, *Economic Policy*, April 1986, 324–77.

Yarrow, G. (1988) Privatisation and economic performance, *Economic Review*, November, 2–6.

Yarrow, G. (1992) *British Electricity Prices since Privatization*, Studies in Regulation No. 1, Oxford, Regulatory Policy Institute.

Yorkshire Customer Service Committee (1992) Minutes and Meeting Papers, Leeds.

Yorkshire Electricity (1991a) *Codes of Practice, Payment of Bills; Provision of Services for Elderly and Disabled People; Efficient Use of Electricity; Statement of Procedure for Handling Customer Complaints*, Leeds.

Index

MARKETS AND MANAGERS
NEW ISSUES IN THE DELIVERY OF WELFARE

Peter Taylor-Gooby and Robyn Lawson (eds)

Over the past decade, the British welfare state has undegone the most fundamental reforms since the Second World War. Much discussion of current policy focuses on the global issues of cuts, privatization and the scope of the state sector. This book argues that the organizational reforms of the 1990s are also of far-reaching significance and will play a major role in setting the agenda for welfare policy into the next century. The new welfare settlement emphasizes decentralization, the use of markets, an autonomous managerialism, a stronger voice for consumers and a greater role for the private sector. Reformers claim that the changes allow a more efficient, flexible and responsive welfare system, while critics argue that they will lead to greater inequality and to discrimination against the most vulnerable groups of service users.

This book differs from other recent publications in its emphasis on the changes in the organization and delivery of services. It examines the emergence of the new managerial ideology in central and local government, considers the similarities and differences between the UK and other European countries and reviews policy change across the range of public services. The concluding chapter evaluates competing explanations of why the transformation has occurred and discusses future developments. The book provides a practical discussion of the issues, and will be of value to a wide range of students and welfare practitioners.

Contents
Markets, managers and the public service: the changing of a culture – Patterns of change in the delivery of welfare in Europe – Contracting housing provision: competition and privatization in the housing sector – A case study in the National Health Service: Working for Patients *– The new technology of management in the personal social services – Social security: the income maintenance business – The new educational settlement: National Curriculum and local management – The legacy of the Manpower Services Commission: training in the 1980s – Where we go from here: the new order in welfare – References – Index.*

Contributors
Pat Ainley, John Baldock, John Butler, Hartley Dean, Ray Forrest, Andrew Gray, Bill Jenkins, Robyn Lawson, Peter Taylor-Gooby.

192pp   0 335 15789 0 (Paperback)   0 335 15790 4 (Hardback)

INFORMATION MANAGEMENT IN HEALTH SERVICES

Justin Keen (ed.)

Health services are set on an inexorable drive for more and better information, and are spending millions of pounds on information technology (IT) in an effort to obtain it. But as the need for information becomes ever more pressing, serious problems have come into focus, ranging from the difficulties of collecting accurate routine data to understanding the role of information in management and clinical processes.

This book seeks to clarify the nature of the problems surrounding information and IT, and point the way to practical solutions. It is divided into three sections; policy overview; views from within the health service; and the views of academic researchers.

Contents

Section 1: Overview: information policy and market – Hospitals in the market – Information policy in the National Health Service – Section 2: The practitioner perspective – Operational systems – Managing development: developing managers' information management – Clinical management – Nursing management – Contracts: managing the external environment – Section 3: The academic perspective – Information for purchasing – The politics of information – A social science perspective on information systems in the NHS – Information and IT strategy – Evaluation: informing the future, not living in the past – IT futures in the NHS – Index.

Contributors

Brian Bloomfield, Andrew Brooks, Jane Clayton, Rod Coombs, Bob Galliers, Wally Gowing, Mark Harrison, John James, Justin Keen, Andy Kennedy, Rebecca Malby, Margaret Marion, Jenny Owen, James Raftery, Ray Robinson, Mike Smith, Andrew Stevens.

224pp   0 335 19116 9 (Paperback)   0 335 19117 7 (Hardback)

CONTROLLING HEALTH PROFESSIONALS
THE FUTURE OF WORK AND ORGANIZATION IN THE NHS

Stephen Harrison and Christopher Pollitt

For twenty years, British governments of both the left and right have tried to improve the management of the NHS. But the distinctive contribution of the Thatcher governments of the 1980s has defined this very much in terms of controlling health professionals: doctors, nurses and others. This volume

- offers an explanation of why this approach was adopted
- examines in detail the various methods of control employed
- assesses the consequences for the future of professional work and organization in the NHS.

The book will be of interest to a wide range of health professionals, including nurses, doctors, health authority members and managers and will also be useful for students of social policy and health students.

Contents
Professionals and managers – Finance for health care: supply, demand and rationing – Challenging the professionals – Incorporating the professionals – Changing the environment – The future of managerial and professional work in the NHS – Notes – References – Index.

192pp   0 335 09643 3 (Paperback)   0 335 09644 1 (Hardback)